W9-CJN-798

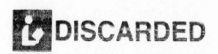DISCARDED

UNIVERSITY OF WINNIPEG
LIBRARY
515 Portage Avenue
Winnipeg, Manitoba R3B 2E9

THE NEW
INTERNATIONALISM

D
748
.K5
1973

THE NEW INTERNATIONALISM

Allied Policy and the European Peace 1939–1945

F. P. King

DAVID & CHARLES
ARCHON BOOKS 1973

© F. P. King 1973
All rights reserved. No part of this
publication may be reproduced, stored
in a retrieval system, or transmitted,
in any form or by any means electronic,
mechanical, photocopying, recording, or
otherwise, without the prior permission
of the publishers

This edition first published in 1973 in
Great Britain by David & Charles (Holdings)
Limited, Newton Abbot, Devon
and in the United States of America by
Archon Books, Hamden, Connecticut
07514

ISBN 0 7153 5950 9 (*Great Britain*)
ISBN 0 208 01399 7 (*United States*)

Set in eleven on twelve point Imprint
and printed in Great Britain
by Butler & Tanner Limited, Frome and London

To Norma, Tara and my Parents

Contents

Introduction

AT LEAST on the left, the last seven years of the 1930s in Europe have often been lamented. Germany metamorphosed from a disarmed, feebly democratic republic into a triumphant, aggressive, national socialist Reich. Italy, the prototype European fascist state, moved from the margin of world affairs into the centre, acquired an empire in the process, and established a dangerous, expansionistic precedent for other nations. States in the Baltic, Balkan and central regions regressed from post-revolutionary bastions of anti-communist reaction to super-nationalistic, territorially acquisitive satellites of the axis alliance. Two of the exceptions to the general European swing to the right, Spain and Czechoslovakia, were crushed by the emerging forces of fascism while the democratic powers acted as handmaidens. The League of Nations atrophied while failing to keep the peace. In the United States, inevitably affected by events in Europe, a Congressional obsession with what was perceived to be the world's overwhelming complexities resulted in the passage of a series of potentially debilitating neutrality acts which threatened to make a deadweight of the most powerful nation in the Western Hemisphere.

If one accepts the notion that 'a foreign policy is primarily a *defence*, a means by which the social organism defends itself against encroachments and seeks to achieve the international environment within which it can prosper',[1] then one must conclude and generalise that the politicians of the non-fascist states were unsuccessful during this period. Ideologically they were confused: they were both repulsed and attracted by fascism while they feared the alternatives. Consequently they allowed forces to develop which threatened their nations and made the second great international war of the century likely—as surely as they

9

showed a singular incapacity to control those forces once they
had fully matured.

President Franklin Delano Roosevelt was an exception. While
he was one of the first statesmen to be unsentimentally suspicious
of the League of Nations' usefulness, he was continually ready and
eager for the United States to play a leading role in international
affairs.[2] In pursuance of this end, he firmly wished to see the
traditional powers of the Presidency enhanced by means of a dis-
cretionary arms embargo in the interests of creating a more active,
effective, and resolute international community.[3] As early as May
1933, he proposed a form of international co-operation involving
the quarantining and identification of errant nations which if
welcomed by other states might well have changed the history
of the period.[4] The responsiveness of the non-fascist European
powers had not improved more than four years later, in October
1937, when he reiterated the proposal during his Quarantine
speech in Chicago.[5]

Forced into waging a running battle with isolationist opposition from 1933 onwards, with little support from putative pro-
gressives, even within his own party, Roosevelt was compelled to
defend both the nation's traditional neutrality rights and his own
efforts at further enmeshing the nation in foreign affairs. His
reversals in part stemmed from the lack of support for his proposals from leading French and British politicians who in many
ways were as incapable of utilising the semi-released powers of
the United States as they were unwilling to collaborate with
others in the interests of creating an anti-fascist alliance. In a
sense, both the USA and the USSR suffered the same misfortune
during the 1930s. They were excluded from European affairs by
politicians who as yet had not accepted the readjustment of power
brought about by World War I and the Russian Revolution—
politicians who were insufficiently alarmed by the rise of fascism
to utilise new coalitions of power imaginatively.

While Roosevelt showed great initiative in mobilising the
slender national resources allocated to him by Congress during
the Italian–Ethiopian War and considerable foresight in resisting
the spirit of compromise with the fascist powers, best typified by
the Hoare–Laval approach to foreign relations, his chief failure
was in not dissociating his brand of liberal international politics

from British and French policy efforts which were manifestly
bankrupt.[6] Perhaps more important, by the end of the decade
Roosevelt had failed to define the nation's policy objectives, even
though this definition by necessity would have challenged traditional alignments and called into question the ideological health
and ends of democratic France and Britain.[7]

Notes to this introduction are on pages 187-8.

Chapter 1 THE ALLIANCE

THE ROOSEVELT administration's skilful and daring manipulation
of the dynamics of the moment following the official outbreak of
war in Europe, which enabled them to secure the repeal of the more
restricting features of the Neutrality Act during October and
November 1939, did little to advance the United States' relations
with her most important connection in the outside world, the
United Kingdom. Chamberlain's War Cabinet of 3 September
1939 was in essence a relic of the 1930s, and as such the passivity
and negativism of the preceding Tory governments remained.
Unlike those from France, British orders for American armaments
stayed 'negligible'. British industry as ever was not to be dislocated,
dollar balances were to be conserved, the English Channel and
the British Navy were to remain Britain's Maginot Line.[1]

With the advent of Churchill's War Cabinet on 11 May 1940,
however, Roosevelt was able to keep pace with the profound
change in mood and even anticipate its direction by constructing
a subliminal alliance. Using the powers of the non-legislative
executive agreement, the President on 3 June 1940 released
surplus arms and supplies to the United Kingdom; and during the
same month he declared defence to be the nation's first priority.
On 3 September fifty old American destroyers were exchanged for
leases of British military installations in the Western Hemisphere.
By 16 September the administration had prodded Congress to
pass the first Selective Service (Draft) Act. Ten days later the
President embargoed exports of scrap iron and steel to all nations
outside the Western Hemisphere but excluded the United Kingdom. By March 1941 the Roosevelt administration had pushed
through Congress what was perhaps the most imaginative and far-
sighted piece of foreign policy legislation ever passed by an

American legislative body, 'An Act to Promote the Defense of the United States (Lend-Lease)'. On 7 July FDR announced that US Naval forces would supplement and eventually replace British forces in Iceland.[2]

As early as Christmas of 1940 Roosevelt expressed a desire to personally meet with the new Prime Minister and First Lord of the Treasury and Minister of Defence, the Rt Hon Winston S. Churchill. As a preliminary step to such a meeting, FDR sent his personal representative, Harry Hopkins, to London in January 1941. For six weeks Hopkins travelled and conversed while he unofficially got Lend–Lease talks started even before the act had become law. As an agent who enjoyed the President's fullest confidence, he left the British, in the words of one observer, 'with the feeling that although America was not yet in the war, she was marching beside us, and that should we stumble she would see we did not fall'. Again during the middle of July, Hopkins was sent to England to confer with the British. Then, after a brief trip to the USSR, he accompanied Churchill and his colleagues to Placentia Bay, Newfoundland. In this fashion, Hopkins became the linking mechanism of the inchoate alliance.[3]

The most significant achievement of the Atlantic conference, which was held at Placentia Bay, resulted from Roosevelt's initiative. The President repeatedly and clearly told Churchill, in the Prime Minister's words, 'that American assistance in money and *material* was not enough'. As Churchill told the War Cabinet on his return from the conference, the President 'was skating on pretty thin ice in his relations with Congress, which, however, he did not regard as truly representative of the country'. As had long been the case in the past, FDR was prepared again to lead public opinion and circumvent Congress. As Churchill phrased FDR's words, 'If he were to put the issue of peace and war to Congress, they would debate it for three months. The President had said that he would wage war, but not declare it, and that he would become more and more provocative. If the Germans did not like it, they could attack American forces.'[4]

While the Atlantic Charter—the joint statement of intention drafted during the Newfoundland discussions—was an incidental product of the conference, within a very short time it came into its own as a significant and unique document. If it failed to acquire the status of a formal agreement (neither the President nor the Prime Minister actually signed the Charter), it easily became the most important press handout the world had ever known. As a lucid and landmark expression of American and British policy in a troubled world it is worth while quoting.

First, their countries seek no aggrandizement, territorial or other;

Second, they desire to see no territorial changes that do not accord with the freely expressed wishes of the peoples concerned;

Third, they respect the right of all peoples to choose the form of government under which they will live; and they wish to see sovereign rights and self-government restored to those who have been forcibly deprived of them;

Fourth, they will endeavor, with due respect for their existing obligations, to further the enjoyment by all states, great or small, victor or vanquished, of access, on equal terms, to the trade and to the raw materials of the world which are needed for their economic prosperity;

Fifth, they desire to bring about the fullest collaboration between all nations in the economic field with the object of securing, for all, improved labor standards, economic advancement, and social security;

Sixth, after the final destruction of the Nazi tyranny, they hope to see established a peace which will afford to all nations the means of dwelling in safety within their own boundaries, and which will afford assurance that all the men in all the lands may live out their lives in freedom from fear and want;

Seventh, such a peace should enable all men to traverse the high seas and oceans without hindrance;

Eighth, they believe that all of the nations of the world, for realistic as well as spiritual reasons, must come to the abandonment of the use of force. Since no future peace can be maintained if land, sea, or air armaments continue to be employed by nations which threaten, or may threaten, aggression outside of their frontiers, they believe, pending the establishment of a wider and permanent system of general security, that the disarmament of such nations is essential. They will likewise aid and encourage all other practicable measures which will lighten for peace-loving peoples the crushing burden of armaments.[5]

The British contribution to the drafting of this statement was not insignificant, and it was a sign that the Churchill government was capable of making ideological affirmations that the Conservative party and the Baldwin–Chamberlain national governments had long avoided. On 10 August, after an evening of preliminary discussions between FDR and Churchill and their advisers, the Permanent Under-Secretary of the Foreign Office, Sir Alexander Cadogan, had presented Sumner Welles with a five-point draft which eventually became the backbone of the eight-point declaration.[6] The first two points of the Charter were taken verbatim from the British draft; the third was only stylistically different; the remaining provisions of the Charter were elaborations of the fourth and fifth points of the British draft.

The most interesting conversation during the conference revolved around point eight of the Charter. FDR had stated that rather than the establishment of a resurrected League of Nations, as suggested in Cadogan's draft, he favoured the creation of an Anglo-American police force to reconstruct the peace immediately after the cessation of hostilities. Despite protestations from both Cadogan and Sumner Welles, Roosevelt insisted that the wording of what became the eighth clause be changed so as to emphasise the importance of international disarmament *before* 'the establishment of a wider and permanent system of general security . . .'. While the phraseology sounded much like the British original, it represented in the President's mind, at least, a promise to terminate the League of Nations concept of international security which FDR for more than a decade had recognised as being inadequate. It was simply not good sense from Roosevelt's view to suppose that an infant international organisation, such as the League had been after the Great War, would be able to wrench order out of chaos after the war. The tasks of enforcing the treaties, of settling boundary disputes, of relocating displaced persons, of enforcing disarmament, of re-establishing economic order—all the problems of a world ravaged by war—could best be accomplished by the victor nations before the construction of a caretaker international organisation. Obviously FDR envisaged a more important Anglo-American role in international affairs than had ever been suggested before.[7]

If there were sections of the Charter that showed hastiness in drafting and a certain disregard for recent historical events, there could be no doubt after its publication that there was a new commonality of purpose between British and American leaders. If Cordell Hull, the American Secretary of State, felt that Welles and Roosevelt 'had sold out the program closest to his heart' by accepting the British proviso in point four protecting the system of imperial preferences,[8] his bitterness about an issue, trade reciprocity, which had become moribund,[9] was a small price to pay for the creation of a joint policy containing their shared ideology, the grounds on which they were prepared to conduct the war, and a hint of the peace they hoped to achieve.

During the Sunday evening of 7 December 1941 both John G. Winant, the American Ambassador in the United Kingdom, and W. Averell Harriman, America's chief expediter of Lend–Lease, were Winston Churchill's dinner guests at Chequers. Upon hearing of the Japanese attack on Pearl Harbor, Churchill immediately telephoned the White House. The President suggested that Churchill and his Chiefs of Staff travel to Washington for consultative talks as soon as possible. What Robert E. Sherwood has called 'the common-law alliance' was fully legitimised on 9 December 1941 when the United States declared war on Japan and on the 11th when Germany and Italy declared war on the US.[10]

STRATEGY

Hopkins and the talks at Placentia Bay had greatly simplified the complex issues confronting the two leaders; consequently, when Churchill arrived in Washington on 22 December for the Arcadia conference, he was prepared, as was Roosevelt, to discuss military strategy and priorities, not politics. At least as early as mid-November 1940, Admiral Stark, US Chief of Naval Operations, had indicated that proper American strategy demanded 'an eventual strong offensive in the Atlantic as an ally of the British, and a defensive in the Pacific'.[11] This suggestion was sustained by joint British–American military discussions, following Hopkins' first mission to Britain, during February and March of 1941, when it was agreed that 'since Germany is the predominant partner of the Axis Powers, the Atlantic and the Mediterranean area is considered to be the decisive theatre'.[12] Even with the passing of the ensuing months, both FDR and Churchill endorsed this policy with alacrity. The thinking behind this decision was uncomplicated: during the conference, Germany was the most resolute and resourceful of the Axis nations; with Germany's defeat the others' will and capacity to resist would cease. There was also the important consideration that a less than vigorous offensive strategy against Germany would very likely result in the defeat of the USSR with results more disastrous in the long run than the possible defeat of China.[13]

In conjunction with a general global strategy, a notable organisational change resulted from the first Washington conference. This was the establishment of the Combined Chiefs of Staff (CCS) which first met in Washington in early 1942. The seven members of the Staff, four Americans and three Britons, were either the sole agents or direct heads of the military services most involved in the conduct of the war; as such they were authorised to implement the decisions made by the group and had powers to act as 'an executive committee for the prosecution of a global war'.[14] The exception to their mandate, of course, was the strong personal relationship that had developed between Churchill and Roosevelt.

What had been constructed during the Atlantic and Arcadia conferences was clearly a closed alliance, which was paradoxically both a strength and a weakness. At best Churchill and Roosevelt spoke only for their own countries. Without a formal treaty the strength of the weld between the two countries was limited to the unanimity of purpose created by the common set of objectives, priorities, and agreed strategy. Rather than a strengthening of these bonds through legalistic means, often in the past an idle occupation, the two leaders decided to reinforce the alliance by casting off its mantle of exclusiveness. On 1 January 1942, twenty-six nations were invited to sign a 'Declaration by the United Nations' which not only reaffirmed the principles of the Atlantic Charter but pledged the signatories to prosecute the war against the members of the Tripartite Pact without making 'a separate armistice or peace with the enemies'.[15] As propaganda this Declaration had great value. As alliance-building it was lacking in substance. The reality of New Year's Day 1942 was that only Churchill and Roosevelt were making effective decisions. United subscription, even to the bitter end, did not create the machinery for collective political and military policy-making.

THE SECOND FRONT

The strategy agreed upon during the Washington conference lacked precision. To a large extent the two leaders and their advisers had merely confirmed the non-political and organisational impulse that the war had already assumed. There had been no questioning the wisdom of the continued bombing of Germany, military and economic assistance to the USSR, the blockade of German and Italian ports, and the support of guerrilla forces in occupied countries. The question of directing the most crippling blow against Germany, however, was different. Here the decision taken had only a superficial hardness: land offensives of a limited nature were to be undertaken during the year; 1943 was to see a return to the European continent by landings in western Europe, the Balkans, or the Mediterranean.[16] The unresolved gritty problems of where, when, and how much were formidable. The residual problems of how these decisions were to be taken were no less impressive.

Well before Arcadia, American war planners had been busily at work and an early consensus had been reached. A relatively obscure assistant to the US Chiefs of Staff, Brigadier General Dwight D. Eisenhower, had expressed the prevalent thinking of the American planners in January 1942 when he called for a concentration of war resources in western Europe 'to be followed up by a land attack as soon as possible'.[17] The British vision, which had been held for decades rather than months, was somewhat different. Whether justified by geo-political facts or not, they saw British interests as an umbilical cord stretching from the homeland through the Mediterranean, by way of Gibraltar, the Middle East and Suez, to India, Burma, Malaya and Singapore.[18] This orientation was to bias British military planning throughout the war. Its absence was to produce an odd quandary for the Americans who had no such historical, political, and psychological predispositions.

From the beginning, many American government officials were unwilling to trust the Combined Chiefs of Staff or the British Joint Staff Mission in Washington to accept plans for the opening of a second front on the European continent as a strictly military proposal. The Secretary of War, Henry L. Stimson, advised the

President in late March that the best procedure was to present the perfected plan directly to Churchill and his military advisers and thus avoid amendments at a lower echelon. Hopkins also agreed that the issue was too important for the newly constituted Combined Chiefs of Staff to consider. When FDR on 1 April agreed with his two civilian advisers on sending a mission to London, he established an important precedent for further Anglo-American discussions. Perhaps it was apparent from the beginning that the question of a second front was not primarily a military question at all.[19]

When Harry Hopkins and General George C. Marshall left for London in early April 1942, they carried with them what has often been called the Marshall memorandum. It was a synthesis of the best current proposals, some from British sources in the US, originating from a memorandum by General Eisenhower which had received FDR's enthusiastic approval in late March.[20] As planned, the invasion was scheduled in three separate phases. BOLERO was the name given to the preparatory build-up of troops and equipment in the United Kingdom. In the event of the imminent collapse of Soviet resistance or the development of weaknesses in German defences in the west, SLEDGEHAMMER, a pre-invasion diversionary landing, was scheduled for September of 1942. The primary invasion, ROUNDUP, was to follow in 1943. While ROUNDUP was to be mainly an American undertaking, because of the logistical situation, SLEDGEHAMMER, the more daring and sacrificial of the two plans, was to be almost exclusively a British undertaking.[21]

From the beginning of the military discussions in London, the British expressed doubts about both the root and branch of SLEDGEHAMMER. On his way to Washington aboard HMS *Duke of York* some five months earlier, the Prime Minister had written a memorandum which called for a series of ambitious Anglo-American commando-expeditionary raids in Norway, Denmark, Holland, Belgium, the French coasts, Italy, and possibly the Balkans with the expectation that 'the German garrisons would prove insufficient to cope both with the strength of the liberating forces and the fury of the revolting peoples'.[22] General Sir Alan Brooke, Chief of the Imperial General Staff, endorsed this view when he held that the holders of predominant sea power should force the enemy with overall land power to disperse and fragment his forces. Thus from the British viewpoint SLEDGEHAMMER was both too weighty and too insufficient. As General Brooke argued to the Americans, the British would be incapable of mustering sufficient forces to hold their positions as a bridgehead during a German counter-attack. More important, he doubted whether it would be possible, as at Dunkirk, to evacuate the troops after their defeat. Vice-Admiral Lord Louis Mountbatten, Chief of Combined Operations, opposed the plan on the grounds that transport was difficult for such a large operation and surprise impossible. Air Chief Marshal Sir Charles Portal concluded that proper tactical air support could not be given to the proposed enclave. The result of this opposition, on both strategical and tactical grounds, was the joint decision that conditions on the Soviet front would be decisive as far as SLEDGEHAMMER was concerned. There was never any serious objection to ROUND-UP from any quarter, and it was accepted by the British Chiefs of Staff on 14 April 1942.[23]

Meanwhile Hopkins' parallel negotiations on the political side followed quite a different tack. Hopkins and Harriman initially presented the American proposals to Anthony Eden, the Secretary of State for Foreign Affairs, and Oliver Lyttelton, the Minister of Production. Both members of the cabinet expressed reservations only about the timing of SLEDGEHAMMER: they favoured early implementation rather than waiting until the end of the year. On 14 April, after the first round of piece-meal talks, Churchill appeared and gave his unqualified approval to the Marshall memorandum before a congregation of the War Cabinet and the Chiefs of Staff. From this time onwards the issue was understood to have been agreed upon; the following day both Hopkins and Marshall cabled messages to their respective bosses, FDR and Stimson, that their proposals had been accepted subject to the conditions raised by the British Chiefs of Staff. After Hopkins returned to Washington and briefed FDR, the President and Churchill exchanged congratulations and confirmations of the decision. And so the matter ostensibly rested for six weeks.[24]

On 8 May 1942, General Sir Bernard Paget, Commander-in-Chief of the Home Forces, Air Marshal Sir Sholto Douglas, and Admiral Mountbatten all reached the conclusion that SLEDGE-

HAMMER was unsound. The Chiefs of Staff supported this view
on the 27th of the month; and on the same occasion the Prime
Minister turned to what he considered a more useful operation,
namely the capture of German airfields in northern Norway. The
following day, Churchill, showing his customary dexterity,
alarmed Washington by extolling the virtues of a French North
Africa invasion (GYMNAST). On 19 June, Marshall talked with
Churchill and immediately warned FDR, since Churchill was
about to embark for the impromptu reciprocal phase of the
Hopkins–Marshall talks of April, that the Prime Minister 'is
pessimistic regarding BOLERO and interested in August GYM-
NAST and another similar movement in Norway'.[25]

The audience for Churchill's second Washington conference of
1942 was familiar, but the script was fresh. The Prime Minister
argued that a successful operation was the only form of aid that
amounted to real coinage for the Free French and the Russians.
A temporary bridgehead was better than none at all, but a permanent one was even better. While Churchill disclaimed any intention
of dropping SLEDGEHAMMER, he did ingeniously question
whether adequate plans had been prepared by the Americans. The
onus had cleverly been shifted: if the Americans proposed they
also were obliged to guarantee the success of all three phases of the
Marshall memorandum. As a fitting conclusion to this masterful
presentation, the Prime Minister praised the possibilities of
GYMNAST. The news of the unfortunate fall of Tobruk, at
approximately the same time, and the surrender of 33,000 British
soldiers was dramatic punctuation—all of a sudden even the most
cynical American military men could see Rommel and North
Africa clearly in the centre of the struggle. None the less, both the
British and American advisers on the military merits alone agreed
on 21 June that GYMNAST should not be undertaken, that
BOLERO should be pursued 'with all possible speed and energy',
and that SLEDGEHAMMER should commence 'only in case of
necessity'.[26]

Even after Tobruk, General Marshall, and others, could see that
an attack on SLEDGEHAMMER, such as Churchill had initiated,
eroded the standing of ROUNDUP. This latter operation was the
fulcrum of allied strategy. If it were, as Churchill had asserted, that
the unanimous weight of British military opinion could see nothing

but disaster in the early cross-Channel invasion, it was equally true that no respectable American military leader was willing to forsake an invasion in western Europe in 1943. A serious impasse had been reached.[27]

After Churchill's return to England, he wasted no time in effecting a resolution. He further politicised the question by gaining the support of the War Cabinet for the North African operation rather than the cross-Channel invasion. This new decision was then forwarded to Washington. The Americans refused to be pressured and reacted, or perhaps over-reacted, with vehemence. Secretary of War Stimson, long a champion of ROUNDUP, now became the author of an unofficial counter-proposal that threatened to change the entire direction of the war.

> A telegram has come from Great Britain indicating that the British War Cabinet are weakening and going back on BOLERO and are seeking to revive GYMNAST—in other words, they are seeking now to reverse the decision which was so laboriously accomplished when Mr. Churchill was here a short time ago. This would be simply another way of diverting our strength into a channel in which we cannot effectively use it, namely the Middle East. . . . This is the third time this question will have been brought up by the persistent British and he [Marshall] proposed a showdown which I cordially endorse. As the British won't go through with what they agreed to, we will turn our backs on them and take up the war with Japan.[28]

When Hopkins and Marshall for the second time went to London for consultations in mid-July, they had been carefully coached by the President. He had specifically rejected Stimson's advice that the gauntlet be thrown down. As he expressed it, 'If we cannot strike at SLEDGEHAMMER, then we must take the second best —and that is not the Pacific.' As secondary targets he proposed North Africa or the Middle East. At the same time, however, he made it clear to Hopkins, on the eve of his departure, that 'we should press forward vigorously for the 1943 enterprise'. In a memo dated 16 July FDR made two other points: that definite plans be made for American infantry action before the end of 1942 and that 'total agreement' be reached in London within a week after the start of negotiations.[29]

Two factors sealed the fate of SLEDGEHAMMER in July.

The first was that while the British were more divided about the merits of a European invasion among the lesser senior officers, at the top the British were politically and militarily, at least in London, unalterably and solidly opposed to the American plan. The second was that Hopkins, who personally was a strong supporter of the Marshall plan, was faithful to his instructions. While Marshall and the other Americans were willing to stand fast, Hopkins, as his deadline approached, showed a willingness to compromise. On 22 July, the Prime Minister and the British Chiefs of Staff irrevocably rejected the American plan for SLEDGEHAMMER. While the British denied that this decision affected the European second front in 1943, the Americans knew full well that in Eisenhower's words its 'death-knell' had been sounded.[30]

THE FORESHADOWED CONCLUSION

Of all the Allied conferences held during the war, the one at Casablanca from 14 to 25 January 1943 was the least tense. General Montgomery's Eighth Army had scored a great victory at El Alamein in late October. In early November General Eisenhower had successfully led landings of British and American troops ashore in Algeria and Morocco. At the time of the conference, the Soviet armies were on the verge of a decisive victory at Stalingrad. Shortly before the conference, Stalin had declined FDR's invitation to attend, expressing his firm wish that the two statesmen would fulfil their promises of a northern European second front in 1943.[31]

The seminal talks carried on in London during the previous July bore fruit at Casablanca. Churchill presented the plan that had long lain close to his heart: from the African shores of the Mediterranean the allies would strike at 'the under-belly of the Axis'. This time his appeal did not fail to receive a hearing. The inescapable fact was that the Anglo-American build-up of troops was in North Africa and not in England. By 18 January the Combined Chiefs of Staff had recommended the invasion of Sicily. By 23 January, when Churchill, Hopkins, and Roosevelt met with the Combined Chiefs, they had prepared a list of priorities which pushed ROUNDUP down the list for 1943.[32]

There were many reasons why Roosevelt and Churchill decided
on the Mediterranean in 1943 other than the obvious military
considerations. Churchill was passing through 'the most disturbed' political period of the war and needed quick victories to
re-secure his position at home. Roosevelt, in turn, was also not
oblivious to the impact of dramatic news on public opinion and
Congressional elections. As General Marshall in later years was
to observe, after serving as Truman's Secretary of State, the
leader of a democratic state 'has to keep the people entertained' for
they demand 'action'. At the time of Casablanca, neither FDR nor
Churchill, had he been so disposed, could afford to wait until
everything was in readiness for the northern European invasion.[33]
None the less, the progression had been too easy, both politically
and militarily; bilateralism had oversimplified the diplomatic
process and more important the diplomatic vision.

Notes to this chapter are on pages 188-9.

Chapter 2 THE THIRD SIDE OF THE TRIANGLE

DURING THE early months of the war, the Americans enjoyed several advantages that the British did not when it came to improving relations with the USSR. First, they had been, and were, more distant—and were likely to remain so. Second, they had more military hardware to dispense. Third, and the most serious of all, the Roosevelt administration had neither appeased fascists nor pursued overtly anti-communist policies during the 1930s. While no less inept and wrong than the British and French during the Spanish Civil War and the Russo-Finnish War, at least the Americans had not taken the initiative in creating policies that resulted in the defeat of the Spanish Republic and had not threatened direct military action against the USSR. More important, in Soviet eyes, the US had not been associated with the humiliating series of anti-Soviet diplomatic rebuffs which had pressured the Soviet government into the ideologically repulsive Nazi–Soviet non-aggression pact of 1939. The President's attitudes toward the Soviet Union as expressed in public also emphasised the degree of variance between the Americans and British. Not only had FDR championed, with little popular support, the diplomatic recognition of the USSR in 1933, but he had dissociated himself from the allied intervention after the First World War. In February 1940, when the Finnish farce was still playing to feverish audiences, Roosevelt, in addition to some distinctly unfriendly comments about the current government, had made some exceptionally enlightened comments about the Russian Revolution.

More than twenty years ago . . . I had the utmost sympathy for the Russian people. In the early days of Communism I recognised that many leaders in Russia were bringing education and better health and, above all, better opportunity to millions who had been kept in ignorance and serfdom under the imperial regime.[1]

In relative terms, these casual comments placed Roosevelt in the forefront of liberal statesmen in the Western world. They were certainly the most favourable and enlightened on the Revolution ever uttered by an American President, before or since, and as such they were noted by the Soviets.[2]

As early as 15 June the Prime Minister had cabled FDR that should the Germans attack eastward 'we shall of course give all encouragement and any help we can spare to the Russians, following the principle that Hitler is the foe we have to beat'. The President had replied that he would publicly support 'any announcement that the Prime Minister might make welcoming Russia as an ally'.[3] It was no accident that Harry Hopkins, Churchill's and Roosevelt's most important agent in their dealings with Stalin, made the first personal contact. He was untainted by past events. While Hopkins had been in Britain conducting the preliminary discussions to the Atlantic conference, he had happened to meet Ambassador Maisky at Chequers; and Maisky had suggested that it would be most helpful if Hopkins could travel to Moscow for first-hand talks with Stalin. Hopkins, Roosevelt and Churchill could all immediately see the merits of the suggestion. Five days later, on 27 July 1941, Hopkins went off to Moscow on his most important unscheduled trip of the war.[4]

The effects of the Hopkins–Stalin meetings reinforced the Anglo-American commitment. In no small part this was the result of Stalin's candour in discussing the Soviet military situation and describing their long-term supply requirements. The impression that Hopkins carried away from these talks was sorely needed. The long-standing Soviet complaint that the Western powers were always willing to believe the worst about their capabilities was not unfounded. Both American and British military reports commonly predicted the defeat of the Soviets by October. Hopkins' report to Churchill and Roosevelt was a strong antidote to this widespread negativism and latent anti-Sovietism. The material results flowed more quickly. On 21 July 1941 President Roosevelt ordered 'immediate and substantial shipments of assistance' to the USSR. On 6 September Churchill offered

Stalin British military aid. Defeatists in the American military mission in Moscow were replaced by more realistic officers. Various Anglo-American supply missions were sent to Moscow during September and October. On 7 November FDR declared that the shipment of Lend–Lease supplies to the USSR was 'vital to the defence of the United States.'[5]

UNFINISHED BUSINESS

The fact remained, however, that except on the material level, where co-operation was always easy to obtain, political connections between the three nations were tenuous. While the supply and technical integration of the war wholesomely developed, Stalin, according to Lord Beaverbrook who had been in Moscow with W. Averell Harriman from 29 September to 1 October, persisted in 'drawing numberless pictures of wolves on paper and filling in the background with red pencil'.[6] Undoubtedly one source of Stalin's uneasiness was the lack of a European second front. As early as 18 July 1941 Stalin had suggested to Churchill that such a front should be established either in northern France or in the Arctic 'not only for the sake of our common cause, but also in Britain's own interest'. He had then gone on to explain that the timing was essential. 'The best time to open this front is now, seeing that Hitler's forces have been switched to the East and that he has not yet been able to consolidate the positions he has taken in the East.'[7] Churchill's cautious reply, dispersed between four messages received by Stalin from 21 July to 1 August, limited British support to air and naval operations against German shipping in northern Norway and Finland.[8] Very likely this extreme caution had been judged by Stalin to be somewhat insincere in the light of British enthusiasm for ground action in Finland—in the face of both German and Soviet opposition—not so many months earlier. By September Stalin saw the military situation, with the arrival of thirty or more German divisions 'with enormous numbers of tanks and aircraft' and the activisation of twenty Finnish and twenty-six Rumanian divisions, as having deteriorated to the point that the Soviet Union was in 'mortal danger'. As the Marshal told the Prime Minister, 'The Germans look on the threat in the West as a bluff, so they are moving all

their forces from the West to the East with impunity, knowing
that there is no second front in the West nor is there likely to be
one.'[9] In November Stalin's depression had been further increased when the British, apparently after having second thoughts,
reneged on a promise made in October to send several divisions
on expeditionary missions to relieve the Soviet position.[10]

Another factor which contributed to Stalin's melancholy was
the lack of any basic and political understanding between the
three powers. Within three weeks of the German attack on the
USSR, Stalin had proposed that such an understanding be incorporated in a UK–USSR political treaty.[11] By November, no
progressive steps in this direction had been taken. Stalin's analysis
of the situation, in a communication to Churchill, was faultless.

> I agree with you that we need clarity, which at the moment is lack-
> ing in relations between the USSR and Great Britain. The un-
> clarity is due to two circumstances: first, there is no definite
> understanding between our two countries concerning war aims and
> plans for the post-war organisation of peace; secondly, there is no
> treaty between the USSR and Great Britain on mutual military
> aid in Europe against Hitler. Until understanding is reached on
> these two main points, not only will there be no clarity in Anglo-
> Soviet relations, but, if we are to speak frankly, there will be no
> mutual trust. To be sure, the agreement on military supplies to the
> Soviet Union is of great positive significance, but that does not
> settle the issue, not does it fully cover the question of relations
> between our two countries.

In the succeeding paragraph, Stalin again indicated the high
priority he assigned to political issues when he warned Churchill
that if he persisted in sending Generals Wavell and Paget to
Moscow to discuss 'military supplies' and other lesser issues, then
he was not interested in receiving them.[12] With characteristic
bluntness, Stalin thus indicated that the preliminary discussions
were over.

Rather than being offended by Stalin's brusque message,
Churchill responded with considerable gusto. He promised Stalin
that Foreign Secretary Eden, with a high-class mission, would be
sent to Moscow in the near future 'and will be able to discuss
every question relating to the war, including the sending of troops
not only into the Caucasus, but into the fighting line of your armies

in the South'. The lure, if needed, had been exposed. The Prime Minister also promised that 'the post-war organisation of peace' and methods 'to prevent Germany, and particularly Prussia, from breaking out upon us for the third time' would be discussed as well.[13]

By the time Eden had arrived in Moscow on 16 December 1941, the Soviets had prepared a powerful brief. Stalin quickly informed Eden that he regarded the USSR's western frontiers 'as the main question for us in the war'.[14] After establishing that important point, Stalin proposed that the future map of Europe should very closely resemble the map that had existed immediately prior to the German invasion of the USSR on 22 June 1941 with exceptions at the expense of Germany. The Baltic states, Bessarabia, northern Bukovina, Petsamo, eastern Poland to the Curzon Line, with variations, and the few safety kilometres on the Karelian Isthmus would all remain part of the USSR. The Poles would get East Prussia; the Rumanians would grant the Soviets military bases and receive their pre-war territory seized by the Hungarians; Britain would get, if desired, military installations and bases in France, Belgium, Holland, Denmark, and Norway. To fragment future German power, Stalin proposed that the Rhineland, Austria, and possibly Bavaria, should all become separate states. The other European states, including Czechoslovakia, would be restored to their original frontiers, and would be free to form whatever federations they desired.[15]

According to Ambassador Winant, who was on excellent terms with Eden and was able to inform Roosevelt and Hull of the Moscow proceedings even before all of the members of the War Cabinet and Churchill had had full details, Stalin also told Eden that the most sensitive problems were those concerning the USSR's frontiers with Finland and Rumania, and the recognition of the USSR's incorporation of the Baltic states. He continued by saying that he thought a three-power agreement could be reached regarding Poland in the future. In conclusion, Winant reported Stalin as having told the Foreign Secretary that 'It is very important for us to know whether we shall have to fight at the peace conference in order to get our western frontiers.'[16]

Apart from a healthy exchange of views, nothing constructive resulted from Eden's Moscow mission. Despite the attractive bait

offered by Churchill in November, the British made no new
military commitments. Eden was sympathetic towards the Soviet
proposals, and impressed by their reasonableness, but he was not
prepared to accept them.[17] Churchill was implacably opposed to
the Soviet proposals both before and after the conferences.

> We have never recognised the 1941 frontiers of Russia except *de
> facto*. They were acquired by acts of aggression in shameful col-
> lusion with Hitler. The transfer of the peoples of the Baltic States
> to Soviet Russia against their will would be contrary to all the
> principles for which we are fighting this war and would dishonour
> our cause. This also applies to Bessarabia and to Northern Buko-
> vina, and in a lesser degree to Finland, which I gather it is not
> intended wholly to subjugate and absorb.[18]

The State Department with FDR's approval on 5 December
had instructed Winant to tell Eden, before going to Moscow, that
in accord with the Atlantic Charter the British should make no
territorial agreements with the Soviets and that the US would
recognise none. After the conference, when consulted about the
Soviet proposals, the Americans had remained 'sharp and negative' and approved of Churchill's above directive to Eden.[19]
Stalin's reaction to Eden's presentation of the American position
was this: 'I thought that the Atlantic Charter was directed against
those people who were trying to establish world domination. It
now looks as if the Atlantic Charter was directed against the
USSR.'[20]

The nadir was not as permanent as it appeared. The Americans
stood firm, the Soviets stood firm, but the British almost immediately began to waver. On 5 January 1942, Sir Stafford Cripps,
British Ambassador to the USSR, told the American Chargé that
he favoured UK and US recognition of the Soviet claim to the
Baltic states, Bessarabia, and Northern Bukovina.[21] Maisky in his
continuing negotiations with Eden in London found the latter
progressively weakening in his resolve. By 6 February the War
Cabinet was deeply divided over the issue.[22]

In Washington, Lord Halifax, Eden's predecessor as Secretary
of State for Foreign Affairs, told both Churchill and the Americans
in mid-February that in his opinion British policy in 1939 towards the Soviet absorption of the Baltic States had been one of

the prime causes of the rapid worsening of Anglo-Soviet relations and the signing of the Nazi–Soviet pact. He also added that 'the attitude of Great Britain with regard to the Baltic states had been the chief reason why the Soviet Union believed that the British policy was insincere and was demonstrating complete lack of appreciation of Russian need for security.'[23]

On 7 March Churchill exhibited one of his more remarkable volte-faces of the war years when he wrote the following to FDR:

> The increasing gravity of the war has led me to feel that the principles of the Atlantic Charter ought not to be construed so as to deny Russia the frontiers she occupied when Germany attacked her. This was the basis on which Russia acceded to the Charter . . . . I hope therefore that you will be able to give us a free hand to sign the treaty which Stalin desires, as soon as possible.[24]

This radical shift in British policy was occasioned by several considerations of varying merit. First, Churchill's reactionary original position had largely been unshared. Second, there were unfounded but real fears on both sides of the Atlantic that the Soviets, who again as in World War I looked to be the real losers, might negotiate a settlement with the Germans and drop out of the war. Third, some of the more enlightened members of the British government felt that to simultaneously deny the Soviets both their defensive frontiers and the immediate opening of a second front— the only two things the Soviets wanted from the US and Britain— was impolitic to an extreme. Fourth, for the optimists and realists alike it looked like the Soviets had asked for no more than they were likely to get in the end anyway. Fifth, there was considerable irritation with the American stand. Sixth, and perhaps most persuasive to those with a diplomatic bent, there was a strong possibility that a 'liberal' attitude on the other territories would strengthen Britain's bargaining hand when it came to Poland.[25]

There were various ranges of complexity within the American camp when it came to opposing the British position. At the simplistic level there was the view expressed in a long memorandum drafted by James C. Dunn and Ray Atherton of the State Department which advanced the nearly classical notion that 'the Soviet Government has tremendous ambitions with regard to Europe' and that acceptance of Soviet demands in the Baltic would result in 'a terrible blow to the whole cause of the United Nations'. Hull, in general, subscribed to these vintage views.[26] At the other extreme there was Roosevelt's position. When Ambassador Halifax had seen FDR on 17 February and expressed what was, in general, to be the new British position, Roosevelt had attempted to explain that timing was everything—the recognition of Soviet absorption of the Baltic states, which he did not oppose, should come after the war.[27] During a long conversation with Welles two days later, which the Under-Secretary of State reported to Halifax, the President had elaborated on his thinking. While the Soviets were 'entitled to obtain full and legitimate security at the termination of the war', the President also wished to discuss this matter directly with Stalin. The President felt the British were being, as he frankly put it, 'provincial' because they were attempting to settle one aspect of a problem before the entire list of negotiable items was known. In short, he felt that it was premature to settle the problem of the Baltic states as a security matter until the three powers had decided, for example, what they were going to do with Germany.[28]

THE PRIZE

After the interesting developments of February and March, Roosevelt showed how tenacious, subtle, and cosmopolitan he could be. At first he attempted to arrange a private meeting with Stalin, which the Soviet leader declined.[29] The War Cabinet on 8 April resolved to invite Molotov to London to negotiate a treaty which would incorporate the Soviet terms on frontiers.[30] The President in turn then proposed to Stalin that Molotov attend the next best thing to a personal meeting, a high-level conference in Washington. The difference in invitations was that FDR's was narrowly and strictly in keeping with his own negotiating axiom: solve secondary issues but delay on major ones until the whole range of pertinent interests and issues can be discussed and reconciled. It was also irresistible: 'I had in mind a very important military proposal involving the utilization of our armed forces in a manner to relieve your critical Western Front.' The rest was no less ingratiating and fascinating: 'This objective carries great weight with me. . . . I wish you would consider sending Mr Molo-

tov and a General. . . . Time is of the essence. . . . 1
advice before we determine with finality the strategic
our common military action.'[31]

At one time it was thought that Molotov's mission to L
was a failure. From the outside it looked as if, after four da
fruitless discussions, a Twenty Years Treaty was signed on 26 May
which in most respects did little more than formally legitimise the
working military agreements reached between the two governments the previous July. We now know, however, that Roosevelt's
'stratagem' had failed in advance. Eden explained it tersely to his
colleagues in October 1943:

> . . . When M. Molotov was in this country in May 1942 His
> Majesty's Government expressed their willingness to sign a treaty
> containing a form of words which, it was agreed, constituted
> recognition by us of the Soviet claim to the Baltic States. The draft
> treaty then under discussion was not in fact signed as it was
> superseded by the Twenty Years Treaty, in which nothing what-
> ever was said about frontiers. But we are fully committed to the
> Soviet Government on this point in the records of the discussion.[32]

When Molotov arrived at the White House on 29 May 1942, however, political issues were not on the agenda. In keeping with the
perimeter established by Roosevelt in his invitation, Molotov told
the Americans that the USSR's security required an Anglo-
American invasion at once sufficient to divert forty German
divisions from the eastern front. At the conclusion of Molotov's
justifiably grim presentation, Roosevelt, with General Marshall's
approval, told the commissar that the Soviets could expect a
second front in 1942. He later confirmed this in their last meeting
on 1 June. To further emphasise his resolve, FDR almost immediately sent a cable to Churchill stating that he was 'more anxious
than ever' that the cross-Channel invasion, SLEDGEHAMMER,
should begin in August and continue as long as the weather
permitted.[33]

There can be no doubt that the first two legs of Molotov's
journey had proved to be unprecedented Soviet diplomatic
triumphs. The third proved no more difficult. During Molotov's
first visit to London, the Prime Minister understandably had been
reluctant to commit his government to SLEDGEHAMMER—

although the official military historian of the period strongly suggests a decision had been taken against it by at least 27 May. Nevertheless, on 9 June Churchill told Molotov, after his return to London, that the UK was planning to send six divisions to France in the autumn with forty or fifty Anglo-American divisions to follow in 1943. The following day, Churchill confirmed to Molotov that preparations for SLEDGEHAMMER were proceeding; on the same day he was given an *aide mémoire* which stated that preparations were under way for a landing in August or September 1942 but that this as such constituted 'no promise in the matter'. The day after, 11 June, the Soviet cause leaped forward, if ever it had lagged, when Roosevelt's office, with the approval of the British, released a statement concerning his recent discussions with Molotov which stated that 'full understanding was reached with regard to the urgent tasks of creating a second front in Europe in 1942'. Regrettably on the same day the Cabinet generally agreed that SLEDGEHAMMER was off.[34]

THE EARLY FROST

General Eisenhower felt that the day the British irrevocably turned down SLEDGEHAMMER, 22 July 1942, would go down as the 'blackest day in history'.[35] Actually as far as US, UK and USSR relations were concerned there were to be several that were worse. Even before the official verdict, Churchill on 17 July cooled the optimism created by Molotov's tour of London and Washington. He notified Stalin that further convoys to northern Russian ports had become prohibitively expensive in terms of both equipment and human life and that all scheduled land and air operations in northern Norway were postponed until the season of winter darkness. The most singularly alarming parts of the message were the oblique references to 'the building-up of a really strong Second Front in 1943', an allusion to Rommel, and the promise of British 'help on your southern flank'.[36] Stalin's reply of 23 July was direct, to the point, and showed that the Marshal had fathomed Churchill's vague prose. He acknowledged that the convoys had been cancelled and, 'secondly, that despite the agreed Anglo-Soviet communiqué on the adoption of urgent measures to open a second front in 1942, the British Government is putting off the operation till 1943'. At the same time, however, he denied that the costly loss of convoy PQ17, which Soviet experts said resulted from 'puzzling and inexplicable' orders from the British Admiralty, justified stopping further convoys.[37] In fact, the demands of the Mediterranean were already beginning to pinch.

The entire matter was discreetly allowed to rest until 31 July when Stalin, at Churchill's prompting, invited the Prime Minister to Moscow.[38] If Churchill's news was already known to Stalin, the Prime Minister nevertheless found that his travelling time was an opportunity for reflection. 'I pondered on my mission to this sullen, sinister Bolshevik State I had once tried so hard to strangle at its birth, and which, until Hitler appeared, I had regarded as the mortal foe of civilized freedom.'[39] Predictably, little resulted from the August conference. Churchill presented what had become an Anglo-American position and denied that the 1943 second front was off. Stalin civilly refused to be persuaded that a northern European second front during 1942 was not best for the allied war effort. He did not bother to mention, as some sort of pathetic appeal, that the Soviets were passing through the worst period of the war and had already suffered great losses.[40] Thereafter, allied relations uneventfully spiralled downward. On 24 October, Churchill notified Roosevelt that he was alarmed at the lack of correspondence from Moscow: for two weeks there had been no news from the Soviets.[41] The freeze had begun that was to result in Stalin's refusal to attend the Casablanca conference.

THE SECOND FRONT RECONSIDERED

After the Casablanca conference, Roosevelt and Churchill informed Stalin that they had decided to launch large-scale operations in the Mediterranean and on the Continent against Germany and Italy during 1943. Stalin bluntly queried the timing and specific operations for a European second front in 1943. There followed a remarkable exchange of messages. Churchill informed Stalin on 9 February 1943 that during the summer Sicily was to be seized, 'promoting an Italian collapse', and the Dodecanese attacked; and at the same time he promised that a cross-Channel invasion would be launched in August or September at the latest. In November 1942, Marshal Stalin estimated that there were 240 enemy divisions on the Soviet front (179 German, 22 Rumanian, 14 Finnish, 10 Italian, 13 Hungarian, 1 Slovak and 1 Spanish). On 16 March 1943 Stalin informed Roosevelt that with the de-acceleration of the North Africa campaign the Germans had transferred thirty-six divisions to the Soviet front. In reply Roosevelt suggested to Churchill, not for the first time, that it would be wiser to 'delay in giving him the bad news' for three or four weeks, that convoys to the USSR would again have to be interrupted because of the operations in Sicily.[42]

By mid-April 1943, if not earlier, the Prime Minister had turned against ROUNDUP. As alternatives, he encouraged his Chiefs of Staff to prepare against German 'incursions' into the Spanish Peninsula. He also warned them that, 'We must not unduly or prematurely disturb our arrangements for defence against invasion.'[43] Undoubtedly many other plans yeasted in the Prime Minister's mind during the short weeks that passed before the third Washington conference (TRIDENT) in May. Aboard the *Queen Mary* on his way across the Atlantic, he had perfected his thinking to the point that he advocated defeating Germany by eliminating Italy from the war in 1943. As a minor matter, given an alternative, he wanted the allies to smite the Axis forces in Greece rather than Sardinia. Spain and invasion defence seemed no longer to be foremost in his mind.[44]

The fundamental divergence of strategic views, which had plagued Anglo-American relations and excluded almost all political considerations since nearly the beginning of the war, was clearly evident during the TRIDENT talks from 12 to 25 May. The question for both leaders was where to thrust after Sicily (operation HUSKY). Churchill presented his penultimate plan for winning World War II. 'The collapse of Italy would cause a chill of loneliness over the German people, and might be the beginning of their doom.' With Italy out of the war, Turkey, having resisted British cajolery for months, would also feel chilled and, after a realistic re-appraisal, would co-operate for the first time with the British and Americans; in the Balkans, where there were currently more than twenty-five Italian divisions, the Germans would either have to withdraw or direct 'large forces from the Russian front to fill the gap'. Roosevelt's attitude, which showed the influence of General Marshall and other American

military leaders, was quite different. The President sa
always shrunk from the thought of putting large armie
This might result in attrition for the United Nations and
Germany's hand.' FDR agreed with Churchill to the ex
since there were already twenty-five Anglo-American divisions in
the Mediterranean a second front in northern Europe would be
impossible during 1943. He insisted, however, that limitations be
placed on Anglo-American activities in Italy and the Mediterranean so that there would be no conflict with the build-up for a
successful cross-Channel invasion (OVERLORD) in 1944.[45]

As usual, throughout the third Washington conference the
Prime Minister had presented his minority case with great skill.
General Stilwell, who was always undiplomatically honest, felt
constrained to comment that 'the inevitable conclusion was that
Churchill has Roosevelt in his pocket'.[46] The agreements drafted
by the Combined Chiefs of Staff, and approved by the President
and Prime Minister on 25 May 1943, nevertheless incorporated
Roosevelt's ideas. The Anglo-American forces in the Mediterranean were to be limited to twenty-seven divisions. After 1
November 1943, seven divisions were to be held in readiness in
the UK as the nucleus of approximately thirty-four British and
American divisions which were to be ready by 1 May 1944 to
participate in OVERLORD.[47]

As was to be expected, June 1943 was a month of recrimina-
tions, evasions and abuse. Stalin complained, with some merit,
that a decision had been reached 'which may gravely affect the
subsequent course of the war' without consulting either political
or military leaders in the USSR. Roosevelt prevaricated and
attempted to divert attention from the second front to aluminium,
bombers and shipping. Churchill counter-attacked Stalin's
claims with considerable asperity and managed to have the last
word on 27 June. 'I am satisfied that I have done everything in
human power to help you. Therefore the reproaches which you
now cast upon your Western Allies leave me unmoved.' Stalin
replied by refusing to meet the western leaders and recalled
Ambassadors Litvinov and Maisky from Washington and London.[48]

THE FINAL ATTACK

Even after TRIDENT, the second front refused to remain stuck. The British still doubted the strategic soundness of American planning, and, especially the Prime Minister, continually had audible 'second thoughts' about the cross-Channel invasion. Secretary of War Henry L. Stimson became so agitated and suspicious of the quality of recent British undertakings that he went to London in July. There his worst fears were confirmed— British strategic thinking had reached the goal it had struggled towards all through the war. While Eden pressed for the Balkans and Greece, Churchill argued mightily for a massive invasion of Italy which would enable the British and Americans to liberate Rome at an early date. When Stimson checked with General Marshall and the Operations Division of the American General Staff, they were unanimous in their opposition to a tedious and costly pursuit of the Germans and Italians up the 'leg' of Italy, which might result in a further postponement of OVERLORD. Faced with this united block of opposition, Churchill burst into a fresh attack on the entire cross-Channel mission and stated that if he were commander-in-chief he would cancel the entire operation—while all the time acknowledging, since he was not, that the British were committed to the operation and good to their word. After a quick trip to North Africa, where Stimson and Eisenhower agreed to stand firm against what Stimson called the 'British conception' of the war, FDR vigorously supported Stimson's endeavours to put the war back on a firm military footing.[49] When the British Chiefs of Staff issued a 'standstill' order on the movement of British troops and equipment out of the Mediterranean, a bitter impasse had been reached which could only be resolved by another military conference.[50]

Churchill's last grand opportunity to derail OVERLORD came in August 1943, from the 14th to 24th, during the Quebec conference (QUADRANT). He faced implacable opposition. The US Chiefs of Staff proposed that 'The Combined Chiefs of Staff reaffirm the decisions of the TRIDENT Conference as to the execution of OVERLORD including the definite allotment of forces thereto and assign to it an over-riding priority over other preparations in the European Theatre.' They then went on to attack the

UNIVERSITY OF \
LIBRARY
515 Portage A\
Winnipeg. Manitoba

tactical bias of Churchill's position by asserting that 'the acceptai
of this decision must be without conditions and without men...
reservation . . . long-range decisions for the conduct of the war must
not be dominated by possible eventualities'. It was too much, too
powerful, too fierce. The Prime Minister's wiles were subtle and
numerous, but his arguments were dated and lacked credibility.
In the end some of his military chiefs defected to the American
side. The Combined Chiefs of Staff concluded that OVERLORD
'will be the primary United States–British ground and air effort
against the Axis in Europe. (Target date the 1st May, 1944)'.[51]
Some observers felt that Churchill secured some important cavils,
but in fact there were too many decisional precedents against him
and support for the second front was too thick and dense to be
dissolved.[52]

In the end all Churchill got was more conferences, discussions,
rebuffs, and even more opposition from within his own supporting
ranks. In October the Prime Minister requested the British Chiefs
of Staff to prepare a staff study of alternatives 'with particular
reference' to the situation in the Balkans. In his words, 'Pray let
this enquiry be conducted in a most secret manner and on the
assumption that commitments into which we have already entered
with the Americans particularly as regards OVERLORD could
be modified by agreement to meet the exigencies of a changing
situation.' If the Balkan campaign were agreeable, it would not be
necessary to 'recant on OVERLORD except as regards emphasis
and the balance of our effort'.[53] A month later the US Joint
Chiefs of Staff with cold blood forestalled Churchill's effort by
strongly recommending to the Combined Chiefs of Staff that 'the
Balkan–Eastern Mediterranean approach to the European Fortress
is unsuitable, due to terrain and communication difficulties for
large-scale military operations . . .'. Instead they recommended
increased military assistance for the partisans in the region.[54] On
22 November Churchill submitted a minute to the British Chiefs
of Staff in which he argued that delay was essential. 'We are now
faced with the prospect that a fixed target date for OVERLORD
will continue to wreck and ruin the Mediterranean campaign: that
our affairs will deteriorate in the Balkans and that the Aegean will
remain firmly in German hands. All this is to be accepted for the
sake of an operation fixed for May . . . .' Specifically he recom-

mended that the build-up for OVERLORD be stopped, that Rome be taken immediately, and that bridgeheads be established on the Dalmatian coast.[55] When the Chiefs considered the communication on the same day, the Chief of the Imperial General Staff, General Brooke, 'pointed out that the minute was inaccurate in respect of a number of items, and in its present form was not therefore suitable for communication to the Americans'.[56] The following day Brooke, Air Chief Marshal Sir Charles Portal, Chief of the Air Staff, and Admiral of the Fleet Sir Andrew Cunningham, First Sea Lord and Chief of Naval Staff, wrote the Prime Minister a joint letter in which they stated that 'Broadly speaking, we entirely agree with your general thesis, but we feel that some of the arguments which you deploy are contestable and that they weaken rather than strengthen our case.' Thereafter they proceeded to refuse to endorse the Dalmatian coast scheme which was at the very heart of Churchill's minute.[57]

Being a man of full character, there was nothing else for the Prime Minister to do but to labour the point again before Roosevelt, Stalin and other important dignitaries at the Cairo and Tehran conferences, on various inopportune occasions between 22 November and 7 December 1943.[58] On 5 December 1943, the Combined Chiefs of Staff concluded that OVERLORD and ANVIL (a supporting operation in southern France which Stalin, among others, endorsed) were 'the supreme operations for 1944. They must be carried out during May, 1944. Nothing must be undertaken in any other part of the world which hazards the success of these two operations.'[59]

THE UNSATISFACTORY RESULT

Very likely there will never be a definite answer to the question whether a successful northern European second front could have been established in 1942–3. The question does not readily submit itself to historical-objective analysis. Even without the benefit of 'an answer', however, it remains one of the most central and critical problems of the war because it revealed important attitudes that coloured subsequent events, relations, and objectives. Some conclusions are unavoidable.

Prime Minister Churchill supplied the motive force beh
everything that is most interesting concerning the diplomatic
aspects of the second front. He suffered, with many of his advisers,
from a variant of Empire mentality which made him see Britain's
strategic and European interests primarily in terms of the Mediterranean. In the interests of furthering this vision, he was willing to
go to great extremes and risk many of the advances his government
had made during the early months of the war in improving relations with the USA. This vision of British interests also made
him singularly indifferent, if not hostile, to the military requirements of the USSR. He never fully shared the conviction, generally held by the Americans, that military planning must to a large
extent be for the purpose of enhancing the Soviet Union's war
efforts against Nazi Germany.[60] This became obvious during the
spring of 1943 when Churchill could begin to see that with the
USSR and Germany locked in mortal combat there were large
strategic gains to be had in the Balkans and southern Europe for
only relatively small losses.[61] He persisted in espousing the merits
of this plan even when it failed to win the support of reputable
military experts on either side of the Atlantic as the most ex-
peditious way of ending the war, and even when it was contrary
to undertakings the British had already made to the USA. Finally
it is obvious that during this period the best efforts of the Prime
Minister were continually frustrated. One military scheme after
another was put aside both in Washington and London. His views
on the question of the readjustment of the USSR's frontiers were
specifically rejected by his own government and by Roosevelt.
In short, Churchill found himself leading, but at the same time
increasingly out of step.

The second front as a diplomatic issue was clearly mishandled
by both the British and Americans. Allied, in the sense of three-
power, planning was never instituted during the war on a permanent basis. Even on the Anglo-American side, after Stalin initially
confused the issue, the second front was treated as both a political
and a military issue when it had best been treated exclusively as
a military matter by the Combined Chiefs of Staff. Roosevelt in his
efforts to forestall British attempts to settle the problem of the
Baltic States compounded the issue, and he and Marshall should
never have promised more to Molotov in May and June 1942

than they could guarantee. There were fewer mitigating factors to justify the misunderstandings caused by the British.

The product of Anglo-American policy failures, which were nearly all avoidable, was that the Soviets were twice bitterly disappointed in their expectations for an early second front; consequently, for most of the period from the summer of 1942 until the Tehran conference in late 1943, they were aggrieved, and for more than a year they virtually withdrew from the 'alliance', ie from approximately September 1942 until the Moscow conference of Foreign Ministers in October 1943.

The most profound result of the uncertainty which plagued Anglo-American planning was that in the interim period Britain and the US had removed themselves from the dynamic centre of the European conflict. As Churchill's mentor, the avuncular Field-Marshal Smuts,[62] wrote him on 31 August 1943, the fact remained that the Red Armies had been on the march:

> While our Middle East campaign was conducted with conspicuous vigour from El Alamein to the end of Tunisia, I sense a slackening and tardiness in operations since then. It took us several months between Tunisia and the Sicilian landing, and there is now another strange pause after Sicily at a stage in our affairs when the urgency is very great. To compare the Anglo-American effort, with all our vast resources, with that of Russia during the same period is to raise uncomfortable questions which must occur to many others. Our comparative performance on land is insignificant and its speed very unsatisfactory . . . almost all the honours on land go to the Russians, and deservedly so, considering the scale and speed of their fighting and the magnificence of their strategy on a vast front.

As Smuts was quick to notice, the Soviets were beyond the danger point and were potentially an unsettling influence in Europe. If the Red Army advances continued 'A tremendous shift in our world status may follow. . . . Unless we emerge from the war on terms of equality our position will be both uncomfortable and dangerous.'[63] This kind of analysis, to which Churchill increasingly turned, undoubtedly helps to account for Churchill's last futile efforts to stop the second front, but more important it helps to explain the new thrust in British policy after the second front had become an inescapable commitment.

Notes to this chapter are on pages 189–92.

Chapter 3 THE QUIET PEACE

WHILE THE British and American leaders were still preoccupied with the problems of military strategy, with their troops engaged in the Sicilian campaign and their commanders preparing for an assault on southern Italy, the Italian government showed the first signs of a crack-up. While it was not totally unexpected, the allies were diplomatically and politically ill-prepared for the event. There was no machinery to ensure consultation, and, if there had been, there was no agency to implement joint policies. The only common political bonds between the three major allied leaders were the Atlantic Charter and the doctrine of 'unconditional surrender' which Roosevelt had unilaterally proclaimed at the end of the Casablanca conference on 24 January 1943.[1]

In Italy, as was later to be the case in Rumania, Bulgaria, Hungary, Finland, and even Germany, right-wing realists with an appreciation of the developing military situation made the first peace overtures to the allies. This was only to be expected: they were the only resident figures at ground-level who wielded the authority to redirect the nation's efforts. Ivanoe Bonomi had started preparations for an anti-Mussolini coup during the first months of 1943 which led to the formation of an action committee in April and culminated in a majority of monarchists, army generals, and other members of the Fascist Grand Council voting for Mussolini's removal on 25 July 1943.[2] It remained patently clear nevertheless that the King, Victor Emmanuel III, who supported the coup, had played a central role in the establishment and consolidation of the Italian fascist state in 1922, and that he had never at any subsequent important juncture felt that Mussolini's actions or political philosophy were inimical to his own or his nation's self interests. There also was no doubt that Marshal Badoglio,

the emergent political leader of the realists, had long been a prominent servant of the fascist state.[3] The simple truth was that not
much had changed: 'The Fascist chiefs hoped to save their
personal positions, and what might possibly be salvaged of
Fascism. The King was primarily concerned with the future of his
dynasty; and the Army Generals, with their careers.'[4]

The new Italian leaders may have lacked the romantic fervour
of the cultists who supported Mussolini to the last, and showed
a more than healthy concern for their own welfare, but they
nevertheless took an inordinate amount of time to settle on a new
course of action. At first they idled in the German camp without
Mussolini, who later in September made an easy escape from his
captors. Then they ceased giving orders, even with a disproportionate number of generals among their ranks, while the military
situation dramatically worsened. At the time of the coup, there
had been only seven German divisions in Italy—three months
later there were more than three times that number. They had
altogether failed to mobilise the Italian home reserve, the population, or the remnants of the Italian army which were still loyal
to the King. At length they removed themselves to southern Italy,
safely behind the allied lines. The Germans then proceeded, as
expected, to fill the political and military vacuum by occupying
Rome and disarming some sixty-one aimless Italian divisions.
No matter how one looked at the balance sheet the allies got a
dubious bargain: they received the surrender of part of the
Italian navy that no longer wished to sail and the dregs of an army
that no longer wished to fight, from a reactionary government
that was incapable of governing either.[5]

The Prime Minister's reaction to the preliminary Italian government was interesting to an extreme. Underlying it was his unique,
highly personalised analysis of the fascist period in Italy. As far
as Churchill was concerned, even in 1952 twenty-one years of
fascism under Mussolini had not been without achievements, for
they had saved the people from the horrors of Bolshevism and
had given the nation 'a new impulse' and an empire in North
Africa. The only inherent evil of Italian fascism had been its
'fatal mistake' in declaring war on France and Britain.[6] According
to Churchill the historian, Mussolini 'had exercised almost
absolute control and could not cast its burden on the Monarchy,

Parliamentary institutions, the Fascist Party, or the General Staff. All fell on him.'[7] In contradistinction to Clement Attlee, the Deputy Prime Minister, who could see the essentially class and economic dimension of fascism,[8] Churchill on 26 July 1943 was already anticipating the fall of Italian fascism.[9] On the same day early in the rush of events, he was able to instruct FDR as to the proper course of action: 'I don't think myself that we should be too particular in dealing with any non-Fascist Government, even if it is not all we should like.' Five days later he added that 'I am not in the least afraid . . . to recognize the House of Savoy or Badoglio, provided they . . . do what we need for our war purposes. Those purposes would certainly be hindered by chaos, Bolshevisation, or civil war.'[10] On 5 August, Churchill was able to unreservedly assure FDR, only two days after the signing of the Armistice, that 'Fascism in Italy is extinct. Every vestige has been swept away.'[11]

American interest in political issues throughout this mid-war period was something less than positive: it was an attitude of bewildered concern. At the same time, if the US were to keep their hands in the area at all, while the British were constructing 'a presence', it required a very carefully delineated arrangement. As described by the then Assistant Secretary of State, the US would have 'equivalent' military and political representation in Italy but 'the authority of the United States should be supplementary rather than equal to that of Great Britain'.[12] Taking advantage of this situation, the Prime Minister on 9 August instructed the Foreign Secretary, who had expressed concern about the application of the phrase 'unconditional surrender', that political considerations did not require a slavish application of the phrase in all circumstances. As an alternative Churchill suggested that the Italians place themselves 'unreservedly in the hands of the Allied Governments', pledge themselves to gaining 'a respectable place in the new Europe', and be granted an ' "honourable capitulation" '.[13] This advice seemed to mesh nicely with the President's sentiments on 26 July when he had written Churchill that he hoped the Italian settlement would be 'as close as possible to unconditional surrender'.[14] In fact, after being notified of Churchill's reservations, on 12 August, FDR agreed to 'an honourable capitulation'[15] even though he had recently, on 28

July, told the American people that 'Our terms to Italy are still
the same as our terms to Germany and Japan—"unconditional
surrender". We will have no truck with Fascism in any way, shape,
or manner. We will permit no vestige of Fascism to remain.'[16]

The Soviet reaction was quite different. As early as 29 July
a representative of the Soviet Embassy in London had called on
Anthony Eden and suggested three-power discussions on Italian
armistice terms. Eden had put him off.[17] Two days later Sir
Archibald Clark Kerr, Ambassador in Moscow, reported to the
Foreign Office that the Soviets were worried that the Italians would
not be required to surrender unconditionally. They were also
'much upset by what they regard as the exclusiveness of the British
and American approach to the whole question of Italy. They claim
that we owe it to them to consult them, inasmuch as on their front
they have fought and beaten as many Italian armies as we have. . . .'[18]
By 9 August Under Secretary of State Breckingridge Long had
become upset when he discovered that FDR and Churchill had
decided upon surrender terms without consulting the Soviets. He
noted in his diary that 'there is a growing feeling on the part of
Stalin that Churchill and Roosevelt are trying to decide the questions of the war without his collaboration and without even notice
to him of decisions having been taken'.[19]

The growing suspicion that Long detected on the 9th became
manifest to all on 24 August when Stalin burst forth with a violent
warning to Churchill and FDR, who were then conversing at
Quebec about the future of the second front. 'Until now the matter
stood as follows: the United States and Great Britain made agreements but the Soviet Union received information about the results
as a passive third observer. I have to tell you that it is impossible
to tolerate the situation any longer.' The Marshal then proceeded
to suggest that a military–political commission be established by
the three nations 'with the purpose of considering the questions
concerning the negotiations with the different governments dissociating themselves from Germany'.[20]

The Foreign Office, which had proposed a commission not
dissimilar to Stalin's in July and the War Cabinet could both see
the merits of Stalin's plan. Attlee on 25 August informed Churchill
that the Cabinet strongly supported the commission because it
established 'the principle of reciprocity'. To deny the proposal

would 'give them an excuse to deal independently with Germany and Eastern Europe generally'. Even more significant the War Cabinet felt that the Russians would regard the Italian settlement 'as a test case which will determine their future attitude towards collaboration'.[21] The Foreign Office in turn supported the plan enthusiastically, believing that it might become a permanent body to deal with other outstanding political problems arising during the war and would healthily 'impinge upon the monopoly at present enjoyed by the Combined Chiefs of Staff in Washington, to whom all armistice questions have to be submitted for approval'.[22]

Churchill and Roosevelt also welcomed Stalin's proposal. Churchill immediately proposed that the French be admitted as a full member of the commission. Within a day Stalin replied that while he had originally envisaged only a tripartite commission, he would accept a representative of the French National Liberation Committee.[23] FDR suggested that Stalin send a staff officer to General Eisenhower's headquarters and that the French be excluded from the discussions relating to the military occupation of Italy. Stalin hinted that he did not care about the French one way or the other and that the matter could be settled at a later date; he stated categorically that the sending of an officer was not a satisfactory alternative to his original plan and that 'Much time has passed, but nothing is done.' FDR suggested that the commission meet in Algiers instead of Sicily as originally proposed. Stalin surprised both the Foreign Office and the State Department by stating that A. Y. Vyshinski, the Assistant Chairman of the Soviet of People's Commissars and Assistant Commissar for Foreign Affairs, and A. E. Bogomolov, the Ambassador to the Allied Governments in London, would arrive in Algiers the last week in September.[24] The American Chargé in the USSR informed the State Department that Vyshinsky, the leader of the Soviet delegation, had been in effect the third ranking man in the Kremlin for several months past and had been serving in effect as the Soviet People's Commissar for Foreign Affairs. He further reminded the State Department that neither the American nor the British representatives to the commission were in the same diplomatic class. The Foreign Office concurred that the Soviets were giving the politico-military commission the highest priority.[25] When Churchill suggested that representatives of the Greek and

Yugoslav governments also be invited to participate in the work of the commission, Stalin did not object. The Foreign Secretary re-emphasised the original intention that the commission should deal 'not merely with Italian interests, but also with the affairs of the other Axis satellites, any one of whom may approach us at any time'. The President seemed reluctant to accept this point.[26]

On 29 September Badoglio signed the Anglo-American surrender document, largely a product of American efforts, which made provision for an Allied Advisory Council for Italy under the general direction of the Allied Commander-in-Chief, but which in no way resembled Stalin's proposed tripartite commission.[27] By 30 September the Foreign Office began to have serious doubts about the politico-military commission because they feared that Vyshinsky supported by the French representative, Monsieur René Massigli, the Commissioner for Foreign Affairs of the French Committee of National Liberation, would attempt to make the politico-military commission dominant in Italian affairs. At the heart of the matter the Foreign Office feared that 'there will be great reluctance on the part of our own and the American military authorities to allow the Russians any real say in the actual organisation of civil affairs within the Anglo-American theatres'.[28] And this was exactly the point. By 8 October 1943, Churchill and Roosevelt were in agreement that in effect they had rejected Stalin's August proposal.[29]

Despite the lengthy, frustrating and complicated negotiations, on 10 November General Eisenhower announced the formation of the Anglo-American Allied Control Commission for Italy. Additionally, an Anglo-American Allied Military Government was created which merged with the Control Commission, after a short life, in January 1944. Until the rationalisation of these two organisations, and the resultant cessation of the overlap of activities, the Military Government theoretically ruled Italy in the name of the occupying powers while the Allied Control Commission worked through the Italian Government. If there was confusion caused by the titles of the organisations as to their specific duties, there was no doubt as to who was making the decisions: the United States and Britain staffed the two groups, shared the financial and legal responsibilities, split the costs of their operations, and issued the orders. On 30 November the Soviets received their unsatisfactory sop when the Advisory Council for Italy was established with its headquarters in Algiers. Initially, René Massigli was its chairman, with Robert Murphy, Harold Macmillan, and Andrei Vyshinsky as its charter members. After the new year, representatives of the shaky Greek and Yugoslav governments joined the Council.[30] There was never any intention that this organisation would move from North Africa closer to Italian operations, and it never did. Stalin's grievance remained outstanding.

Internal Developments

The earliest signs of resistance to Mussolini, prior to the rightist coup of 25 July, came in the form of communist-led strikes in northern Italy during March. Unlike other European nations in 1943, 'the resistance did not exist save as an abstraction, and, of course, as a fear in the minds of the Italian elite and Anglo-American leaders'.[31] In this respect there were initially no anti-fascist military groups to be considered by the royal government. The fear of something more, none the less, persisted. Churchill especially viewed continuing public and union protests in the north with alarm. In August, apparently on the basis of a report from an underling formerly associated with Count Ciano, Mussolini's son-in-law, Churchill was prepared to inform Roosevelt that the worst had already happened.

> Italy turned Red overnight. In Turin and Milan there were Communist demonstrations which had to be put down by armed force. Twenty years of Fascism had obliterated the middle class. There is nothing between the King, with the Patriots who have rallied round him, who have complete control, and rampant Bolshevism.[32]

This fantasy, unsubstantiated by any hard intelligence before or after, failed to reveal that the bulk of the German Army in Italy (and subsequently the Anglo-American forces as well) stood solidly between the strikers of Milan and Turin and Victor Emmanuel and his patriots. Nevertheless this bogus fear, that some sort of red resistance threatened the 'legitimate' authority, was to become the inner spring of Churchill's outlook. While the Prime Minister was looking north, however, there were forces already apparent on the political horizon in the south that had real vigour and substance.

Prior to the defection of the monarchists from the Nazi alliance, the Committee of National Liberation (CLN) had been established in southern Italy by six parties ranging across the political spectrum. From left to right, these were the Communist and Socialist parties, the Action Party (the only one of the six that had not existed before the fascist period), the Democratic Labour Party, the Christian Democrats, and the Italian Liberal Party. While the composition of the CLN was necessarily skewed to the left, in the absence of any outrightly pro-fascist parties, the leadership was safely in the hands of venerable liberals of the pre-fascist period such as Benedetto Croci, aged seventy-seven, and Count Carlo Sforza, aged seventy. With the exception of the Liberal Party and some members of the Christian Democrats, the CLN early went on record as being opposed to any continuation of the monarchy. On 12 November the CLN in Naples, encouraged by mass meetings in other cities throughout Italy, called for the immediate abdication of King Victor Emmanuel and the formation of a non-royal government.[33] While the Bolshevist resistance was not running rampant over the length and breadth of the country, it was obvious that equally powerful forces were. Sooner than expected by some, it looked as if, with the assistance of the CLN, there was going to be an early implementation of the allied pledge at the Foreign Ministers' conference in Moscow 'that nothing can detract from the absolute and untrammelled right of the people of Italy by constitutional means to decide on the democratic form of government they will eventually have'.[34] The monarchists firmly refused to acknowledge or co-operate with the CLN no matter how broadly based or popular it was.[35]

As has been noted, the British position, due to Churchill's dynamism, had definition. By comparison the Americans groped. In one corner were spokesmen who saw in Italy, perhaps as in no other post-war situation, an opportunity for creating a liberal democratic government. Hopkins, as one of the pre-eminent members of the inner circle, in August expressed serious doubts about the democratic instincts of Badoglio and the King.[36] Hull, that quixotic liberal, felt on this occasion that the King had 'to all intents and purposes, gone along with Mussolini' and that Badoglio was not 'adequate for the purpose of governing Italy'.[37] There were others in the administration, like Stimson, who advised the President in September that 'It would be a mistake for us to try to impose from outside too hastily a modern democracy upon a government which has had such a history of free parliamentary government.'[38] There were also those in Washington, the supposed realists, who put forward the seemingly reasonable argument that the military situation justified the postponement of all political questions. Without any clear idea of what was wanted for the future, Roosevelt met this latter group and the British at the realist position which could easily be justified in patriotic terms having to do with the saving of American and British lives. On 22 September Hull cabled Robert D. Murphy, the State Department's representative on Eisenhower's staff, that the General 'should make recommendations from time to time to lighten the provisions of the Italian armistice in order to permit the Italians to wage war against Germany within the limit of their capacities'.[39] The expected profits flowing from such a policy undoubtedly seemed humane and honest.

Hopkins remained unconverted. On 20 September he again advised FDR to insist on unconditional surrender. 'I cannot see that a declaration of war by Badoglio gets us anywhere except a precipitated recognition of two men who have worked very closely with the Fascists in the past.'[40] Ironically at the very time of Hopkins' warnings, allied military authorities had decided independently that the common effort would be best advanced without Italian military help. Only four days earlier an informed member of Eisenhower's staff noted in his diary that 'Outside of the acquisition of the Italian fleet we have virtually nothing to gain, certainly, from the Army, except as the soldiers may be used as labour at ports and on our line of communication.'[41] In fact with the exception of one Italian motorised unit which saw action in December 1943 after re-training, no units of the Italian Army were engaged in the allied cause until November 1944; and even then they amounted to only some five combat groups.[42] None the less, despite these early warnings, the diplomatic machine continued to whirr and on 13 October 1943 the status of the oldest and closest ally of Nazi Germany was re-established when the US and UK recognised the royal Italian government 'as a co-belligerent in the war against Germany'.[43]

The leaders of the CLN continued to press ahead with demands for internal reform. In early November Count Sforza, acting on behalf of the CLN, presented the King with abdication papers which named the King's six-year-old grandson as the successor until a national referendum could be held. The King refused to sign. The CLN remained united and on 13 November Marshal Badoglio acknowledged to the nation that he had failed to form a government of 'the more outstanding representatives of all political parties, none excluded, so that the Government could assume a completely democratic aspect'. He also announced that Count Sforza and Benedetto Croci refused with other CLN leaders to participate in his government until the King abdicated in favour of the Prince of Naples. Concluding on a positive note, Badoglio stated that he was forming a government of non-political 'experts' as an alternative to a democratic government.[44] And so the first in a series of transparent delaying tactics was used.

Churchill's attitude throughout this period remained as constant as the northern star. He was convinced that King Victor Emmanuel and Badoglio would be able to do more for what had now become the common cause than any Italian government formed from the exiles or opponents of the Fascist regime. On 1 October he attempted to warn FDR about Count Sforza and implied that his republican activities on behalf of the CLN were somehow subversive and contrary to the war effort. A month later he again counselled Roosevelt against allowing the 'King–Badoglio show' to be broken up and further advised that allied support should be given to the royal government until Rome had been captured and 'a really broad based Italian Government can be formed'.[45]

The Promising Start

During the last days of January 1944, the Bari Congress of the CLN passed a resolution calling for the summoning of a constituent assembly at the end of hostilities and the immediate delegation of the King's powers to a collegiate regency, which was to appoint a cabinet composed of CLN representatives.[46] Churchill's answer to the Bari resolution came in messages to FDR on 3 and 13 February. Despite evidence to the contrary, he linked the existing government with the war effort and attacked the CLN as 'the worn-out debris of political parties, none of whom have the slightest title by election or prescription'. Later in the month, before the House of Commons, he returned to his theme that politically all had been contaminated in Italy except the monarchy. On 11 February, even before the full weight of Churchill's rhetorical efforts had been felt, Roosevelt notified the Prime Minister that he had ordered the Department of State not to effect or encourage any change in the present government until the military situation had improved. By mid-March, however, the President had allowed himself to be guided by Hopkins and occasionally by Hull towards a more daring course of action, which in effect got his administration out of the Prime Minister's wake, when he informed him that 'I did not at any time intend to convey to you agreement that we postpone all political decisions until after Rome had been taken.' Continuing in this spirit—while bolstering his presentation with the argument that all respectable military opinion, including that of General Sir Henry Maitland Wilson, supported political change—Roosevelt boasted that for the first time military and political considerations had been harmonised. In brief, the President announced that his administration was taking note that public opinion 'would never understand our continued tolerance and apparent support of Victor Emmanuel' and was immediately supporting the CLN's programme. After a hurried meeting which failed to support the Prime Minister's earlier claims of solidarity, the War Cabinet, within two days of receiving FDR's last message, also decided to support the CLN's proposals for a more democratic government. A cruel blow had been struck.

During the course of 1944 the locus of Italian political activity moved gradually from the south to the north. By January the poorly organised resistance movements in the north had formed the Committee of National Liberation of Upper Italy (CLNAI) and begun to show signs of political cohesion. During March the CLNAI instigated the most successful general strike of the war in Nazi-occupied Europe. As an associative branch of the CLN, the CLNAI greatly enhanced the bargaining power of their political associates in the south. Even after the creation of Mussolini's Republican Fascist Party and the intensified control of the northern area by German troops, the numerous massive strikes in the north, especially in Turin, gave a ring of authority to the CLN that it had never had before. Even though the allied represen-

tatives and Badoglio refused to integrate CLNAI partisan units
into the remnants of the Italian army, and gave them a low
priority in terms of equipment and training, their movement
became the illegitimate government of northern Italy.[47] By
October the Earl of Selborne, Minister of Economic Warfare,
reported to Churchill that CLNAI units comprised 150,000
members, a number which could be doubled with sufficient
supplies, and that 'they have done a magnificent job . . . in fact,
just as good as the French did'. Churchill agreed and they were
kept in the field.[48]

During the last week in March, with the CLNAI beginning to
exert its influence, Palmiro Togliatti, the long-exiled leader of
the Italian Communist Party (PCI) arrived from the USSR and
rapidly demonstrated that he was prepared to unpack the political
deadlock. On 1 April 1944, the National Council of the PCI and
Togliatti declared that they were prepared to enter the Badoglio
government as part of a liberal anti-fascist front in the interests
of a maximum national effort against the fascists in the north.[49]
Independently Roosevelt increased the pressure on the King
and Badoglio by recalling Robert Murphy to Washington and
empowering him, if necessary, to insist on the King's abdication.
On 10 April, Murphy pressed the King to accept the CLN's
long-standing plan. Two days later Victor Emmanuel III declared
that he would abdicate in favour of his son 'on the day on which the
Allied troops enter Rome'.[50] While less than the CLN asked for,
it was a significant step forward.

Ten days later, Badoglio formed his third government. All the
chief military posts were retained by the old guard, and the
former 'technicians' still held prominent positions. Croci, Sforza,
Togliatti, and other prominent CLN members were forced to
serve as ministers without portfolios. The centrifugal forces
working against the government from the start were considerable.
Badoglio became increasingly unpopular when it was known that
his earlier governments had failed to implement effective de-
fascistisation programmes.[51] The Action Party and Pietro Nenni's
Socialists exacerbated the situation by proclaiming radical and
popular reform proposals.[52] The leader of Churchill's red menace,
however, played a quiet game. Rather than exploit the manifest
weaknesses of the Badoglio government, the PCI adopted a

thoroughly collaborationist policy and in general 'carefully
avoided getting involved or committed on questions of principle
and ideology, preferring the substantial political advantages to be
achieved by viable tactics'.[53] As a result, whatever stability the
short-lived third Badoglio government enjoyed was largely the
product of PCI tactics. There was nothing incidental in the fact
that between 'the end of 1943 and July 1944 the party's membership quadrupled, as it did again over the next year and a half'.[54]
Unquestionably the quiet game paid spectacular dividends.

The liberation of Rome on 4 June marked the end of the old
order and of the transition period. The following day Prince
Umberto appointed Ivanoe Bonomi, chairman of the Rome
Committee of National Liberation and the leader of the Labour
Democrats, to head a new government. This time, on 18 June,
all the cabinet positions but one went to CLN politicians.[55]
Churchill was 'astounded' even before the government was
formed and complained to Stalin, almost as if to a personal friend,
'that we have lost the only competent man we had to deal with and
one who was bound to serve us best. The present cluster of aged
and hungry politicians will naturally endeavour to push Italian
claims and might be the greatest possible inconvenience to us.'
Stalin was also astounded that the change could have taken place
'regardless of the will of the Allies' but asseverated that 'In any
case, if for you and the Americans circumstances suggest that it is
necessary to have another government in Italy and not the Bonomi
Government, then you can count on there being no objection to
this from the Soviet side.'[56] These were all fitting comments.

On balance, the Italian peace settlement was successful. While
it was in no way an allied one, there can be no doubt that Roosevelt
and his colleagues had achieved a victory for liberalism in Italy.
Despite the considerable obstacles placed in their way by the old
order in Italy and its supporters in the British government, the
Americans in accord with the mood of the times played a part in
allowing the monarchy to be dealt a series of blows from which it
never recovered. At the same time the rightists were squeezed
out of office and representatives of the legitimate anti-fascist
parties, including the CPI, were encouraged to assume control of
the government. At least as important, while Churchill had
attempted to bolster the pre-war order by raising a stentorian

anti-Bolshevist cry, Roosevelt had remained realistically calm and had eventually pursued an independent policy of his own.

The history of the pre- and post-war Russo-Finnish settlement is a study of restraint on the part of the victor.[57] During Anthony Eden's visit to Moscow in December 1941 Stalin frankly told him that the Soviets wanted a re-establishment of the pre-war Finnish–Soviet frontier.[58] Ambassador Cripps shortly thereafter stated that he had heard the Soviets also wanted control of Petsamo in the far north.[59] Nothing of any significance had changed during the next two or three years. At Tehran Stalin reiterated his earlier terms and further clarified the details for his allies: the Finns were to expel units of the German army from their territory and then reduce the size of their armed forces to their peacetime strength; reparations were to be fixed at fifty per cent of the damage caused to the peoples of the Soviet Union and paid over a five-to-eight-year period; in exchange for the reversion of long-term Soviet interests on the Hanko Peninsula the Finns were to give Petsamo to the USSR.[60] All of this was proposed before the bitterly destructive German–Finnish blockade of Leningrad had been broken (in January 1944)—at a time when anti-Finnish sentiments in the USSR were probably at their height.[61] As Stalin told a prominent Finn after the war, his carefully calculated policy was 'not kindness, but common sense. We must not repeat the mistakes of the Old Czars.'[62]

No less than the Soviet leaders, the Finns could see but a straight line. Only a few months after Britain had severed relations with Finland, but prior to declaring war in November 1941, Churchill had made a proposal to Marshal Mannerheim that remained good for the Americans, British, and Soviets up until the last few weeks of the war. 'It is not necessary to make any public declaration, but simply leave off fighting and cease military operations, for which the severe winter affords every reason, and make a *de facto* exit from the war.' The Finns rejected this proposal, and the many others that followed, on the deceptive ground that without continued military actions their 'security' interests could not be fulfilled.[63]

During February 1944, after the Finns had shown the first signs of mild curiosity about the effects of an allied victory, Madame A. M. Kollontay, the Soviet Ambassador in Stockholm, told Dr Juho Kusti Paasikivi that the Soviet Government would accept an armistice without any prior agreement having been reached between the two governments on Petsamo, reparations and demobilisation, on the single pre-condition that Finland 'break off relations with Germany and intern German troops with her own forces or, if it were required, with the help of Soviet troops'. The Finns quickly rejected the terms.[64] The British and Roosevelt, informed by the Soviets of these diplomatic discussions, were satisfied with the terms offered, but the Foreign Office undoubtedly thought them lenient in comparison to their own pre-planned terms.[65] The Chiefs of Staff felt the Soviets should have asked for occupation of the strategically important Aland Islands at the northern approach to the Gulf of Finland. The Foreign Office disagreed: 'The Russians have been making a point of the moderate nature of the terms which they have put forward as preliminary to negotiations, and the fact that they do not include a demand for the occupation of Finnish territory is welcomed by His Majesty's Government and has made an excellent impression on world public opinion.'[66]

On a different issue, the Foreign Office felt that the Soviets should include some safeguard in their terms against continued Finnish–German trade since '. . . Germany gets no less than 70% of the nickel supplies and a small but valuable quantity of molybolenum from Finland and the cessation of this source of supply would have a considerable effect on the German war effort.'[67]

On 9 June 1944, the Red Army began its first offensive action against Finnish troops since the end of the Winter War in 1940. Eleven days later Soviet troops had re-captured Viipuri, the hub of Finland's coastal defence, on the Karelian Isthmus. Finland's leading military authority considered the war lost On 22 June, von Ribbentrop, the German Foreign Minister, arrived in Helsinki. After four days of negotiations, President Risto Ryti without parliamentary consultation made a written pledge to Hitler that Finland would make no peace with the USSR without German approval. The internal rot in the government was so great that even after the terms of Ryti's executive pact became known the Social Democrats, the nation's leading liberal party, decided not to withdraw their support from the government.[68]

With a nice sense of timing, the State Department on 16 June requested Finland's Minister in the US and three of his counsellors to leave the country. On the 30th, Hull made the US's position explicit. 'The American Government is not unaware of the fact that the infiltration of German troops into Finland, with the consent of the Finnish Government, and German infiltration into the councils of the Finnish Government have deprived Finland of liberty of action and reduced the Government . . . to the condition of a puppet of Nazi Germany.'[69] The warning from Washington was clear. There was to be no repetition of the Winter War fiasco when the Finns diplomatically played the USA and Britain off against the USSR. On 1 August, mounting criticism at home, the news of the American denunciation and the successes of the Red Army in Estonia forced Ryti to resign. Three days later Marshal Mannerheim succeeded him as President of the Republic.[70]

As had been the case in Italy, the transition period proved difficult for the emergent realists. In mid-August Mannerheim received Field-Marshal Keitel and informed him that Finland was going to pursue an independent foreign policy. On 2 September, Mannerheim penned one of the most painful letters of his long career to Hitler:

> I regard it as my duty to lead my people out of the war. The arms which you have generously given us I will never of my own accord turn against Germans. I cherish the hope that . . . you will share my wish and the wish of all Finns, that the change in our relations may not give rise to animosity.[71]

The Finns and Soviets had renewed their discussions on 25 August. The Soviets reiterated their earlier precondition and insisted that the Finns officially express their intentions by 15 September. Undoubtedly the military problems posed by this demand were considerable: Finland by consent harboured the 20th German Alpine Army of nine divisions plus specialist troops—200,000 in total. Subsequently the Soviets proposed that the Finns expel the German forces as an alternative to their internment. Perhaps with an appreciation of Mannerheim's inclinations, the Soviets eventually allowed the armistice to be signed on

19 September even though the pre-condition had not been fulfilled.[72]

The only refinements on the earlier armistice terms were that Allied (Soviet) High Command required the use of various airports on Finland's southern and south-western coast and of Finnish merchant ships for the duration of the war against Germany. The Aland Islands were to be permanently demilitarised. Moderate reparations of $300,000 were to be paid in commodities over a six-year period (which the Soviets later extended to eight years). The only political provisions called for the dissolution of all 'pro-Hitler organisations' and the apprehension–trial by Finnish authorities of all war criminals.[73] Working from the Italian precedent, an Allied Control Commission was established to oversee the implementation of the armistice terms under the direction of the Allied (Soviet) High Command.[74] There was no penetration of Finnish territory by Soviet troops, no meddling in Finland's internal politics,[75] and not even a vigorous purge of Finnish war criminals.[76]

THE DIPLOMATS' PEACE: CZECHOSLOVAKIA

The Czechoslovakian situation was unlike that of other east and central European nations and certainly different from that of Finland or Italy. The legitimate government had neither collaborated with the Axis nations nor authorised aggressive acts against the allies. There were several historic advantages which helped to account for the Czechs' unique situation. Firstly, they had successfully escaped the 'white terror' which swept over Europe after the Russian Revolution and World War I and had built strong democratic institutions. Secondly, they had intellectually, emotionally, and culturally accepted the permanence of Marxism and socialism without any harmful repercussions. Thirdly, they enjoyed, perhaps as a product of the other two factors, political leadership of the highest quality.

As the last democratically elected President of the Republic of Czechoslovakia, Dr Eduard Beneš constructed a provisional government in London that became the model wartime government-in-exile. Under his guidance, it became a caretaker government representative of the healthy democracy that had existed before the war. There were thirteen ministers and a State Council of some forty members. By 1942, five communists sat in the State Council in London and a sixth served *in absentia* from Moscow. This was a balanced number considering that the various communist parties had consistently held ten per cent of the seats in the Chamber of Deputies since the 1925 elections. Unlike the Poles, the Czechs created a political atmosphere which allowed contacts between communist and non-communist politicians, as had been the case before the war.[77]

When Klement Gottwald, a prominent communist, predicted a massive 'revolutionary shift' during the war among the Czech peoples, Beneš, a moderate socialist, anticipated the radical left's legitimate demands in some situations, and in others neutralised their position with the government by co-opting the best of their domestic programmes. When the communists, Social Democrats, and National Socialists formed a National Front within the State Council, Beneš welcomed the opportunity to secure representation for the non-socialist Catholic People's Party. When it became obvious that the ultra-rightist Agrarian Party no longer enjoyed popular support, Beneš did not hesitate to ban it. In this fashion the problems of factionalism, endemic among other exiled governments in London, never arose within the Provisional Government or with its partisan supporters in Czechoslovakia because Beneš had the perception to read the signals.[78]

His genius was even more apparent in his conduct of foreign affairs. Well before any other statesman in Europe or America, Beneš realised that the dismemberment of his own country and the Molotov–Ribbentrop pact had been caused by the western policy of isolating the USSR from the rest of Europe. 'I was always aware of the fact that Munich with all its catastrophic consequences would not have occurred but for the hostility of Western Europe towards the Soviet Union and the differences between them.'[79] Beneš sought to establish what the pre-war world had so sadly lacked, an anti-German regional alliance that included the USSR. As he expressed it 'This same war has proved that . . . real, friendly and loyal co-operation between Poland, Czechoslovakia and the Soviet Union is essential. If we succeed in bringing this about, the whole future of Poland and of Czechoslovakia will be guaranteed.'[80]

Prior to discussions between the USSR and the Czechoslovak Provisional Government, from August to October 1943, Beneš travelled to the United States for consultations with Roosevelt. Following these talks, although there were some people within the State Department, including Ambassador Harriman, who were less than enthusiastic about the proposed treaty,[81] Beneš gained the impression that the Americans supported his activities.[82]

In his preliminary negotiations with the Poles, Beneš was less fortunate. They remained profoundly anti-Soviet in their attitude and refractory about the return of Teschen which they had seized from the Czechs before the war. Besides, the Poles had plans of their own for a Polish-led federation of central European states which was to be both anti-German and anti-Soviet.[83] Despite this rebuff, Beneš decided to persevere without them.

The Foreign Office looked on Beneš's efforts with ambivalence. They did not want to create a situation where the UK and USSR were openly vying for the friendship of minor European states, but neither did they want to appear overtly anti-Soviet by opposing the treaty. While they did not favour the proposed Czech–Soviet treaty because it threatened to cramp their diplomatic style as well as that of the Poles, they also did not want to be seen obstructing the efforts of a respected western statesman. The Foreign Office reminded Molotov of a non-specific agreement he had reached with Eden in November 1942 that neither Britain nor Russia would conclude unilateral agreements with smaller nations. When they lost confidence in the strength of that approach, however, they planned to accept the treaty with the provision that the Poles be permitted to subscribe to it at some later date. Before this latter proposal could be put to the Czechs and Soviets, however, Beneš informed the Foreign Office that the Soviet Government had already suggested postponing the treaty's conclusion and Dr Beneš's Moscow visit.[84] The influence of the second front was evidently powerful: and in fact it was the first item on the Soviet Union's agenda for the forthcoming Foreign Ministers' conference in Moscow.[85]

After the British had had an opportunity to present their reservation at the Moscow conference, events proceeded smoothly. On 12 December 1943 the Czechs and Soviets signed a simple agreement, the heart of which provided that the two nations would render mutual assistance during the present war. A protocol signed at the same time stated that 'any third country having common frontiers with the Czechoslovak Republic or Union of Soviet Socialist Republics and having in this war been an object of German aggression' could also adhere to the treaty.[86] In this somewhat oblique manner the Foreign Office was satisfied, and the Poles were given a second chance to enter into a political and military alliance with their neighbours. On 6 January 1944 Churchill was able to report to FDR that the Czechoslovak–Soviet situation was encouraging.[87] This was one of the Prime Minister's rare uses of litotes.

With this promising background, in May 1944 an additional agreement was reached between the Czechs and the USSR on liberation and occupation problems. While this document inevitably entailed a risk for the smaller nation—a risk that would have been minimised if the Poles had entered into the earlier agreements—Stalin accepted Beneš's suggestion that Czech Army units operating in the USSR be allowed to take the major responsibility, with resistance forces, for the occupation of their homeland.[88] Obviously Stalin felt the Czechs had earned this dividend as a result of their earlier diplomatic efforts.

When Beneš formed a National Front Government in March 1945, the National Socialists, Social Democrats, (Catholic) Populists, Czech Communists, Slovak Democrats, and Slovak Communists all participated. The price had been small. Both communist parties held only eight out of twenty-five posts; two of the most important ministries, foreign affairs and defence, were held by independents. Dr Beneš had negotiated his government so that there was abundant room for the moderate right, centre, and left to operate without internal or external opposition.[89] This was no inconsiderable personal achievement.

THE RESIDUAL PEACE: THE BALTIC STATES

In pre-war Europe, Estonia, Latvia and Lithuania 'stood in a class by themselves as the weakest representatives of the sovereign independent species of polity with the sole exception of Albania'.[90] What had been tolerable weakness before 1934, became a European liability with the re-emergence of Germany as a great power. The signing of the Polish–German non-aggression pact of 26 January 1934 dealt a severe blow to any possible Czech–Soviet–Polish–Baltic alliance against Germany. As the decade progressed, the significance of this event grew, as the three states became more authoritarian and wretched, more susceptible to indirect aggression, and more entangled in the German net.[91]

As a result of these developments, A. A. Zhdanov, before the Eighth Soviet Congress in November 1936, issued a warning which was to remain the keystone of Soviet policy in the region, if not for all of eastern Europe, for at least the following decade:

> As you know, the Leningrad region marks the Soviet frontier with Finland, Estonia, and Latvia, countries with whose peoples the USSR has normal peaceful relations. And if, in some of these little countries . . . feelings of hostility to the USSR are being kindled by larger and more adventurist countries, and preparations are being made to make their territory available for aggressive action by fascist Powers, in the long run it is these little countries alone which will be the losers. It does not pay for little countries to get entangled in big adventures, and if fascism dares to seek military victories on the north-west frontier of the Soviet Union, then we in Leningrad, placing at the service of defence all the technical strength we can command, shall deal it such a crushing blow that the enemy will never again turn his eyes on Leningrad.[92]

With the passing of the years, while some of the iron went out of Zhdanov's speech, the view remained the same.

When the Germans occupied Prague, declared a protectorate over the remainder of Bohemia and Moravia, and forced Lithuania to cede Memel in 1939, conventional diplomatic modes ceased to be adequate. The British temporised by entering into vacuous treaties with Poland, Rumania, Turkey, and Greece which carried no specific promises of military assistance. At the same time Chamberlain weakly wished to support these tender advances by bringing the USSR and Poland into the Anglo-French partnership, such as it was, to resist future German encroachments in eastern Europe. The Soviets welcomed the idea, but the Poles would have nothing to do with a pact which included the USSR. After rejecting a Soviet proposal for talks in March as 'premature', the British on 15 April approached the USSR and suggested they become the junior partner in a three-power alliance to defend their commitments in East Europe, which meant primarily Poland and Rumania but not the Baltic states. The Poles were never abandoned, just ignored. The Soviets demanded full equality and reciprocity. Two days later Litvinov counter-proposed an original new approach to old problems: the United Kingdom, France and the Soviet Union would guarantee for the foreseeable future the autonomy of all eastern European states from the Baltic to the Black Sea. The British rejected this plan ostensibly as defenders of the independence of small states. In reality they were staked to the barren middle ground of irreconcilable interests where the UK was mainly concerned in not antagonising Germany, Poland and Rumania, and less interested in building good relations with the USSR. From May onwards, after Molotov succeeded Litvinov, the Soviets insisted on an agreement which would contain three items: (1) A binding commitment among the UK, France and the USSR to defend one another. (2) A promise by these three powers to guarantee, after negotiations, what eventually became a long list of nations: Finland, Estonia, Latvia, Poland, Rumania, Turkey, Greece and Belgium. The guarantees were to provide against both direct and indirect aggression—by which Molotov meant that action would be taken, even in the absence of overt German interference, if a nation 'voluntarily' violated its own independence and neutrality. In short, the Soviets wanted the UK, France and themselves to agree on action to stop the drift of East Europe towards the fascist right. (3) Immediate military collaboration and planning among the three nations, and the implementation of a range of measures which included, as examples, the dispatch of British ships to the Baltic and the securing of bases in Finland, Latvia and Estonia. In principle, the French agreed to all three points. Even after Molotov consented to strike the Baltic states from the list of guaranteed nations, the British could agree only to the first point.[93]

It was only after Anglo-Soviet differences became irreconcilable that the USSR turned to the Germans. The open pact signed on 23 August 1939 called for mutual non-aggression. A secret protocol signed at the same time gave the Soviets partly what they had wanted all along—the exclusion of German influence from the Baltic states and eastern Poland—and something that they had never asked from the western powers: exclusive protectorate rights over eastern Poland to the Curzon Line, Estonia and Latvia. The alternatives were war without support from any European country or the expansion of German suzerainty right up to the throat of Leningrad.

After the signing on 25 September of an amendment to the earlier protocol which placed Lithuania in the Soviet sphere, a series of bilateral agreements were signed between the USSR and the Baltic states which gave the Soviets naval, army and air bases in these countries without compromising their political and economic sovereignty—a generosity which must have caused some difficulties in Moscow considering that it allowed the dictatorial regimes in these countries to flourish while Baltic communists in appreciable numbers still remained imprisoned.[94]

Even after Denmark, Norway, Belgium, Holland, Luxembourg and France had fallen, the Soviets proceeded to concern themselves with sovereign rights that had no immediate relevance. Only in mid-June 1940 did they demand that the Baltic states politically reform themselves and then only to the extent of casting out the more notorious pro-Germans and Red-baiters. The majority of new faces in the reformed governments were socialists and liberals rather than communists.[95] By the end of June 1940, the German Minister in Estonia was able to report to Berlin that the pro-Nazi president of the country, Constantine Paets, was still in contact with him and providing useful military intelligence. Paets, at least, remained certain, in the words of the dispatch, that 'sovietization and unification with the Soviet Union need not be expected of the present Government'.[96] It was not until 8 August 1940 that the Baltic states, patently incapable of bringing about internal reforms consonant with external realities, became the fourteenth, fifteenth and sixteenth Soviet Socialist Republics, after a hasty referendum.[97]

Neither the British government nor the Roosevelt administration ever seriously proposed that Latvia, Lithuania and Estonia be restored as sovereign states. While the annexation of the three republics seemed severe, there was no satisfactory alternative. It was obvious to all that the Baltic region had been a hotbed of fascist sympathy before the war and a festering breach in the Soviets' defensive perimeter. By 1942 Lord Halifax in Washington was not the only one to have serious doubts about the efficacy of

Britain's attitudes towards the Baltic states and the Anglo-French-Soviet negotiations of 1939. In May 1942, the British government, reflecting this critical re-assessment, became fully bound to recognise the Soviet claim to the Baltic states. There is also considerable evidence that FDR disapproved only of the timing and circumstances of this recognition.[98] British planners could see that 'The USSR's chief aims in the Baltic are, we consider, directed to secure herself against any future German invasion through the Baltic States or Finland and to prevent German domination of the Baltic.'[99] The British were not alarmed at this prospect, and there is no reason to suppose that the Americans saw the problem and solution in any different terms.[100]

Notes to this chapter are on pages 192–6.

Chapter 4 THE GRAND DESIGN

THE INVENTIVE ALTERNATIVE

As WE have seen from the selected peace settlements already discussed, Soviet negotiations for the post-war period were based on remarkably uncomplicated and limited objectives. As most national policies tend to be, Soviet efforts were grounded in an amoral and visceral regard for the national interest. These efforts were almost exclusively confined to those regions and countries immediately surrounding the USSR. As a result, for security and historical reasons, there were important areas of Europe, such as Italy, which were beyond Soviet concern and capabilities. Flexibility and a spirit of accommodation were significant means to their ends. While it was true that the USSR had seized the Baltic states, for want of a better alternative, it was also true that where nations were capable of reforming themselves the USSR was perfectly willing to negotiate sane and unpunitive treaties. When it had proved necessary to work with non-communist and even non-socialist politicians, the Soviets had been realistic. It was all a matter of the most enlightened variety of political pragmatism. At the same time, any sort of restoration of the old order under the guise of some newly discovered anti-German sentiment was an impossibility. It was a mixed, somewhat conflicting but not overly complex set of interests. It all returned to Zhdanov's warning in 1936.

The British and American positions were considerably less consistent and perhaps more obscure. By early 1944 their problems were compounded by the growing realisation that things were not progressing as well as had earlier been hoped. The promise of a grand peace, as guaranteed by the Atlantic Charter, was looking less attainable all the time. The difference between restoration and reconstruction was going to mean incalculable delays, errors and uncertainties. It was also becoming increasingly clear that the work of the Versailles diplomats had been imperfect and hasty, and that many of their efforts were being, and were going to be, altered without the benefit of a general peace conference. It was also obvious that millions of displaced and misplaced persons would be flowing in disturbing currents and eddies throughout Europe as soon as the first signs of liberation appeared. Even more worrying was the mounting evidence that there was going to be a crisis at the very centre of what had been considered civilised society. Party politics as a game was going to be played with different rules in practically every European country. With the discrediting of the fascist and semi-fascist parties of the right, and a remarkable upswing in the fortunes of the left, the familiar status quo was under heavy attack. For these and other reasons there came the awareness that past efforts had been insufficient.

The tripartite Foreign Ministers' conference, which was held in Moscow from 18 October until 1 November 1943, temporarily helped to dispel some of the uneasiness that had arisen. It was very likely the most successful gathering of foreign ministers from the US, UK and USSR that there has ever been. Eden and Molotov secured the establishment of the European Advisory Commission, which placed future discussions about the fate of Germany and Austria securely within a three-power frame of reference. Hull, at his first and last major inter-allied conference of the war, obtained what was closest to his heart, a declaration which sounded akin to the Atlantic Charter and promised the creation of 'a general international organisation'.[1] Roosevelt was enthusiastic about the conference 'not only from what has been accomplished in the way of definite items of agreement, but also in the spirit of it'.[2] Nevertheless, Richard Law, Minister of State at the Foreign Office, realised even before the conference, that it would be seriously flawed if it failed, as it did, to deal with such substantial issues as the Balkans and eastern and south-eastern Europe.[3] Even after the Tehran conference in December 1943, the most important pre-Yalta conference where Roosevelt, Stalin and Churchill had talked seriously about many vitally important questions, including the future of Germany and Poland, the remainders were significant.[4]

The concept of 'unconditional surrender' was the first part of the patchwork to be questioned. The British led and the Soviets followed not far behind. With the Italian example and the Soviets' terms for Finland in mind, the Foreign Office by 25 March 1944 informed the State Department that they no longer considered the principle applicable to the Axis satellite states. Under the stress of drafting and negotiating real armistice terms, FDR's Casablanca pronouncement had become distant.[5] The Soviets concurred. The demand, if continued, would have the negative effect, in their view, of strengthening Germany's hold over her satellites. What was needed was three-power consultation to formulate applicable terms in each unique situation.[6] FDR refused to be convinced, with the result that practically the whole question of eastern Europe and the Balkans remained unattended.[7]

As it became increasingly unlikely that the British would be able to directly build a military presence in southern Europe, because of the Americans' insistence on a northern European second front, the British began to contemplate and explore other methods of achieving their objectives. An early plan proposed by L. S. Amery, the Secretary of State for India, among others, called for the invention of a series of European federations and the 'remodelling of Europe immediately after the German collapse in the interest of its own peace and our security . . .'. The most important point was this: 'If we are first in the Balkans we should push on the setting up of a Balkan Confederation then and there, while things are malleable and our influence at its highest. Similarly, we should try to bring about a Danubian–Polish Federation, if the Russian position allows it.'[8]

During May 1943, the Prime Minister, who warmly embraced this plan, presented it to a group of high-ranking Americans (Vice-President Henry Wallace, Secretary of War Stimson, Secretary of the Interior Ickes, Under-Secretary of State Welles, and the Chairman of the Senate Foreign Relations Committee, Tom Connally) as part of a British proposal for the future united nations organisation. The Americans had been favourably impressed.[9] With the passage of time, however, the idea lost some of its charm: important political developments were taking place and would not wait until the German collapse; and it began to appear unlikely that the British would be the first to penetrate the Balkans. By the

end of the year, both Molotov and Stalin had separately disapproved of the project.[10]

By 1944, the British were beginning to toy with a more promising approach. Since it was almost certain that the Soviets were
going to liberate and occupy Rumania, a further spread of their
influences must be checked. If the Americans would occupy
Austria and Hungary, the British would occupy Bulgaria and the
Dodecanese Islands. Control of Bulgaria was felt to be decisive for
it would insure British influence in Greece, which the Soviets had
already agreed was to be an area of British responsibility, and in
the Dardanelles and Turkey.[11] Almost immediately counter-
blows were struck which caused adjustments to be made. The
USSR expressed an interest in participating in the occupation of
Austria, as had been agreed at the Moscow conference, and
implicitly in the occupation of Hungary and Bulgaria. The
President and the US Chief of Staff informed the British that
American forces would not under any circumstances participate
in the occupation of south-east Europe and would be withdrawn
from Europe 'as soon as possible'. Faced with these developments,
British policy planners hoped at best for a predominant influence
in Bulgaria.[12] During April the Foreign Office passed a memorandum to the State Department which made their intentions known.

> Our interest lies in preventing the extension of Soviet influence
> towards the Straits and the Mediterranean. It is therefore sug-
> gested that, in addition to British membership of any Allied control
> machinery in Bulgaria, a British force should be sent to Bulgaria in
> order (a) to 'show the flag' by participating in any military occupa-
> tion there may be; (b) to demonstrate British interest in that part of
> Europe; and (c) to ensure if necessary that Bulgarian forces
> evacuate and do not re-occupy Greek and Yugoslav territory of
> which they are now in possession.[13]

This was the generative proposal that resulted in what was to be
a very grand design indeed.

While the Foreign Office plan was well intentioned, it had
several serious weaknesses: (1) If the way were not carefully prepared, two could play the same game and the Soviets in the long
run would have enough players, unlike the British, to compete all
over Europe. (2) It made for extremely complicated diplomatic

and military negotiations for each country involved. (3) It in no basic way altered the underlying geo-political realities about to be shaped by the successes of the Red Army. (4) A bit of flag waving was going to be hard pressed to stretch beyond a very short half-life. (5) In an all out competitive race with the Soviets not only would they very likely gain more territory than Britain, but in the process many more dangerous and lasting problems would become unravelled, which Britain without US assistance would have to solve alone. (6) Britain's share was too vague and small.

It was Churchill, the wily statesman of the old school, who first proposed a memorable alternative to the pattern of peace already under way. If there were no other fragments of his diplomatic wit scattered over the historical landscape of the period, this single proposal would have ensured his immortality. In late May, the Prime Minister suggested to the President 'as a practical matter' that the USSR should 'take the lead in Roumanian affairs, while we would take the lead in Greek affairs, each Government giving the other help in their respective countries'.[14] Without waving a single useless flag, Churchill had devised a plan whereby Soviet expansion could be stopped at the gap by political and contractual means alone. This was no mean trick by any standards. It was a creation the Prime Minister was loath to share in full with any man; consequently, the first glimpse was but a carefully timed and lighted teaser.

Flawlessly directing the proper advances, Churchill instructed Halifax to approach Hull on 30 May about the exciting news. The long neglected Secretary of State, as expected, responded negatively:

> I was, in fact, flatly opposed to any division of Europe or sections of Europe into spheres of influence. . . . It seemed to me that any creation of zones of influence would inevitably sow the seeds of future conflict. I felt that zones of influence could not but derogate from the overall authority of the international security organisation which I expected would come into being.[15]

On 11 June, Roosevelt cabled Churchill that while it was inevitable that occupying forces would make 'decisions required by military developments' it was likely that the military leaders would tend to define their powers, as in Italy, rather broadly and for rather long periods of time.[16] Despite this parry by Roosevelt and Hull's perceptive fears, the Americans without any alternative plan of their own were left in a very cramped position.

Wasting no time, Churchill sent a message to Halifax on 8 June 1944, giving a brief, but revealing, look at the package's contents.

> There is no question of spheres of influence. We all have to act together, but someone must be playing the hand. It seems reasonable that the Russians should deal with the Roumanians and Bulgarians, upon whom their armies are impinging, and that we should deal with the Greeks, who are in our assigned theatre. . . . I have reason to believe that the President is in entire agreement with the lines I am taking about Greece. The same is true of Yugoslavia.[17]

Hull, informed on the same day, liked the proposal no better for the inclusion of Bulgaria and Yugoslavia. On the 12th and 17th he sent disapproving telegrams to Churchill, and on 22 June, circulated a warning memorandum to the principal American diplomats in Europe. The major objection was the one FDR had voiced earlier: that military control tended to become political control.[18]

By 11 July 1944, despite Hull's persistent efforts to counter such a move, Churchill, with FDR's approval for a three-month trial period dated 13 June in hand, felt secure enough to approach Stalin directly. After seeing the larger terms of the proposal as forwarded to Halifax, and indirectly to Hull, on the 8th, Roosevelt had succumbed. Hull had been ignored.[19] In his initial proposal to Stalin, the Prime Minister suggested a division of south-east Europe on the basis that it would 'avoid as much as possible the awful business of triangular telegrams, which paralyses action', although this point had never been raised in any settlement to date. He held out the promise to Stalin that the USSR would have a guaranteed foothold. In Churchill's words, Stalin's reply to the new design was 'non-committal'.[20] More accurately Stalin's reply showed a strong unwillingness to proceed on a bilateral basis. 'One thing is clear to me, that the US Government has certain doubts about this matter, and we shall do well to return to the matter when we get the US reply.'[21]

For Eden, as he notified the War Cabinet, the problem was a non-ideological product of the war. 'It is doubtful whether in actual fact there is any deliberate "communising" of the Balkans at the present moment. . . . Nor can any accusation be levelled against the Russians of organising the spread of communism in the Balkans.' The indigenous communists in the region had been the most active elements in fighting the Axis, and the US and Britain had supported them in the interests of winning the war. 'The Russians have merely sat back and watched us doing their work for them.' In his view and that of the Foreign Office, it was time to counter this disequilibrium by traditional diplomatic means.[22] For Churchill and Smuts, however, the securing of an acceptance of the Prime Minister's proposal had become a mission of great moral significance.[23] When Churchill arrived in Moscow on the afternoon of 9 October 1944, it was almost a foregone conclusion that Marshal Stalin, ever cognisant of the Soviet Union's security interests, would accept Churchill's apportionment of five nations—using Churchill's percentages, Churchill's paper, with the whole scheme written in Churchill's hand. That night, the British acquired a ninety-per-cent interest in Greece, a half interest (with the US) in Yugoslavia and Hungary, a quarter interest in Bulgaria, and a ten-per-cent interest in Rumania. The balance belonged to the USSR.[24]

After quietly accepting Churchill's grand scheme, which denied self-determination and the Atlantic Charter, the evident problem for Roosevelt, now that Churchill had carved out a role for Britain, was to find cards to play in what had largely become a two-man game.[25] The US could join Britain in literally fulfilling the terms of the Churchill–Stalin agreement or somehow the US could find room to play the difficult Italian role. It proved a most difficult choice to make.

THE CONTRACTED PEACE: RUMANIA

Fascism, that tragically perverse alternative to socialism, liberalism, conservatism and communism, had come early and left indelible marks on Rumania's pre-war history and institutions.[26] From the formation of Ion Antonescu's National-Legionary State on 15 September 1940, which succeeded King Carol's dictatorship, the Iron Guard was declared the only legal party. The pro-German political and economic bias of the government, which originated with Carol, was further accentuated when 120,000 German troops entered the country in October. At the same time Antonescu guaranteed his supremacy by casting the old guard Carolists out of the government, with German approval, and dissolving the dated Iron Guard. By January 1941, Antonescu had transformed Rumania into a modern fascist state.[27]

If an enlightened left had survived the thirties, it undoubtedly would have protested Rumania's joining the Axis alliance in June 1941 and the eagerness with which Rumanian troops joined the Germans for the invasion of the USSR. Instead, even Constantin Bratianu and Iuliu Maniu, leaders respectively of the National Liberal and National Peasant parties, favoured a 'short war' against the Soviets to recapture the provinces, Bessarabia and northern Bukovina, which Carol had yielded to the USSR the previous summer. It is interesting to note that they never called for military action to recapture northern Transylvania and southern Dobrudja, which had also been lost to Hungary and Bulgaria. Very likely the democrats would have found that a lesser provocation would have served as well.[28]

Rumania's assistance to the Third Reich was vigorous. In addition to massive shipments of oil, grain and other foodstuffs, the Rumanians also contributed the output of their sizeable munitions industry. In 1941 alone, they offered the assistance of some thirty divisions. By July, Bessarabia and northern Bukovina had been reoccupied. Thereafter the Rumanians aided the Germans in overrunning Soviet territory from the Dniester to the Bug and annexed a large area east of the Dniester which they renamed Transnistria. By October, in the operations which resulted in the capture of Odessa, the Rumanians had lost 70,000 men compared with German losses of 117,000 along the entire front. When it came to genocidal antisemitism, the Rumanians were surpassed only by the Germans themselves. Killing centres were quickly established in Transnistria and by the end of the war at least 270,000 Rumanian Jews had been destroyed.[29]

By 1944, the Rumanians had already shown signs of wanting to withdraw from the Axis cause. The British had rejected an approach from Iuliu Maniu, leader of the National Peasant Party, on the grounds that proper negotiations would have to be conducted with the USSR as well. By February the State Department had prepared a draft armistice document which contained harsh terms: all Rumanian military and para-military forces were to be disarmed and demobilised; Bucharest and other major cities were to be occupied; restitution and an unspecified amount of reparations were to be made. Soviet claims to Bessarabia and northern Bukovina were not to be honoured until after a general peace conference, and these territories were to be occupied in the name of the united nations, even though the US had never recognised Rumania's seizure of Bessarabia after World War I. The British had their own thoughts. Since they were in the process of encouraging the Soviets and Poles to settle their territorial disputes, they were eager for the Soviets and Rumanians to do the same. For quite some time the Foreign Office had endorsed Stalin's territorial claims made to Eden in 1941; these included both Bessarabia and northern Bukovina, and the return by Hungary to Rumania of Transylvania, with its 1·25 million Rumanians.[30] By March the State Department had come to the position that while Soviet claims to northern Bukovina were obviously based on strategical grounds, since the USSR desired a common frontier with the eastern border of Czechoslovakia, there were supporting ethnical arguments as well. The State Department also felt that, since the juridical confusion over Bessarabia was so great, it might be able to 'contemplate' the claim.[31]

During the same month, March, Prince Barbu Stirbei, representing the quasi-governmental person of Iuliu Maniu, appeared in Cairo and began discussions with the allies. He said that if they would grant Rumania co-belligerent status, such as Italy had, elements within the army, with the support of Carol's resident successor, King Michael I, would stage a *coup d'état*. They wished to retain Transylvania, were willing to let Bulgaria keep Dobrudja, and wanted a plebiscite in Bessarabia. From the beginning, the Soviets were suspicious of Stirbei and regarded Maniu not as an opposition figure but as Marshal Antonescu's creature. As if to substantiate this allegation, Stirbei attempted at the end of March to contact the British and American representatives separately, but again was rebuffed by the Foreign Office.[32]

During April the Soviet government made its armistice terms known. The frontier claims were familiar and the military clauses were unexceptional, apart from the provision that the Rumanian divisions were either to attack the Germans or surrender and immediately, after rearming, be placed under the command of Marshal Antonescu and Maniu. General Marshall and the joint Chiefs of Staff quickly approved the terms. A State Department official noted that they varied 'drastically' from the earlier American terms and the principle of unconditional surrender. The Soviets accepted Churchill's amendment that the terms regarding the Vienna Award of 1940 and Transylvania be made conditional on the holding of a general peace conference. Secretary of State Hull informed the US Ambassador to the Yugoslav government-in-exile, Lincoln MacVeagh, that on the 'merits', but not the principle, the Department favoured the Soviets' position on Transylvania and the other two provinces. Officially Hull's position remained the same: all difficult questions, including those touching on frontier changes, should be postponed until the conclusion of hostilities. By June all opposition parties within Rumania were reported to have accepted the Soviet terms.[33]

By the end of August, two Soviet armies were making their final preparations for a push forward that threatened to annihilate the last of the German and Rumanian defenders along the Jassy defence line. Ion and Mihai Antonescu, with true German stoicism not shared by their colleagues, refused to negotiate with the Soviets and were prepared to withdraw their shattered armies to the Carpathians and form a defensive citadel. On 23 August 1944, General Constantin Sanatescu, the President of the Council of Ministers, and other prominent army officers accepted the Soviet armistice terms and placed the Antonescus, their chief aides and collaborators under arrest. The take-over, unlike that in Italy, was well planned and executed. The King on the day of the coup explained to the people over the radio that hostilities against the allies had ceased and that Transylvania would be liberated from Hungary and Germany. The Germans responded immediately on 24 August by bombing Bucharest. By the time Soviet troops entered the city a few days later, the Rumanians had established an effective defensive line against the Germans. Almost immediately after the coup, Molotov informed the US and UK that his government, in order to enhance the Sanatescu government's prestige, would not introduce major new armistice terms. And so the soft surrender terms of April became the basis of the future peace.[34]

Between the Soviets and Rumanians a bargain was struck. In addition to the earlier terms, the Rumanians were to provide no fewer than twelve infantry divisions to serve under the Allied (Soviet) High Command; all discriminatory legislation was to be repealed; reparations, as the Soviets had made clear in June, were to be equivalent to one-fifth of the damage caused— approximately $300 million payable in commodities over six years; an Allied Control Commission under the direction of the Allied (Soviet) High Command was to supervise the fulfilment of the surrender terms.[35]

At the top level of British Government and in the liberal corners of the Roosevelt administration, there was general satisfaction with the terms.[36] As early as June, Churchill had indicated in a letter to FDR that he had seen the Soviet proposal and approved of it.

> It seems to me, considering the Russians are about to invade Rumania in great force and are going to help Rumania recapture part of Transylvania from Hungary . . . it would be a good thing to follow the Soviet leadership, considering that neither you nor we have any troops there at all, and that they will probably do what they like anyhow. Moreover, I thought their terms, apart from indemnity, very sensible, and even generous. The Rumanian Army has inflicted many injuries upon the Soviet troops, and went into the war against Russia with glee.[37]

At other levels there followed a short and rancorous period of haggling. Ambassador Harriman increasingly became vicious in his dealings with the Soviets and at times called for using Lend–Lease as a weapon for securing petty points. Hull and the Foreign Office in turn grasped at several points of doubtful merit which made the Soviets extremely suspicious of western intentions. First Hull and the Foreign Office quibbled about the size and complexion of the Allied Control Commission; then they refused to accept a specific sum in connection with reparations, even though they had offered no calculations themselves. Molotov informed Harriman that the USSR considered the fixing of a definite figure, with provision for reparations to other united nations as well, to be one of the essential components of the document.[38] On 5 September the State Department and the Joint Chiefs of Staff finally approved the instrument, while orally disapproving of the reparations sum. On the following day Molotov informed Harriman that the Rumanian Control Commission was fully modelled on the Italian example. Harriman irrationally informed Hull that 'the Soviet Government intends to keep a tight rein on Rumanian affairs during the period of military operations'.[39]

On the following day Hull informed Harriman that for the first time the State Department had decided to participate on the Rumanian Control Commission, which showed the depth of their concern about Rumanian affairs. Bolstered by this announcement, the Foreign Office proposed a protocol which called the $300 million a 'non-revised figure'. The Americans in turn decided that the figure was acceptable but not as a precedent for future settlements. At nearly the same time George F. Kennan, the US Chargé in the USSR, with no technical expertise and little reliable information from Rumania, began a campaign to defend the inviolable property rights of the Romano–Americana Company and other firms in which the British and Americans had large holdings. The Soviets explained that the Germans had operated the oil companies and fields for the past four years and that the Soviets were seizing as war booty substantial stores of surplus equipment which had been intended for use by the Germans in Soviet oil fields. The Soviets produced data and technical reports. Kennan issued unsubstantiated warnings from his Moscow office. Nevertheless on 13 September, the armistice with the British protocol was signed. Harriman could only see evil ratified.[40]

By the end of the year, however, the early days of pygmy diplomacy were over. The Combined Economic Warfare Agencies at General Wilson's headquarters in Caserta had done their sums, confirmed an earlier State Department estimate, and had concluded that the Rumanians could meet the Soviet figure by devoting only half of their export surpluses for six years to reparations. Coming last instead of first, Harriman in December asked that a tripartite commission of petroleum experts be formed to survey the Rumanian scene.[41] In fact the people at the top, Roosevelt and Churchill, who could still see the big picture, had never shown signs of being dissatisfied.

In the more significant area of domestic politics, developments were more regular. In the second Sanatescu government, formed on 4 November, the Liberal and Peasant parties gained ten of seventeen ministries. An avowed anti-communist was given the powerful position of Minister of the Interior and as such exercised control of 'the police, the rural gendarmerie, and the appointments of local prefects and mayors'. The National Democratic Front, a rapidly emerging coalition of anti-fascist parties, had yet to get representation.[42]

Increasingly Sanatescu was unable to control the rising tempo of public and trade union agitation against the government and the Minister of the Interior. On 2 December 1944, Sanatescu resigned and was succeeded by the former Chief of Staff, General Nicholas Radescu, noted for his anti-German and anti-Soviet views. As was the case in Italy, the radical left decided to enter the government, with Soviet encouragement, but paid an unrealistically high price in the process. Radescu as a precondition demanded that the communist militia be disbanded and all agrarian reform be postponed until the end of the war. While Radescu kept the major posts beyond party politics, Petru Groza, a wealthy landowner, industrialist and leader of the Ploughmen's Front, became Vice-Premier. British representatives in Bucharest felt that any danger of the Soviets 'communising' the country was past and that the Radescu government represented a conservative triumph.[43]

Nevertheless, by 24 February 1945, Rumanian troops were firing on demonstrators in Bucharest and Radescu had called on the army to support him against the populace. Three days later he showed himself incapable of governing in this situation, even though his government was still visibly in control, and sought asylum in the British Embassy. In the midst of this chaos, Andrei Vyshinsky, who had spent a month in Rumania in late 1944, familiarising himself with local conditions, arrived again and demanded that troops in the vicinity of Bucharest be sent to the front lines. During a mass demonstration, an irreversible step towards a pacific transition away from the old order was taken when the King complied with Vyshinsky's directions and called on the Vice-Premier, Petru Groza, and the National Democratic Front to form a new government. Considering the influence the old order retained within the unpurged army and the popularity the monarchy still enjoyed, it was a most moderate settlement that easily ensured the British their ten per cent interest.[44]

On 1 March 1941, Bulgaria became a member of the Three Power Pact. Although the nation's leaders attempted to publicly maintain a posture of neutrality towards the allies, they were openly hostile towards their pro-western neighbours and enthusiastically set about securing the rewards resulting from adherence to the pact. Their country was never properly occupied by the German army, but the Bulgarian government willingly furnished important staging areas for the invasion of Yugoslavia and the USSR, and granted the Germans naval facilities at their Black Sea ports. Initially the Bulgarians incorporated only Yugoslavia, Macedonia and Greek Thrace; later in the war their troops occupied parts of Serbia and Greek Macedonia as well.

Unlike the situation in Rumania, the left had never become subservient to the royal dictatorship which had been established in 1934. While small in comparison to the Yugoslav and Greek partisan movements, the radical left did succeed in spasmodically opposing the national government. During the first nine months of 1941 alone, over 12,000 persons were charged with resistance crimes of sufficient magnitude to carry the death penalty. In February 1942 the resistance boldly succeeding in assassinating General Lukov, the chief proponent on the general staff of a Rumanian style invasion of the USSR. By July 1942, a coalition of representatives from the Workers' Party, the Agrarians' Union, the Zveno Group (a political club which favoured a semi-socialist republic), and the Bulgarian Communist Party had formed the Fatherland Front which had its roots in the partisan movement.[45]

There were several reasons why the Fatherland Front in Bulgaria was successful while the Rumanian National Democratic Front achieved only moderate success. Firstly, the fascist movement in Rumania, as in Hungary, had been highly organised and enjoyed widespread popular support. In contrast, large sections of the Bulgarian population were historically neither anti-semites nor pro-German. Secondly, the Communist Party, although illegal, had long enjoyed strong local support and first-class leadership. Thirdly, the majority of the Bulgarian people were pro-Russian, which strongly influenced the government's alleged non-belligerency towards the USSR. Fourthly, the Bulgarians had had no frontier disputes with the USSR.[46]

By May 1944, the government was prepared to negotiate its way out of the war. As a preliminary step, a new government was formed on 1 June by Ivan Bagrianov, a former member of the Agrarian Party with monarchal sympathies. While the cabinet still contained pro-German, anti-Soviet members, the new government made moderating changes in the personnel of the political police, relaxed some anti-Jewish laws, released 15,000 political prisoners, and freed some relatives of resistance members who had been held as hostages. On 22 August the Foreign Minister stated that troops would be withdrawn from some areas in Yugoslavia and Greece, but not from Macedonia and Thrace which were still regarded as Bulgarian territories.[47]

By the time representatives of the Bulgarian government arrived in Cairo on 30 August, to negotiate an armistice with British and American representatives (Bulgaria had never officially been at war with the USSR), an explosion of events was welling up. The American and British diplomats seemed perfectly willing to ignore FDR's strictures about unconditional surrender and offered the Bulgarians terms, which had been negotiated in the European Advisory Commission (EAC) from US and UK drafts, and were aimed at satisfying Bulgaria's desire for general neutrality. The Bulgarians were to sever relations with Germany, disarm and intern Axis troops, withdraw from all foreign territory, free allied prisoners and repeal all discriminatory legislation. Beyond these basic measures nothing more was required, and no steps towards assisting the allied war effort were suggested. Somewhat surprisingly in light of their opposition to similar Soviet claims, the US and UK had decided that the province of Dobrudja, with a majority Bulgarian population, was to remain part of Bulgaria even though Rumanian–Bulgarian negotiations for the province had taken place, in September 1940, under Axis auspices.[48]

Throughout the negotiations the Soviet representative on the EAC, Ambassador Gusev, had resisted suggestions, such as those by the British Treasury, that more stringent economic controls be forced on the Bulgarians. Soviet tactics remained the same, in

Bulgaria and elsewhere: armistice terms were to be moderate if not generous. Four days after the EAC terms were completed, Gusev informed the Americans that the USSR desired to fulfill the same role in regard to Bulgaria as the US had in Finland—that of an interested observer.[49]

Meanwhile in Bulgaria, on 2 September, the establishment further attempted to appease the Fatherland Front and the western allies by again reshuffling the cabinet and appointing a right-wing agrarian as head of the government. While the Muraviev government refused to accept the Anglo-American proposals outright, to break relations with Germany and to renounce all territorial gains, they did show themselves to be great believers in the bargaining process when they unilaterally declared Bulgaria to be no longer at war with the US and Britain.[50]

Here was á potentially dangerous situation for the USSR. The US and UK had made no political demands on the Bulgarians and shown no interest in that aspect of the problem. The government remained unreconstituted, essentially a wartime administration, and excluded any representatives from the Fatherland Front. Furthermore, representatives of the US and UK, with the free hand given them by the Soviets, continued to make no military demands on the Bulgarians as far as their future participation in the war was concerned. The Soviet response, after months of pursuing an obscure policy line, was decisive: on 5 September 1944 the USSR declared war on Bulgaria. On the following day, in a desperate attempt to satisfy the exigency of the moment, Muraviev declared war on Germany. Two days later Soviet troops entered Bulgaria. On 9 September, the Fatherland Front, assisted by members of the war ministry and army units near Sofia, swept the regency, the Muraviev government, and all former ministers who had served in the government since 1941 into prison. On the same day, the necessary political changes having taken place, the Soviets ceased all military operations within Bulgaria.[51]

The new government formed at the time of the coup was led by Colonel Kimon Georgiev and three other members of the non-communist Zveno group; the remainder were independents (2), Social Democrats (2), Agrarians (4), and Communists (4). Georgi Dimitrov, the most famous Balkan politician of the time, did not return to Bulgaria until almost fourteen months later. The composition of this government, which looked to the east before the west, was such that the negotiations in Cairo became superfluous.[52]

The conclusion of the Bulgarian peace continued painlessly, with the Soviets supplying many of the elements lacking earlier. The Bulgarians quickly became co-belligerents. The Fatherland Front's resistance groups joined Tito's partisans in operations against the Germans. A month after the coup, the Bulgarians concluded a pact with Yugoslavia which provided for formal military collaboration and the peaceful settlement of territorial questions. The Bulgarian army played its part and under Soviet command fought unstintingly through Croatia and Hungary to Vienna. On 28 October 1944 the Bulgarians signed an armistice in Moscow, prepared by the EAC, which resembled in all essentials the terms earlier proposed by the American and British representatives in Cairo, with the addition of military terms mainly supplied by the Soviets. Since no Bulgarian troops had attacked the USSR, no provision for reparations was contained in the armistice. In a separate protocol, the Bulgarians promised to supply foodstuffs to Greek and Yugoslav victims of Bulgarian military operations. As in Rumania, an Allied Control Commission was established under the general supervision of the Allied (Soviet) High Command. By the end of the year the US and UK had political representatives in Sofia and US–UK military officers had made an inspection tour of Macedonia and Thrace to verify the fulfilment of the armistice terms. Again it was difficult to see how the British and Americans received less than their quarter interest.[53]

THE CONTRACTED PEACE: HUNGARY

To a greater extent than that of any other European state, except Germany itself, the history of Hungary from 1938 until the end of the war showed an escalating progression towards fascist purity. Without producing a leader of the stature of Hitler, Mussolini or Franco, Hungary developed a native brand of fascism as distinguished as any in Europe. By the spring of 1943, however, the romance was wearing thin. While spiritually and territorially the country's alliance with Germany was felt by its leaders to have been profitable, the Hungarians had seen their newly formed Second Army shredded during operations in the

USSR and reduced to a purely defensive role. When Admiral Horthy visited Berchtesgaden in April, Hitler voiced his own complaints: the Hungarians' martial spirit was too low, their living standards too high, their Jewish laws too lax, their tolerance of political dissent too great, and their interest in getting out of the war too obvious. When Horthy denied these charges and returned to Budapest, Hitler, using Nazi supporters within the government, began to apply political pressure on Horthy and Count Micklas Kallay, the Hungarian Premier, to reform.[54]

By September 1943, Horthy and Kallay had made several diplomatic advances to the Anglo-Saxon powers. The terms were similar to those put forward by all right-wing realists throughout Europe. If the US and Britain would save Hungary from the Bolshevists, guarantee her pre-war territorial gains and tolerate the existing dictatorial regime, Hungary would join an anti-communist federation of Danubian nations and cease close collaboration with Nazi Germany. Although the British and Americans responded with some uncertainty to the more suggestive aspects of these advances, they did stand firm on the most immediate issue when they demanded that all Hungarian troops be withdrawn from the Soviet front.[55]

During March 1944, Kallay paid for his earlier prevarications by being swept out of office by Hitler's most trusted Hungarian protégé, General Ferenc Sztojay, the former Hungarian Minister in Berlin. The new government stated their intention of 'bringing to fruition the ancestral virile and martial qualities of the Hungarian people'. The consequences were disastrous for Jews, workers, and liberals alike. With Germanic dedication, the Sztojay regime announced a total economic mobilisation which entailed not only increasing numbers of conscripted Hungarian labourers being sent to Germany but a great many Germans being transported to the most ravaged areas of Hungary to revitalise the war effort. The rededication also meant the shipment of enormous quantities of Hungarian goods to Germany, for the first time, on a purely credit basis. Most calamitous of all, despite public assurances by Adolf Eichmann and other 'technicians' that no harm would come to them, the slaughter of Hungarian Jews entered its worst phase, ultimately exceeding 450,000 victims.[56]

The least tragic effect of these Draconian measures was on the country's enfeebled reactionaries. Regent Horthy, the strongman of Hungarian politics since the white terror of 1919 had destroyed Bela Kun's Hungarian Soviet Republic, roused himself from semi-retirement to reassert his authority. He feared developments in Italy, Yugoslavia, Poland and Bulgaria. He feared future retaliation by the Hungarian people and the Soviets against Sztojay's excesses. With the collapse of Rumania, he could see Hungary stripped of her outlying political and military defences.[57] At this point, Horthy and his followers, with their backs nearly against the wall, resolved to move.

By 12 October 1944 Horthy's agents in Moscow had signed preliminary armistice terms prepared by the Soviets. The Hungarians were to withdraw their troops from Czechoslovakia, Yugoslavia and Rumania to their own 1937 frontiers, to cease hostilities against the allies and to declare war against Germany. In all other respects the document was similar to those presented by the allies to Rumania and Bulgaria. The clause concerning reparations specified $400 million to be paid in commodities over a five-year period. Since Churchill and Eden were already in Moscow and quick agreement on the terms seemed a certainty, Harriman requested that the State Department send him instructions. Hull's response was negative and disappointing. He expressed disapproval of the reparation figure, the unspecified list of commodities, and the constitution of the Control Commission which he felt should give the US and Britain a larger voice. As usual, Hull was opposed to any territorial settlement even though pre-war Hungarian seizure of Czechoslovakian and Rumanian territories, which included parts of southern Slovakia, Slovakia-Ruthenia and Transylvania, had neither legal nor ethical justifications. None the less, Hull empowered Harriman to provisionally accept the terms.[58]

Unfortunately, Admiral Horthy had waited too long. When he announced on 15 October that negotiations for an armistice would commence, he was immediately denounced by Sztojay and others. With the deportation of Hungary's Regent and Supreme War Lord to Germany, the old order not only destroyed the 'realist right' but delivered their country to the Germans for total annexation at a moment when the war in Europe was rapidly coming to a close. The confusion following Horthy's precipitous actions

prepared the way for Hungary's first post-war government.
Receiving no support from his fellow commanders, the commanding general of the Second Army, General Bela Miklos, defected to
the Soviets and was permitted to form what Hungary so sadly
lacked, an alternative to the fanaticism of the ruling government.
In due time a provisional government was established in Moscow
with Miklos as Minister President and Minister of Defence. As
was the case in all the other East European nations, the Soviets
approached the reconstructing of Hungarian politics in a non-
partisan fashion. Their aim was to work with politicians of any
stripe who were sincerely interested in reversing the country's
anti-communist and expansionistic tendencies. Despite the fact
that the State Department considered Miklos to be a conservative,
the Soviets permitted him to take the lead in the restructuring
process.[59]

The interim period following the debacle of 15 October provided Hull and his supporters with a belated Indian summer. On
17 October, after Molotov had offered to set aside twenty per cent
of the $400 million for Czechoslovakia and Yugoslavia, Stalin
proposed a reduction of the reparations sum to $300 million of
which a third would be allocated to satisfy the claims of other
countries. Eden and Churchill had agreed subject to American
consent. The Americans were not satisfied. Standard Oil of New
Jersey was worried about its $58 million investment in Magyar
Amerikai Olajipari R.T., which it felt had great potential; so too
was the State Department. At a meeting presided over by Assistant
Secretary of State Dean Acheson, it was decided that opposition
should be phrased in general terms to emphasise the crippling
effect of large reparations on the Hungarian economy, rather than
in specific terms concerning the adverse effects of reparations on
American investment and trading interests in Europe and Hungary.
It was all to be very delicate and diplomatic.[60]

On 2 November the new Secretary of State, E. R. Stettinius,
sent Kennan his instructions. If the mention of a specific sum
could not be excluded from the terms, the Americans were to
accept Stalin's last offer. The important consideration was that
normal trade relations were not to be disturbed by the collection
of reparations and the Soviets were not to be allowed to set up in
the oil distribution business in Europe using Hungarian oil. By

the end of December the Soviets, having compromised by extend-
ing the period from five to six years, had produced their figures.
According to these, which no one disputed, the annual reparations
only amounted to one-third of Hungary's average pre-war output,
or three and one-half per cent of the nation's pre-war annual
income. In terms of European trade and the actual devastation
caused by the Hungarian armies, the reparations figure was of
little significance. Harriman for one was convinced that $50
million a year was not excessive. As an alternative, he favoured
settling on the sum, lest the Soviets ask for more in the future,
and, using Lend–Lease as a weapon, he advocated beating the
Soviets into accepting sizeable American trade concessions and a
larger Anglo-American share in the Control Commission. The
State Department rejected the use of the weapon, but approved
of the objectives. Ultimately neither the Americans nor the British,
who reluctantly followed the American lead, approved of the
Soviet reparations claim. In the long run and the large picture, the
objections were meaningless.[61]

The most significant event in Hungary's rehabilitation came
during the last days of 1944 when underground local committees
throughout the still-occupied country sent 230 representatives to
liberated Debrecen to form a Hungarian Provisional National
Assembly. Of the total membership of the Assembly, the communists, who had a very strong pre-war following among industrial
workers and urban intellectuals, contributed only seventy-two
members who played a rather insignificant role in the Assembly's
deliberations. With this liberal composition, the Assembly passed
a resolution calling for the preservation of private capital and
extensive land reform. General Miklos was elected Minister
President on 21 December 1944, his cabinet being composed of
members of the Communist Party (2), Smallholder Party (2),
Social Democratic Party (2), Peasant Party (1) and five non-party
politicians. When non-communist politicians from abroad, such
as Michael Karolyi, attempted to return to Hungary, the Soviets
welcomed them. The most threatening opponents of the Miklos
government were the radical socialists and not the communists
who, as in Italy, assiduously worked to be more Hungarian than
the Hungarians. Neither the Debrecen Assembly, the Miklos
government, nor the Hungarian Armistice of 20 January 1945

imposed a less than democratic settlement on Hungary or seriously prejudiced the possibility that Churchill and the Americans might not secure their half interest.[62]

The Axis invasion of Yugoslavia was an ugly act of euthanasia. The nation had been incurably ill before the first German, Bulgarian, Italian or Hungarian ever crossed the border.[63] Within hours of the government's inking of the Axis Pact on 25 March 1941, elements of the Yugoslav army, with strong Serbian backing, overthrew the government, forced Prince Paul to flee the country, and installed the young King Peter in his place. As well as a violent reaction to the pro-German leanings of Prince Paul's government, the *coup d'état* indicated a resurgence of Serbian nationalism. The Germans, taken aback by the sudden change of governments and suspicious of the new régime, bombarded Belgrade on 6 April 1941, an act of aggression heralding a massive fifty-two division Axis invasion. By 10 April, royalist resistance had ceased to be effective, and the Independent State of Croatia under the leadership of the fascist Ustashas was proclaimed. The Germans annexed two-thirds of Slovenia; the Italians, Hungarians and Bulgarians took the rest. Almost before King Peter could reach London, his kingdom was no more than a brief memory.[64]

Early in 1942, the King's government-in-exile appointed Dražă Mihailović as Minister of War and Commander-in-Chief of the scattered remnants of the army in Yugoslavia. It was a bold attempt to get back into action. The appointment was extremely popular with the anti-communist, pro-Serb exiles in London, while the Allies welcomed him as a comrade in arms. In Yugoslavia, however, something completely different was shaping.

Although the Yugoslav Communist Party had been outlawed since 1921, it had managed, like the Bulgarian Communist Party, to survive with strong roots underground. Numbering under 27,000 at the time of the Axis invasion, the members were disciplined and well trained, some as participants in the Spanish Civil War; and its leadership was unmatched anywhere in Europe. Ultimately of greater significance, the party was able to identify its own objectives with a great patriotic revival which gradually became a nationalistic movement of liberation. Unlike Mihailović's *chetniks*, the partisans welcomed all Yugoslavs, from whatever minority group, to join them for the express purpose of defeating the nation's enemies. These incentives more than compensated for the lack of recognition and supplies from outside sources, including the USSR. It was a phenomenon of the war. Communist Party membership grew to 140,000 by 1945 (although of the original 12,000 adult members only a quarter lived to see the end of the war). Partisan membership, which was no less risky, expanded even more impressively to 200,000 by 1942, 300,000 by 1943, and 800,000 by the end of 1944.[65]

The communists were not satisfied to see the multiplier effect stop with the transformation from party to national partisan movement. From the beginning, the end was in sight. At Bihach in November 1942, representatives from partisan groups all over the country assembled for the first congress of its kind to be held by any of Europe's resistance movements. In amoebic form, the Bihach Congress produced the Anti-Fascist Council of National Liberation of Yugoslavia (AVNOJ), whose first president was the non-communist Dr Ivan Ribar, a former chairman of the 1921 Constituent Assembly and a member of the Democratic Party. The first affirmation was expressed in multi-partisan and organisational terms.[66]

It was not until the second plenary session of AVNOJ, held at Jajce in Bosnia, that the Yugoslav resistance movement developed a truly political dimension, at least in the context of international politics. During a busy two-day session at the end of November 1943 the congress declared itself to be Yugoslavia's sole legitimate government, prohibited the King from returning to the country prior to a plebiscite, resolved that henceforward there was to be a federation of Serbia, Croatia, Slovenia, Macedonia, Montenegro, and Bosnia–Herzegovina, and created a National Committee of Liberation (NLC), with Josip Broz as its president, to act as AVNOJ's executive arm.[67]

The allies were beginning to take AVNOJ into their policy calculations. The British, who had twenty-nine Special Operations Executive (SOE) missions in Yugoslavia, had been receiving reliable information from their agents since the autumn of 1941. Even before the end of that year, there was strong evidence to

suggest that the partisans were waging anti-Axis warfare throughout the country while Mihailović's *chetniks* were centring their
activities in Serbia where they had collaborated with the quisling
regime of General Milan Nedic, the former Minister of Defence
and Chief of the General Staff. During 1942 there had been
reports that some of Mihailović's commanders had collaborated
with the Italians and Germans as well. In the early part of 1943, the
British had set Mihailović a series of specific tests which his forces
failed to pass. On 27 May, Captain F. W. D. Deakin, an Oxford
don and one of Churchill's literary assistants, was parachuted to
the partisans to establish a mission with Tito. Deakin's wireless
messages confirmed earlier intelligence reports and in June the
Prime Minister ordered the despatch of massive supplies to the
Balkan resistance groups and especially to Yugoslavia. In August,
the first American agent, Major Melvin O. Benson, was sent and
the following month Brigadier Fitzroy Maclean, accompanied by
Major Linn Farish of the Office of Strategic Services (OSS),
arrived at Tito's headquarters to substantiate Deakin's findings,
while Brigadier Armstrong was sent into Mihailović's area for
confirmation of his collaboration.[68]

These drops came at an opportune moment, when partisan
activities were at a peak. With the collapse of the Italian war effort,
the partisans were able to disarm several Italian divisions and
outfit an additional 80,000 of their own men. By mid-October the
SOE estimated that there were 180,000 partisans, with an equal
number in reserve, containing nine German divisions plus perhaps as many Bulgarian, Serbian, Hungarian and Croatian
divisions. Milhailović's forces were estimated at 20,000, with
perhaps 50,000 in reserve. By the end of October, Major Farish,
the OSS agent, confirmed in a perceptive report the root cause of
Mihailović's defection:

> . . . Mihailovitch made the fatal mistake of allowing his political
> beliefs and his plans for the future to overcome his better judge-
> ment. He feared communism more than he feared the common
> enemy. He and his leaders were more concerned with their plans
> for themselves after the war than with the actual ending of the war
> by defeating the Axis.[69]

In November 1943 Brigadier Maclean flew to Cairo to consult
his superiors. He handed Eden a report dated 12 November for

the Prime Minister, which substantiated earlier information. Mihailović's *chetniks* were hopelessly compromised, inactive and weak. In contrast, the partisans were a permanent factor. He stressed that any reconciliation between the *chetniks* and the partisans was a political impossibility. At the same time, the report predicted, at least as interpreted by the Foreign Office, that to switch support from Mihailović to Tito would mean Yugoslavia would be placed in the grasp of a communist regime which would either consolidate its power through terrorist means or be challenged in a bloody civil war. Churchill presented this evidence before FDR and Stalin during the Tehran conference and the three leaders recognised the partisans as an allied force. Notwithstanding any trepidations resulting from the Jajce Congress, the British in December withdrew their support for Mihailović and subsequently recalled their *chetnik* missions. In this light, the decisions taken by AVNOJ at Jajce looked very bright indeed.[70]

During the early months of the war, the Soviets were no less enthusiastic about the supposedly heroic exploits of Mihailović than the exiled Yugoslav government in London. Thereafter they seemed unwilling to recognise the radical changes that took place. When the partisans requested the Soviets in 1942 to expose Mihailović as a traitor and a collaborator on their Yugoslav radio broadcasts, the Soviets refused. As late as the Moscow conference Molotov told Eden that the Soviets were considering sending a military mission to Mihailović. At Tehran, whilst Vyschinski agreed with Harriman that the *chetniks* were not doing all that they should against the Germans, Stalin refused to believe that Tito's partisans were as important as Churchill and his advisers claimed. A few days later Stalin was furious with Tito when he learned of his successful instigation of AVNOJ's break with King Peter's government.[71]

Obviously there was more to the Soviets' unresponsiveness than faulty intelligence. It was the result of a narrowness founded on ideological grounds—of the sort that prompted Stalin at one time to call the Chinese revolutionaries 'margarine communists'. Partly this was caused by the Soviet understanding of their own unique revolutionary experience which made them unwilling to accept outside authority. Partly it was an unwillingness to allow

goslav Communist Party, AVNOJ or Tito to endanger
,iet security interests by exacerbating the USSR's relations with
the US and Britain. If this was true, as Milovan Djilas and
others have suggested—and the general pattern strongly supports
it—then it was a conscious decision which kept the Soviets from
sending Tito a military mission until February 1944. By then it
was too late for the team, led by an unusually high-ranking expert
in guerrilla warfare, to mend the hard feelings caused by earlier
Soviet indifference.[72]

If the outside world was slow to grasp the magnitude of the
changes taking place within Yugoslavia, the Americans showed
that they were impervious to them. Although American intelligence on the spot, as typified by Major Farish's reports, was
excellent, there was a certain density in Washington which
prevented it from being converted into sensible policy. As late as
July 1944, more than six months after the British at the highest
levels had become convinced of Mihailović's defection and several
months after the Yugoslav government-in-exile had dismissed
him as commander-in-chief, the United States were still dropping
arms to his troops. Up until August, only a few months before
Belgrade was liberated, the State Department, the Joint Chiefs
of Staff and Admiral Leahy all persisted in building up Mihailović's
Serbian collaborationists in an effort to offset Tito's influence. The
rationale for this course of action can only be interpreted as
an overt sign of anti-communist sentiment in the lower echelons
of the Roosevelt administration during this period which had as
its only antidote the futility of the entire exercise.[73]

The negotiations following the military and political developments within Yugoslavia during 1943 were relatively uncomplicated. The Americans had taken themselves off the playing field.
The Soviets seemed uninterested in granting Tito recognition.
Churchill, more directly concerned in salvaging something from
the wreckage, accepted the task of chief allied negotiator; but
as Brigadier Maclean has suggested all the cards but one were
Tito's. On 9 February 1944, Marshal Tito informed Churchill
that AVNOJ and the NCL would co-operate with the government-
in-exile in the establishment of a post-war coalition if the King
and the allies would unconditionally repudiate the *chetniks*,
whose number had slipped to 15,000, and accept the Jajce Con-

gress's resolutions. While Churchill felt that generosity would guarantee influence, the young King from the beginning caused him no end of trouble. Rather than accept this proposal, which was generous, the King intended to wait for something better. Churchill undoubtedly knew that Tito's Army of National Liberation had grown to over 290,000 men in the past six months alone. By 1 April he informed Eden that the King was surrounded by 'fatal millstone advisers'. As the result of sustained British pressure, to which the Americans were sympathetic, the King finally dismissed his chief minister and on 1 June redressed the blatantly Serbian bias of the government by appointing Dr Ivan Shubashich, a leader of the Croatian Peasant Party, as head of a new government.[74]

Shubashich, the first Croat to become Premier, moved to support Churchill's negotiating position by entering into talks with Tito on his island fortress of Vis. Shubashich bravely proposed that the royal government should absorb the NCL. Josip Smodlaka, the National Committee's spokesman on foreign affairs, replied with honest bluntness that 'You have neither people, nor army, nor territory.'[75] By 16 June, Shubashich had accepted the NCL proposals in total. The government-in-exile was to wholeheartedly support the National Liberation Army, issue a declaration acknowledging the achievements and sovereignty of AVNOJ and NCL, and recognise the right of the Yugoslav peoples to settle the question of the monarchy by means of a plebiscite. The NCL in return agreed to co-operate with Dr Shubashich in the construction of a coalition government. For an exiled cabinet in London with only a promise it was an excellent arrangement.[76]

Churchill agreed to meet with Tito in Naples in mid-August in an effort to secure the best terms. The most that could be done was attempt to awe Tito with General Wilson's sophisticated war room as though he were some barbarian chieftain from a bygone age, to council moderation and urge him consider the advantages of a constitutional monarchy. A few days later, after unceremoniously leaving Churchill in the lurch, Tito also rejected Stalin's suggestion that the monarchy be restored and the NCL tone down its demands. Even in Moscow, the partisans' war lord showed an independent spirit.[77]

By 1 November, a final solution seemed near at hand. In mid-September King Peter had appealed to the Yugoslav people to unite behind Tito. On 1 October, some three weeks before the liberation of Belgrade, Tito and Shubashich had concluded a second agreement creating a temporary three-man, non-communist regency to act for the King. The two leaders also agreed that Shubashich would become Foreign Minister, that additional room would be made in the NCL for other prominent politicians in exile, and that Marshal Tito would become Premier and Minister of War. In January 1945, when all seemed settled and very likely encouraged by the negative reaction of the Americans towards Tito and the NCL, King Peter repudiated both Shubashich and his agreements. Churchill, always master of a loose situation, quickly proposed to Stalin, who had approved of the Tito–Shubashich agreements in late November, a terminal solution: the two leaders would validate the agreements and bypass the King. It was the wisest move and secured for the US and UK the closest to a half interest in Yugoslavia that the situation allowed.[78]

In the meantime, a grand opportunity, from what should have been the American point of view, was lost. In April 1944, various members of the NCL, AVNOJ and the Yugoslav Communist Party began considering a scheme with possibilities such as Churchill's Danubian Federation never had. The plan envisaged a closer union between Yugoslavia and Bulgaria and the eventual creation of a Balkan confederacy. Such a scheme had been proposed at various times since the nineteenth century as a means of offsetting Austrian and Russian influence in the region, but none the less it had current potential. During December 1944 talks took place in Sofia. The Bulgarian representatives were divided in their reactions to the plan since in its initial form it would have given them federation only on an equal basis with six other republics to be carved out of Yugoslavia, Albania, and Greece. But the internal dynamism of the scheme was not to be lightly dismissed. The Bulgarians did agree, during the December talks, to the establishment of a south Slav council in Belgrade to begin discussions of practical matters such as trade, tariffs and cultural exchanges.[79]

Here was an area where there was room for creative diplomacy between the unyielding right and the inflexibility of the old left.

In three of the countries involved, Albania, Greece and Yugo-slavia, the Soviets had only the slightest interest either politically or militarily. Of all the USSR's western neighbours, Bulgaria, with the possible exception of Finland, enjoyed the longest and loosest tether, if that is an appropriately descriptive term. From a diplomatic point of view, such a confederation had none of the objectionable features of Churchill's Danubian Federation or the London Poles' proposals for a 'third force' in eastern Europe, since it did not propose the formation of an anti-communist bloc or the restoration of the pre-war order.

During the spring of 1944, when it was first being considered, the Soviet press gave the idea its blessing. In fact, however, Churchill was so busily preoccupied with his own grand scheme that he never seriously considered the plan. The Foreign Office opposed it because they feared that it would isolate Greece, en-courage the Bulgars to claim an Aegean outlet, and increase Soviet influence in the region. The Americans had lost a great opportun-ity to create a manageable alternative in south-eastern Europe. For a nation that publicly supported a policy of self-determination while opposing the creation of large blocs and spheres of influence, it was a disappointingly inept performance. Instead of pursuing an independent policy, the State Department and FDR first threw obstacles in the way of Churchill, who was obsessed with only the smallest corner of the problem; then tried to fragment the revolutionary trend by backing Mihailović and King Peter; finally, with greater persistence, they resorted to legalistic trickery in Hungary, Rumania and Bulgaria in a desperate effort to delay the natural development of events. In this strange fashion the best opportunity of the war in eastern Europe to shape an alternative to Churchill's grand design was lost.[80]

Notes to this chapter are on pages 196–200.

Chapter 5 THE BALKAN ANOMALY:
GREECE

GREECE WAS the fifth tile in the mosaic that Churchill and Stalin laid during 1944. For the British it was the most important piece of the pattern, and the one closest to Churchill's and Eden's hearts; for the Soviets it was a matter of little concern. For the Americans it was a further opportunity to reassert their liberal commitments and redefine their European policies. Despite this seeming lack of underlying international tension, Greece proved the most difficult of the five pieces to fit satisfactorily.

Like the Italian monarchy, King George II and his family had tainted themselves in liberal eyes by countenancing and encouraging a pre-war dictatorship as an alternative to an anti-fascist united front. This was a difficult blot to obliterate and continued to be a complicating factor during the war, and even afterwards. Fortunately, in January 1941, before the British, in April, and the royalists, in June, were driven from Greece by the Albanians, Bulgarians, Germans, and Italians, General Ionnis Metaxas, the pre-war dictator, dropped dead. After much serious thought, encouraged by the Foreign Office, King George declared the Metaxas era at an end in October and promised a restoration of the Constitution of 1936 which he had helped Metaxas to suspend.[1] None the less, many of the pre-war blemishes remained.

Events during the war followed a familiar pattern. In September 1941, the National Liberation Front (EAM) was organised in occupied Athens. Its modest programme emphasised a return to constitutionalism and an active resistance to the fascist invaders. Its political drive came from socialists, agrarians, the left-wing of the trade union movement, left liberals and communists. Like the FCNL and AVNOJ, EAM had impressive support from all segments of society and included six bishops, several hundred priests, thirty university professors and two members of the National Academy. In April 1942 EAM announced the formation of its military branch, the People's Liberation Army (ELAS).[2]

Initially there were no royalist groups in Greece. The only alternative to the broadly based EAM–ELAS was the Greek National Democratic League (EDES), led by Colonel, later General, Napoleon Zervas. Like its Albanian counterpart, the *Balli Kombetar*, EDES was essentially a non-ideological coalition, republican in sympathy, which was to become increasingly anti-communist in thought and action. It was not surprising that EDES remained organisationally and militarily backward. Colonel C. M. Woodhouse, one-time Chief of the British Military Mission in Greece, was eventually compelled to note that EDES survived only because of its British connections. At the time of liberation, EDES controlled no more than a small part of Greece, some twenty-five by thirty-five miles, with 12,000 men. Despite these deficiencies and Zervas's objections, the British early on supplied material aid and military missions to both EDES and ELAS.[3]

By contrast, EAM generated local support and an effective political-military apparatus rivalling that of Tito's partisans. By the summer of 1943, ELAS had at least four times the strength of EDES; and the efficiency of its underground political network, a society within a society, was comparable to those of the Yugoslav partisans, the Viet-Minh, and the Chinese communists. While EAM's claim of 1·5 million adherents may be inflated, the British Foreign Secretary estimated that EAM had 500,000 to 750,000 followers and ELAS some 50,000 regulars. Out of a population of 7 million in an occupied country either figure was significant and meant that EAM controlled from two-thirds to four-fifths of the countryside.[4]

During March 1942 the first public conflict between the government-in-exile and the Greek people occurred when an apparently non-affiliated group of what Churchill conceded were 'prominent politicians in Athens' drafted a manifesto counselling the King not to return to Greece until a national plebiscite had been held. The response from the royalists was less than enthusiastic. The British reaction was outright hostile. As the monarchy's chief prop, the British government instructed its liaison mission in

April to pay particular attention to the needs of pro-monarchist factions. King George II, for his part, on 4 July broadcast a promise to hold free elections for a Constituent Assembly not less than six months after the liberation of Greece; beyond that mildly progressive step he would not go. The Foreign Secretary endorsed this pronouncement in the Commons three days later and Brigadier Edward Myers, Britain's chief liaison officer in Greece, meanwhile arranged a meeting between the conflicting resistance groups which resulted in the signing of the National Bands Agreement. This, in brief, avoided all political problems but did manage to apportion Greece into operational zones, based on existing control, with future operations to be planned and executed by a Joint Greek Headquarters working in consultation with British liaison officers.[5] The impact of these events on the anti-EAM cause was considerable: the King had expectations of becoming a constitutional monarch; ELAS was showing a willingness to compromise and co-operate with EDES; the British had secured a toe-hold in Greek military planning.

THE MUTINY

By 10 August the EAM, in spite of the setbacks of July, had reappeared under the auspices of the Special Operations Executive (SOE). On that date Brigadier Myers shepherded six EAM representatives to Cairo where they presented a memorandum containing their views to Premier Emmanuel Tsouderos. The result was the first Greek crisis. The EAM representatives asked for the King not to return to Greece until a plebiscite had been held and that EAM politicians be given the portfolios of the ministries of the Interior, War and Justice. The Foreign Office on 12 and 15 August advised the King 'to play for time' and avoid making any promises. This he gladly did and refused to make any concessions beyond those offered on 4 July. The Tsouderos Cabinet, all royal appointees with no public mandate, then proceeded to embarrass the monarchy and the British by supporting the EAM proposals. British officials on the spot reacted vigorously on 22 August, before the EAM representatives had completed their mission, and ordered them to return immediately to Greece.

General Sir Alan Brooke, Chief of the Imperial General Staff, was profoundly disturbed by these events and questioned the entire drift of his country's policy towards Greece. The General could not see how the government was to reconcile the discrepancy between its military obligations and political inclinations. The facts were simple. The King's popularity was 'doubtful'. EAM controlled more than half of Greece even when opposed by fourteen Axis divisions. The Tsouderos government controlled none of Greece and was 'little known or supported in Greece itself'. If the British government were to lose the EAM's confidence, 'the chances of restoring the King or the Tsouderos Government except by force after the war would be indeed slender'. In support of General Brooke's analysis, the Chiefs of Staff reminded the Foreign Office at the same time of the following crucial point: 'As you know our present strategy in the Mediterranean does not dictate that we should attack and capture Greece with an Allied Expeditionary Force.'[6] Reason now seemed to dictate a Yugoslav settlement.

Even before General Brooke's request for a re-examination, policy-makers were calling for a closing of the ranks and a speedy resolution of contradictions. On 20 August General Smuts, who apparently had his own sources of information, warned Churchill that 'There appears to be strong suspicion that British Intelligence agents who brought Greek Patriots and other party representatives to Cairo are anti-Royalist, and that Patriot representatives even have Communist leaning.' After calling for a purge of the undesirables, Smuts recommended that the implementation of the Atlantic Charter by means of a plebiscite would only lead 'to civil strife, if not to civil war . . .'. Continuing in much the same vein, he warned that 'With politics let loose among those peoples we may have a wave of disorder and wholesale Communism set going all over those parts of Europe.' His suggested solution was 'food and work and interim Allied control'—by which he meant British and American control, or at least the former.[7]

Buttressed with such sound advice, Churchill counter-attacked on 30 September. With more enthusiasm than he had ever shown for the second front, he suggested to the Chiefs of Staff that 'we must certainly be able to send 5,000 British troops with armoured cars and bren-gun carriers into Athens. They need have no transport or artillery.' He need not have added that the troops would be used for riot control and seizure of the capital. As it defended Foreign Office policy, Eden approved of this course of action. He notified Churchill that even a small British force would be sufficient to deter EAM because the troops would enjoy overwhelming popular support.[8]

The first step towards preparing the way for this action required a mixture of sweet and sour psychology. For the unconvinced Chiefs of Staff, the Foreign Office prepared a message, on 8 October, reminding them that, while the EAM leaders were militarily helpful, in all other respects they were 'brigands', communists and terrorists. For the troops, both British and royalist Greek, the Foreign Office prepared implausible propaganda material on the King of the Hellenes and even on the good dictator Metaxas. After two trips to Athens, Eden admitted to his colleagues in mid-November that the going would very likely be difficult: British support for the King was unpopular, Italian co-belligerency was bitterly disliked, and EDES continued to support a republican line. He observed that 'The undeniable connexion of the King with the Metaxas régime and the campaign of vilification which EAM have carried on for the past two years have resulted in turning at least 80 per cent of the Greek people against the King.'[9] It was time to pull together and pull together hard.

Within a few days, Eden presented the government with a comprehensive political policy to complement the Prime Minister's new military plan of 30 September—in the face of warnings from military and intelligence advisers. The power of EAM and ELAS leadership was to be destroyed. EDES, under General Zervas or General Plastiras (who was in exile in Vichy France), was to be strengthened in its efforts to rival EAM. Archbishop Damaskinos was to be advanced as a regent; and Damaskinos, Zervas, and the King were to be reconciled and politically welded together.[10]

With such impressive solidarity at the top, the lower ranks had little chance of holding out. None the less, Richard Casey, Minister of State in the Middle East, continued to feel that EAM supporters 'were not left-wing in outlook' but only anti-monarchists. Air Chief Marshal Sir Charles Portal and General Sir Alan Brooke continued to question the new policy on military grounds. But further down the rolls, results were more evident. By the end of January 1944, SOE agents, who earlier had been at odds with

Reginald Leeper, Britain's Ambassador to the Greek Government in Cairo, began to recommend drastic reductions in supplies and equipment to EAM. At the same time some British liaison officers in Greece, according to Leeper, showed such enthusiasm for the anti-EAM policy that they made contact with the less ostensibly pro-Nazi elements within the Evzone and Rallis security battalions recently recruited by the Germans.[11]

The last serious challenge to government policy came in mid-February 1944 when General Sir Henry Maitland Wilson, the new Supreme Allied Commander in the Mediterranean, supported by the unrepentant Chiefs of Staff, requested that EAM be given unrestricted support in its efforts to defeat the Germans. This request got no further than General Brooke's earlier one. The Foreign Secretary warned Churchill that this last move 'would almost certainly lead to the resignation of the Greek Government, and possibly even to the abdication of the King'. Faced with the loss of these two possessions, on 15 February Churchill rejected General Wilson's and the Chiefs' recommendation. The dissidents in the middle were vanquished. As if to underline this point, at the end of the month the Prime Minister insisted that Brigadier Myers, Maclean's counterpart in Greece, should not be allowed to return to the Greek mainland 'as he is the chief man who reared by hand this cockatrice brute of E.A.M.–E.L.A.S.'. With the loss of Myers the British soldiered on without their best link with the EAM; in his place they got the more orthodox Colonel Woodhouse, a supporter of the new policies.[12]

In conjunction with the attempt to subvert EAM's authority in Greece and to construct an anti-EAM political front, the British for several months past had tried to strengthen monarchist support overseas among the Royal Hellenic armed forces. There had been small problems shortly after the King's speech of 4 July 1943. During April 1944 the whole carefully constructed fabric almost unravelled. The 1st Brigade, the chosen unit for flag waving in Italy, and intended eventually for service in western Greece, mutinied. More than a hundred men had to be placed in an 'isolation camp'. A large section of the Royal Hellenic Navy came out for the resignation of the government and a republic. On the 4th, General Kallergis, the former Director-General of the Army, was arrested as a trouble maker. On the 8th, the crew of a Greek destroyer refused to steam out of harm's way until a government including EAM representatives was formed. Dissidence spread to elements within the Royal Hellenic Air Force. Then the entire 1st Brigade of some 4,500 men revolted and spoiled any chances they had ever had to win glory for their king and country. Churchill's reaction was predictable. On the 22nd, in his most statesmanlike fashion, he instructed General Sir Bernard Paget that when the shooting became necessary he should make certain that 'the onus should lie to the account of the British rather than of the slender, tottering Greek Government'.[13]

Some of the *post-mortems*, after the second Greek crisis, were interesting. Premier Tsouderos believed the cause of the unrest was the problem of the monarchy. Admiral Alexandris, the Greek Commander-in-Chief, thought that 'strong feeling was running amongst the lower decks on the subject of lack of co-operation between the Cairo Government and guerrillas in Greece'. Taking their lead from Ambassador Leeper, the British felt it was time to find a strong replacement for Tsouderos.[14]

The American reaction to all this was surprisingly distant. In a letter written during the worst of the trouble, FDR expressed hope, sympathy and warmth for the Prime Minister's plight, which revealed neither understanding nor curiosity about the situation's underlying causes. On the 26th, after the suppression, the President simply noted that 'I am very pleased indeed by your success in handling the Greek naval and military mutiny.'[15]

THE UNIVERSAL ATTRACTION OF LAW AND ORDER

Politically the situation remained non-progressive. During the last months of 1943 the British had attempted to get King George of Greece to accept Archbishop Damaskinos as regent. This was done even though he was known to be unpopular in Greece since he had risen to power under Metaxas and had received his latest position with German approval. Roosevelt, who at Quebec in August 1943 had promised to support British efforts to militarily tranquillise the situation in Greece before the holding of elections, unexpectedly counselled the King to reject the proposal. On his own initiative, the King again turned down the suggestion in March 1944.[16]

After the military reversals of April, May 1944 surprisingly produced political dividends for the British. On 7 May, in occupied Greece, the National Council, the Greek equivalent of a plenary meeting of AVNOJ, began its session. The two hundred and fifty members, remarkably representative of class and regional interests within the society at large, showed their non-revolutionary character. On the 27th they passed a resolution providing for the dissolution of EAM's Political Committee of National Liberation and the National Council in the event of EAM achieving representation in the Cairo cabinet. Meanwhile, in the Lebanon, Tsouderos' successor, George Papandreou, a well-known anti-EAM monarchist, cleverly drafted a National Charter which provided for the creation of a unified government within the existing Cairo framework. After a temporary delay when EAM repudiated the work of their delegates at the Lebanon meetings, by 2 September EAM agreed to enter the unity government and accept six ministries. What the British had failed to achieve by intimidation, the EAM had succeeded in doing without external interference. The first signs of Soviet interest in the domestic affairs of Greece occurred at this time, when Moscow encouraged their supporters within EAM to accept Papandreou's offer.[17]

By 26 September 1944, EAM had all but liquidated themselves, in a spirit of compromise, when they agreed to place their units under the control of the Supreme Allied Commander in the Mediterranean, General Sir Henry Maitland Wilson, and the unofficial designate Commander-in-Chief of the army of the Greek Government of National Unity, Major-General Ronald Scobie. The only member of the ELAS high command to oppose this contractual arrangement was the non-communist General Saraphis. After exhaustive discussions, the EAM had surrendered with shockingly little of any substance having been settled. The question of a future government was undecided and the continuance of the present arrangement, which granted EAM much less representation than it was entitled to by any intelligible standard, augured ill for any continuing success. Even more threatening, no agreement regarding the formation of a unified national army had been suggested.[18]

By July 1944 the military stake had gone up. The Chiefs of Staff, who had never had much confidence in the pro-British sympathies of the Greek people, estimated that it would take 80,000 troops to control the major areas of the country and 10,000 to control Athens and Salonika. For practical reasons, the lesser number had been agreed upon by August. By the end of the month, Churchill had tactically decided that 'It is most desirable to strike out of the blue without any apparent preliminary crisis. It is the best way to forestall the E.A.M.' There was to be no consultation with the Greek government and operation MANNA was to be ready to strike by mid-September. It had also been decided by the end of the month that the 'stabilising force' should 'be sponsored by British Headquarters and not by a combined Anglo-American Headquarters'. General Sir Bernard Paget, hero of the Greek mutiny and commanding officer of MANNA, was to have a free hand to plan his operation in consultation with Leeper. The problem was that the British had insufficient transport to get their troops across from Cairo. The Americans were obviously going to have to be brought into the operation at some point.[19]

The Prime Minister asked the Americans for transport on 17 August. On the 26th, FDR replied that the US would supply transport to make MANNA operational and save Greece, in Churchill's words, from 'a tyrannical Communist Government being set up'. The British then approached General Eisenhower for the use of one hundred transport planes for a week or ten days. On 14 September Hitler ordered German troops to fall back in such a manner, as General Alfred Jodl was to describe it, as to 'kindle and fan strife between communist and nationalist forces'. MANNA started at Patras on 4 October and proceeded smoothly. From the 13th to the 18th the American 51st Troop Carrier Wing transported 10,000 British troops to Greece; by 1 November the entire country had been liberated.[20]

Despite the speed with which MANNA had been effected, the shadow of the Papandreou government hardly extended beyond the presence of the British army which in turn was mainly confined to Athens and Pireaus. The modified royal government faced a period of lengthy re-negotiations if it was to establish its authority over the ELAS bands which controlled nearly all the country. Rather than accept this state of affairs. Churchill girded his loins for battle. As he wrote Eden on 7 November, 'In my opinion, having paid the price we have to Russia for freedom of action in Greece, we should not hesitate to use British troops to support the Royal Hellenic Government under M. Papandreou.' He added the sincere hope that 'the Greek Brigade will soon arrive, and will not hesitate to shoot when necessary'.[21]

The vital problem facing the Papandreou government was not that of satisfying politically the various semi-autonomous guerrilla chieftains but the disarming of some 55,000 to 90,000 EDES–ELAS troops, which stood anywhere from three to seven to one in favour of ELAS. On 5 November, with the liberation barely completed, Papandreou and General Scobie ordered both ELAS and EDES units to disarm by 10 December. Immediately the inadequacies of earlier agreements became apparent. No provision had been made to disarm the anti-EAM Security Battalions hastily recruited by the Germans to fight ELAS units, or the hand-picked royalist Sacred Squadron and the Greek Brigade, the only units not to be affected by the mutiny of April 1944, which were being brought into the country from Syria. Nor had any provision been made to form a new national army.

EAM took the position that a national army should be constructed on a proportional basis reflecting the *status quo*. After initially agreeing to this, Papandreou on 22 November, when the process of disarming was well advanced, argued that some units such as the Greek Brigade should not be disbanded because they were officially under the command of the Supreme Allied Commander, General Wilson. While the last few hours of the 10 December deadline were literally ticking away, EAM counter-proposed, in a typically conciliatory fashion, that the national army should be composed of two brigades with the ELAS brigade equal in size to the government's. Papandreou replied by defending a scheme whereby the one ELAS brigade would be half the size of royalist units.[22] The question was whether Papandreou and the British would accept the creation of a military establishment incompatible with the political gains they had already achieved. The answer was never really in doubt.

DEAF AND DUMB

When the six EAM ministers resigned on the night of 1–2 December, calling for a demonstration on Sunday, the 3rd, and a

general strike on the 4th, it was for the express purpose of bringing
the Papandreou government down. Giving permission on the 2nd
for the demonstration to take place, the government then arbitrarily
called it off at almost 7 pm the same day, after it had received wide
publicity. It was then too late. On Sunday, 3 December, the Athens
police fired on a crowd of unarmed EAM demonstrators, killing
about twenty and wounding 140. It was only on the 5th, when
Churchill, through Leeper, expressed his opposition to any
change of Prime Ministers, that Papandreou resumed the office
from which he had just resigned. Coupled with a provocative
warning by General Scobie that any ELAS units around Athens
would be treated as hostile forces, this contributed to the inevitable
clashes between British and ELAS units.[23] The King, Papandreou
and British strategic interests in the Balkans and the Eastern
Mediterranean were safe, but the Greek civil war was on.[24]

American foreign policy during this period reached its nadir:
there was no reassessment of FDR's decision of 26 August 1944
to support the British nor of its consequences. The US Ambassador
to the Greek government-in-exile, Lincoln Mac Veagh, collaborated with Leeper, the King, and Papandreou, but was ignorant of
what was happening inside Greece. When Leeper complained to
Mac Veagh in June 1944 that American intelligence agents in
Greece were pursuing an anti-British line, Mac Veagh took the
matter up with the Commanding General of American Forces in
the Middle East and the heads of OSS and the Office of War
Information and had the dissident voices quelled. On 16 June he
seriously reported, after talking to the King, that 'only extreme
Leftists and a couple of radical Republicans without any real
following in the country' opposed the monarchy returning prior
to a plebiscite.[25]

The real problem, however, lay in Washington. On 30 November
1944, the American Chiefs of Staff, who never showed any curiosity about British policy in Greece or any willingness to oppose it,
informed the British that they were prepared to equip 40,000
Greek troops. On 5 December it seemed the Americans might be
prepared to cross the British when Hull's successor, Edward
Stettinius, publicly criticised Britain's interference in Italian
affairs. On the 10th the Americans appeared to be taking an
independent line when Admiral Ernest J. King revealed in a news

summary that he had informed General Wilson that American landing craft were no longer to be used to carry British supplies to Greece. The administration and the US Chiefs of Staff, however, quickly reversed this decision. In Hopkins' view, Admiral King's action was 'off base from an organisational point of view'.

> I told Leahy that I thought King was getting into the political arena and that we would undoubtedly hear from the British about it. I told him, furthermore, that I felt that, while we should keep our troops out of Greece, and let the British do the policing, withdrawing the LSTs was like walking out on a member of your family who is in trouble. Under any circumstances, we had told the British that they could use our airplanes to send their paratroopers into Greece and the action of Admiral King did not jibe with that.[26]

This sentimental nonsense from the normally realistic Hopkins suggests that the Americans simply pursued a course of institutional convenience. After General Scobie's call on 11 December for reinforcements from Italy, there was no second hesitation. During the following two weeks, American troop planes transported from Italy two British divisions, an Indian brigade, and several other battalions, all of which very likely saved the military situation for the British.[27]

A second source of external support for EAM, or at least for an equitable peace, was the USSR. However, as had been the case with Yugoslavia and Albania, the Soviets showed no interest in internal Greek affairs until the war was practically over. The first Soviet Military Mission did not arrive at ELAS headquarters until the end of July 1944, months after the British and Americans. The Soviets unquestionably were keeping their eyes on the larger picture and did not want Greece to become a source of conflict between themselves and their allies. They allowed Tsouderos and other monarchist politicians to use Radio Moscow during the early weeks of 1944; were quietly helpful during the April mutinies; seemed to get most of their information about the internal situation in Greece from the British; and encouraged their supporters within EAM to be co-operative.[28]

None of this should have been surprising, for after the Moscow conference of 1943 Eden was able to report to the Middle East Defence Committee that the Soviets were definite 'that they had no interest in, or contact with, Greece, which they apparently regarded as within our sphere of influence . . .'. On 11 December 1944, at the height of the tension in Athens, Churchill wrote Eden that '. . . Stalin has kept off Greece in accordance with our agreement . . .'. Later, in his history of the Second World War, he was to comment that Stalin, who 'adhered strictly and faithfully to our agreement of October [1944]', was so co-operative that, unlike *The Times* and the *Manchester Guardian*, 'during all the long weeks of fighting the Communists in the streets of Athens not one word of reproach came from *Pravda* or *Isvestia*'.[29]

Emboldened by the absence of any opposition from the Americans or Soviets, and alarmed by the prospect that without Greece Britain would lack political influence in south-east Europe to maintain her post-war strategical position in the eastern Mediterranean, Churchill and Eden would undoubtedly ask for a strictly British peace.[30] On 5 December, the Prime Minister reminded General Scobie that the immediate objective was to defeat EAM. 'The ending of the fighting is subsidiary to this.' He advised Leeper on the same day that the best diplomatic approach was to ignore EAM, freeze it out of the government and treat the whole matter exclusively in law and order terms. 'This is no time to dabble in Greek politics . . .You should not worry about Greek Government compositions. The matter is one of life and death.' Three days later, after EAM had proposed peace talks, the Prime Minister wrote Scobie that he was perfectly willing to stand pat and keep the EAM's ministers, 'with their hands wet with Greek and British blood' outside the Greek government.[31] In situations such as these, it is difficult to deny inevitability a part in the historical process.

While encouraging the exclusion of the leftists from the political centre, the Prime Minister realised that he needed to trim some embarrassingly loose ends on the right if the game was going to be played to the end. When on 13 December, Churchill and Eden approached the King, he refused, for the third time, to accept Archbishop Damaskinos as anything other than prime minister. Two days later, the British threatened to cut off all military, financial and political aid to the royalists. The King temporised, offering something that no one wanted, a three-man regency. Churchill in turn responded much as he had when King Peter of Yugoslavia had been obstructive.

When he and Eden arrived in Athens on Christmas Day, they began direct negotiations with the Archbishop and soon reached agreement. As regent, Damaskinos would refuse EAM's latest terms (half the government's portfolios, an anti-fascist purge of the army, police and civil service, and an immediate plebiscite on the future of the monarchy) and form a small non-EAM government headed by General Nicholas Plastiras. With the last prop withdrawn, and no encouragement forthcoming from the Americans, the King had no option but to accept the regency plan and promise not to return to Greece until after a national referendum. On 3 January 1945, General Plastiras succeeded Papandreou as head of the new government. The loose ends, at least the ones most susceptible to foreign and internal criticism, had been knotted.[32]

By the end of the first week in January, the British still controlled only Attica. ELAS, however, had lost heart and decided not to pursue what had become a lonely battle against a major power. By 4–5 January the battle for Athens was over and ELAS ordered a general withdrawal. The losses were high: after some thirty days of fighting 11,000 had been killed, more than half of whom were non-combatants. On 3 February, the Varkiza Agreement was signed. The EAM and the Communist Party were recognised as legal but non-governmental parties. In return for an amnesty for 'crimes' committed during the 'rebellion', ELAS agreed to disarm and disband its component groups and accept royalist units from the Middle East as the nucleus of the national army.[33]

If it is true that 'the Varkiza Pact brought not the promised peace but a chain of events that have culminated in the present dictatorship',[34] it is also fair to say that British strategic interests were kept very safe.

Notes to this chapter are on pages 200–1.

Chapter 6 THE UNATTENDED PEACE

ONE OF the least credible monarchs of the pre-war period was Zog of Albania who from September 1928 until April 1939 ruled his kingdom in quiet obscurity, paying little attention to reform, prosperity or the outside world. There were no universities, few ideologies and no political parties. The country folded very quickly when the greedy Italians invaded it on 7 April 1939, their vulture hearts quickened by Hitler's annexations. When Count Ciano, Mussolini's son-in-law and Foreign Minister, went to Tirana on the 12th, the Albanian assembly, well disciplined by Zog over the past decade, heartlessly turned against their former master, voted to abolish the Royal Constitution of 1928 and offered the crown to Victor Emmanuel. Except for a brief and angry outcry from Cordell Hull, the old Albania and its monarch slipped quietly from the scene.[1]

During November 1941 two representatives of Tito's partisan movement slipped across the border to help the two or three thousand Albanian communists organise a resistance movement. As a result of this mission, Enver Hoxha became the party's first provisional secretary and the National Liberation Movement (LNC) was formed during September 1942. The LNC found their chief supporters among the landless peasants in the south and among urban intellectuals. Their leaders were a nationalistic mixture comprising a communist, a leader of an obscure Moslem sect, a guerrilla–outlaw with extensive pre-war experience, and an anti-Italian landowner who later defected to the German puppet government. The National Front, or *Balli Kombetar*, gathered together the conflicting elements of the right: those who were frightened of the communists, the Germans, and the Italians; the landowners of the north, the Westernists, the Zogists, and the rightist republicans.[2]

During the first days of August 1943, representatives of the National Liberation Movement and the National Front tentatively formed a coalition committee of National Salvation. Their history was as short lived as similar experiments in Yugoslavia and Greece. With the collapse of Italy and the rapid disintegration of the five and a half Italian divisions in Albania, the Germans parachuted troops into strategic areas in an attempt to salvage the situation. Their two and a half divisions secured them the major urban areas and main transportation lines, but their political efforts yielded more spectacular results. A puppet government was formed, and sufficiently vague promises were made to hearten and placate the motley collection of interests on the right to secure the old order's support. Faced with the increasing successes of the LNC, the National Front proved consistent with the general European experience and turned collaborationist. With assistance from the Germans, National Front units were rearmed and retrained, and by May 1944 some were fighting alongside the Germans.[3]

The remainder of the story is quickly told. On 24 May 1944 the LNC established a National Congress and an Antifascist Council of National Liberation. During October a provisional government was created with Enver Hoxha as its premier. By December 1944 the National Front had receded far into the background. The LNC, with a partisan army of more than 70,000, liberated Albania without allied military assistance.[4]

With the exception of the Germans, Italians and, to a limited extent, the Yugoslavs, the outside world was hardly aware of internal developments in Albania. Of the three major leaders, Churchill came nearest to expressing concern. During July 1943, he reminded General Sir Harold Alexander, of the North Africa command, that the Albanian resistance had developed, 'with no more aid from Britain than the dropping of a few bundles by parachute'. From October 1943 until January 1944, resistance groups in Albania received but 100 tons of supplies which was only a 57th of what the Yugoslavs were receiving. Even after Churchill's urgings, very little was done to improve this situation. The Americans were neither interested nor informed. As late as 15 November 1944, when the LNC had all but triumphed, acting Secretary of State Stettinius was clearly uncertain about what was happening. All he could tell the nation was that there were two or three Albanian resistance groups and at present the US intended to recognise none of them. The Soviets were no more enlightened. By the spring of 1946, neither Tito nor Stalin had met Enver Hoxha, and Stalin was still uncertain whether he was a communist or not. With the amount of attention given to the Balkans by the allies, it seems strange that Albania should have been a diplomatic oversight.[5]

IBERIA

Although Britain and the USA had recognised Franco's government following his victory over the Republic in 1939, thus greatly easing the establishment of the new regime's economic and diplomatic ties with the non-fascist world, Franco never responded with anything approaching full-blooded gratitude. On 20 February 1939, even before the Republic was finished, Franco had signed the Anti-Comintern Pact with Germany, Italy and Japan. The full-scale slide from there into the Axis camp, however, never occurred. First, the signing of the Nazi–Soviet treaty in August 1939 acted as an icy dash of water on the pro-fascist ardour of Catholic Spain. Second, Franco and the Falangists always maintained that Spain's unique cultural and religious institutions made it unsuitable as a Nazi satellite. Third, Franco and his cohorts were still sitting on a potentially explosive internal situation. Fourth, and most important of all, the Germans failed to satisfy Spanish territorial ambitions. During mid-June 1940, Franco submitted his shopping list to the Germans: in return for Spanish participation in the war against the allies, Spain wanted various select properties on the west and north coasts of Africa and Gibraltar. Since Italy, Vichy France and Germany all had designs on these territories, no satisfactory arrangement had been reached. As an alternative, in July 1940 Franco and Dr Salazar of Portugal, who was in much the same frustrating position, decided to fashion a profitable, middle-road, Iberian bloc.[6]

While both Spain and Portugal during the early stages of the war posed as neutrals, with Germany's invasion of the USSR in June 1941 Franco's approval of the Axis course perceptibly quickened. On the Russian front, the Spaniards played as active a part as their uncertain domestic situation and their modest means allowed.

The Blue Division, supplemented by a Spanish air squadron, eventually numbered more than 18,000 regular troops. After the Blue Division was ostensibly withdrawn from the front in October 1943, the air squadron remained with a number of volunteers, reinforced by Falangist recruits, and these were incorporated into an unofficial Spanish Legion under German command. At times, especially during the allied invasion of North Africa in November 1942, even the British and Americans were uncertain of Spanish neutrality. With approximately 150,000 Spanish troops in Morocco during the invasion and a cloudy political picture, allied military authorities felt justified in keeping the US Fifth Army in readiness in the event of a Spanish sneak attack. This precaution seemed especially timely after the Spanish Ambassador in London had candidly warned the Foreign Office in October that Spain viewed any prolongation of the war as dangerously favourable to international communism and other revolutionary elements. Even after the surrender of Italy, when Axis power in the Mediterranean had been severely diminished, Spain defied the allies by accepting fourteen Italian merchant ships, one cruiser, three destroyers and two torpedo boats—all much needed by the allies—which had refused to surrender with the balance of the Italian fleet at Malta. As of 1 November 1943, the US Chiefs of Staff modestly considered Spain's policy to be one of 'non-belligerent adherence to the Axis'.[7]

While Spanish policy remained constant throughout 1943, Portugal was carefully nudged by the US and UK into a more co-operative stance. Salazar and Portugal did not easily relinquish their pro-Axis bias. Restricted rights granted to the British in the Azores in June 1943 were the product of pressurised negotiations. As late as mid-May 1943, Harry Hopkins and others had felt that military operations against these islands would be necessary. Similar facilities in the Azores were accorded to the Americans only after considerable delays and with outrageous conditions attached.[8]

The real game, however, was played with money. The prize was wolfram, widely used in the manufacture of high grade steel, armour plate, and armour piercing projectiles for anti-tank weapons. At the time, Iberia produced ninety-five per cent of Europe's supplies of this ore. On 1 January 1942 Germany had no more than 500 tons. Production in Axis Europe amounted to another 250 tons. During the course of the year, the Axis nations consumed 5,800 tons of wolfram. The conclusion was inescapable. Between 1941 and 1942 Spain increased shipments of minerals of all kinds to the Axis by more than fifty-two per cent. Widespread smuggling pushed the figure higher. Portugal also had a great flush of economic health from trade with the Axis, shipping large quantities of tungsten, tin, wool, skins and olive oil. For the second half of 1943, the Portuguese contracted to deliver nearly half of their sardine catch to Germany. When the British and Americans attempted to purchase these strategically important commodities to keep them from the Germans, the Spaniards rejoiced. They falsified their trade figures, continued their exports to Germany and allowed prices to soar. Dr Salazar, a former professor of economics and minister of finance, also appreciated a stabilisation of the nation's economy with guaranteed high levels of production and prices. As a matter of principle he refused to allow the allies to create an unfavourable balance of trade between his country and Germany and honoured his prior commitments. Failing to deflect Spain and Portugal from their course, the British and Americans toyed, ineffectively, with the idea of economic retaliation.[9]

During the last months of 1943, various spokesmen called for a more positive Anglo-American policy towards the two countries. Robert P. Patterson, a US Under Secretary of War, called for a closing of the petroleum lifeline without which the Iberians would be incapable of fulfilling their internal and shipping needs. General Marshall supported Patterson. Churchill opposed the plan. The US Chiefs of Staff were in favour. The British Chiefs of Staff backed the Prime Minister. None the less, during January the US suspended all shipments of oil to Spain which was singled out as the major offender. General F. G. Jordana, the Spanish Foreign Minister, who was always more willing to negotiate with Sir Samuel Hoare, the British Ambassador, than the Americans, presented his terms on 17 February. In return for the resumption of oil shipments, the Spaniards would close the infamous German consulate in Tangier, expel all known German spies in Morocco and Spain, withdraw all Spanish units on the Soviet front, release the Italian ships and reduce wolfram exports to Germany.[10] While the British were eager to agree to this proposal, the American Ambassador on 28 February told General Jordana that the US would accept nothing less than a suspension of exports for six months and a reduction of the total figure to one-tenth of 1943 exports.[11]

By March the tension between Madrid, London and Washington had reached a very fine pitch. The Americans wanted an embargo on wolfram to Germany and a reduction in production. Hoare told Ambassador Hayes that the American terms were unacceptable and turned to the War Cabinet and Churchill for support. The following day General Jordana rejected the proposed embargo. When Spanish oil supplies had all but dried up, Jordana attempted to bluff his way clear by threatening to abolish all restrictions on the German trade. Finally a British–American compromise, with FDR's full backing, was presented to the Spaniards: oil shipments would be resumed if there were no further wolfram shipments until July and thereafter no more than 300 tons. This time Franco personally rejected the offer.[12]

Until mid-April the Americans appeared to remain firm. Then Hull, who publicly had been taking a firm line against pro-Axis neutrals, proposed that the British take the lead in the negotiations and the resumption of oil shipments. Britain viewed this diplomatic line as a typical American attempt to get the necessary job done while giving the British a bad press as appeasers of Franco. Whatever the interpretation placed on Hull's remarks, Churchill, towards the end of the month, accepted Hull's onerous gambit. Before the Prime Minister could release a statement to the press and publicly air the differences between the two governments, however, Hull instructed Ambassador Hayes in Madrid to fully co-operate with the British. The moment passed, and Franco again was spared the embarrassment of changing his course once it had been set.[13]

Obviously something was stirring in the British camp. No sooner had a private Anglo-Spanish agreement been reached which allowed Spain to enjoy the fruits of the whole world, than Churchill on 24 May hyperbolically praised Franco's Spain, in the House of Commons, for the grand service she had rendered to the Allies in refusing to intervene on the Axis side during the dangerous moments of November 1942. As was the case in Italy,

Rumania and Greece, the Prime Minister was generous when forgiving past authoritarian indiscretions. But there was more to it than that. On 4 June 1944, Churchill made it clear that Britain wanted nothing more than a friendly Iberian peninsula after the war. There was nothing subtle about the progression; Salazar and Franco were being refurbished in the public eye for a future junior partnership.[14]

On 30 May 1944, Mr Duff Cooper, the British Representative with the French Committee of National Liberation, had written Anthony Eden a personal letter which powerfully argued for a confederation, under British tutelage, of France, Belgium, Holland, Norway and Denmark, which would subsequently embrace Sweden, Portugal, Spain and Italy. Eden considered the presentation to be 'masterly', but he also was concerned that the Soviets might see something more harmful in the plan than an anti-German front. As he warned Duff Cooper, 'unless we are very careful we shall find that the natural corollary to a Western group under our aegis is the creation of a similar group under Russia's aegis, implying the division of Europe into spheres of influence with Germany as a no-man's-land in between'.[15]

Regardless of Eden's misgivings and the tact required, on 27 July 1944 the British Chiefs of Staff approved the plan in principle. As part of the parcel, on 9 October the Chiefs noted the views of Cooper and Hoare and stated that Britain required post-war military facilities in Spanish Morocco and the friendship of Spain to maintain British interests in Gibraltar and the Straits. By the end of the month, the Foreign Office had started talks with all the countries concerned. By November, after tabulating the latest results, the membership had changed slightly to include Iceland and exclude Italy.[16] Again the Chiefs of Staff approved of the plan 'not only for security purposes against Germany, but also to draw together the countries concerned, and thus increase their influence in world affairs'.[17] Things were shaping nicely. Since the British conducted their negotiations *in camera*, the Americans did not see beyond the immediacies and their record throughout this last phase of the peace plans remained smirched. By callously failing to precipitate a crisis which would have resulted in a break with Spain, the Roosevelt administration enabled Franco to escape the peace settlement. Equally important, the administration allowed itself to be closely associated with a policy which showed the greatest disdain for the USSR and the professed ideals of American liberalism. For little, if any, advantage, the Roosevelt administration let slip the opportunity to rectify one of the more egregious international lapses not only of the late 1930s but of the mid-1940s as well.

FRANCE

After the fall of France in June 1940, there developed a fundamental divergence in attitudes between the Americans and the British towards that nation. Churchill and the Foreign Office, who were not always at one on many issues, were welded in their conviction that Vichy should not be allowed to play the profitable Iberian game. Because the British demanded that the French government unreservedly serve the anti-fascist cause, at least during Britain's grimmest months, direct relations with Vichy were never established and, ineffectual as it may have been, the British Navy in 1940–1 attempted to blockade and impose trade controls on North Africa and France. The rationale for these actions was simple: until proved otherwise Vichy was to be treated as a potential enemy state. As an early alternative, the British on 28 June 1940 recognised General de Gaulle as the leader of the anti-fascist French.[18]

In direct variance with this attitude, well before the United States entered the war, the State Department and Roosevelt had decided that the Vichy French were worth reclaiming; accordingly Fleet Admiral William D. Leahy arrived at Vichy as the US Ambassador to France in January 1941. His tasks were to keep the Vichy leaders from actively joining the Axis and to ferret out those personages within the government who would best further allied war aims. From the beginning, the Ambassador, Roosevelt, and Stimson felt kindly disposed towards Marshal Pétain, Admiral Darlan and General Weygand. All three were authoritarian figures with seemingly impeccable, if conservative, records; Pétain and Weygand had the additional advantage of being World War I heroes. As if to reinforce this preference, Robert D. Murphy, the State Department's peripatetic specialist on France, concluded a trade agreement with Vichy, the Murphy–Weygand Agreement, in

February 1941. It was an arrangement that seemingly had much to recommend it: not only did it give America for the first time an influential position in the economy of French North Africa, but also bestowed an unofficial mark of approval to the activities of Pétain, Darlan and the President's favourite, Weygand.[19]

The British continued to protest futilely against American policy. During March 1941 it became known that Admiral Darlan's response to America's gesture of friendship had been to conclude an extensive trade agreement with the Germans. During May the Vichy government generously granted Germany naval and air bases in North Africa and Syria for use against the British in Egypt and Iraq. From then on the gale never subsided. Even Leahy, who ordinarily defended his first impressions, was forced to conclude that Darlan was an unsuitable ally. Before the end of the year the casualty list had grown even longer. During November General Weygand, the Americans' first choice, was painlessly and permanently dismissed as Pétain's deputy in North Africa for lack of ideological purity. And suddenly there was only the Marshal.[20]

In the meantime de Gaulle unwittingly complicated everyone's relations. During the summer of 1941, British and Free French troops executed a successful campaign in Syria. At its conclusion, the British commanders in the field, without consulting London, negotiated an extremely generous armistice on 14 July with the defeated Vichy leaders. De Gaulle was publicly enraged by Britain's leniency. In retrospect, the Foreign Office agreed with de Gaulle; nevertheless, bad feelings on both sides were caused by this incident. On 11 November, in an effort to diplomatically hedge the administration's bets and spread their risks, Roosevelt granted the Free French Lend–Lease assistance. This was a considerable concession, for the President as early as September 1940 had formed the impression that General de Gaulle's ambition exceeded both the best interests of France and the allies. On Christmas Eve 1941, Free French naval forces seized St Pierre and Miquelon islands off the coast of Newfoundland from their Vichy defenders. The United States had previously objected to the operation on the grounds that it would damage US–Vichy relations. The Free French had then promised the British that it would be postponed. Only after de Gaulle began to suspect that the islands, with American approval, would remain permanently under the control of Vichy had he broken his undertaking. The State Department reacted violently against the action and the British began to have serious doubts about de Gaulle's integrity.[21]

During January 1942 the administration suffered yet another reversal. While Vichy held that invasions from whatever source would be gallantly repelled, Leahy was obliged to inform Washington that, when the Germans decided to move in that direction, Vichy would not exclude Germany from French Colonial Africa. In mid-April, Pierre Laval, the most pro-German of all the Vichy politicians, assumed effective control of the government. At this critical juncture, in May, Leahy was permanently recalled to Washington. And then, all of a sudden, there were none.[22]

At this time, as never before, Roosevelt stamped his own personal ideas on the policy-making process and shifted the diplomatic emphasis and military swing away from metropolitan France to North Africa. Obviously American efforts had so far failed both as a deterrent to the pro-Nazi drift of the Vichy government and in uncovering pro-allied supporters for a reversal of Laval's influence. Increasingly Roosevelt and his advisers became convinced that there was a residue of good feelings among North African leaders created by past American efforts. First-line policy called for a continuation of the Leahy tradition with a change in venue. With the aim of obtaining safe passage for American troops, Murphy and others conducted lengthy and secret negotiations with high level French commanders and politicians in North Africa during the fall of the year. The second line of policy was also an offshoot of Leahy's lead as adapted by Roosevelt. Originally favoured by OSS agents as a counter to Darlan's North African influence, General Giraud was selected by the administration as the new leader. A military hero, like the others, he had impressive business, financial and military connections. Unfortunately the General also had a close association with Pétain and little popular support.[23]

This last American personnel discovery came too late to be of any use before or during operation TORCH. Twelve hours before the landings in North Africa on 7 November, Giraud in Gibraltar graciously gave his approval for the invasion to take place. He also, however, insisted on being named the operation's supreme

commander. With this last minute surprise, Giraud's approval
proved to be more unfortunate than useful. When Giraud arrived
in North Africa on 9 November, it became apparent that the *colons*
still danced to the Marshal's tune and Giraud was powerless to
influence the stream of events. It again became obvious to many
members of the Roosevelt administration that only Darlan, once
rejected, could salvage the situation.[24]

Darlan's colleagues in Vichy, along with Marshal Pétain,
regarded the allied invasion of North Africa as nothing less than
an act of aggression. When Pétain called on Vichy soldiers to
resist, scattered units did so at Casablanca, Oran and Algiers.
Laval quickly severed relations between Vichy and the US.
Darlan's reaction to the invasion was in the Italian mode: until
time and events cancelled his options, he wavered. On 9 November, he ordered his commanders in Tunisia to resist with the
Germans. The following day, when threatened with arrest, he
ordered a cease-fire but no French operations against the Germans.
On 12 November, Darlan chose to survive: with the assistance of
Generals Clark and Eisenhower, the Admiral assumed political
control of French North Africa while Giraud relieved him of his
military duties. Despite an additional blemish that allowed the
Germans to take Tunis and Bizerta without French opposition, it
could be said that American policy efforts had brought about
stability. It mattered little that Sir William Strang, perhaps not a
lonely voice in the Foreign Office, felt that Roosevelt was 'losing
the moral leadership of Europe . . .'.[25]

The Emergent Outsiders

The British meanwhile continued to struggle with de Gaulle
who refused to believe that Vichy was rehabilitable. He preferred
to put his trust in the quasi-revolutionary resistance groups
associated with the French National Committee. The Americans
continued to regard de Gaulle as 'an embryo dictator' and a
democratic *poseur* 'who would upset their plans for working
through the "respectable" elements at Vichy'. De Gaulle for his
part considered the Americans to be hopelessly wedded to French
reactionary traitors. The Foreign Office attempted to mediate. On
6 June 1942, de Gaulle telegraphed three Free French generals
that 'he was not disposed to remain associated with Great Britain

and the United States, that the Free French should form a united front against all comers and have no relations with the Anglo-Saxons, and must warn the whole world, and the French people, against Anglo-Saxon imperialist designs'. After intercepting the telegram in Cairo, the British had no compunctions about occupying Madagascar without consulting the French National Committee. In keeping with strong American prejudices in the matter, de Gaulle was not given advance warning about the Anglo-American invasion of North Africa. In public de Gaulle masked his emotions, and on 8 November he broadcast his approval of the action. In private, he was disgusted by the Americans' dealing with Darlan. In all it was a trying relationship for the British and a difficult one for de Gaulle.[26]

Churchill, although faced with a *fait accompli*, persisted in refusing to co-operate with Darlan, who successively had been Vice-Premier, Foreign Minister, and Minister of the Interior at Vichy, until such time as Darlan delivered the French fleet to the allies. The Americans, annoyed by the Prime Minister's insistence that the Admiral deliver some sort of tangible proof of his new allegiance, hurried to secure a more permanent understanding with Darlan. By 22 November, Murphy and H. Freeman Matthews of the State Department had helped draft an agreement which was signed by General Mark Clark and Darlan. In its most important particulars, it did no more than confirm the existing situation: the allies were given military rights they had already assumed; Darlan was given a free hand to deal with local political matters. No provision was made for any Vichy forces to operate under allied command; nor was there any mention of the plethora of fascist organisations in French North Africa or the impressive number of anti-semitic and anti-communist laws on the books. In December the Foreign Office approached the State Department and insisted that pro-Axis officials be discharged, that allied sympathisers in jail be released, that pro-fascist legislation be repealed, and that government representatives, not allied commanders, deal with political and civil affairs. The proposal was rejected.[27]

In general US policy makers received the news of Darlan's assassination on Christmas Eve 1942 with relief. The relationship had been neither popular nor profitable. Politically he had persecuted pro-allied sympathisers; tolerated the growth of a number

of fascist societies and used police-state methods of law enforce-
ment. Militarily he had saved no Anglo-American lives; he
allowed Admiral de Laborde to scuttle the major part of the
French fleet at Toulon; he permitted Admiral Jean Esteva to
defect to the Germans with the remainder. The meeting of the
Imperial Council, called immediately to name the Admiral's
successor, must have disappointed those statesmen in Washington
and London who were looking for a new face and a more defensible
political configuration. The Council selected Darlan's fellow
Pétainist, the familiar Giraud. Not surprisingly the deciding
weight had not come from the ultra-rightists but Eisenhower who
had insisted, on FDR's instructions, on Giraud's appointment.[28]

Under Giraud's stewardship the rightward swing of North
African politics continued, if not quickened. During January 1943
it was announced that the infamous Marcel Peyrouton, the former
Vichy Minister of the Interior, was to become the Governor-
General of Algeria. In the interests of political stability, the State
Department approved of this appointment. The British viewed it
as one of many signs of Giraud's patent inability to govern. The
Foreign Office called for a transfusion of talent and popular
leaders from the French National Committee. Roosevelt and the
State Department, who were subject to a degree of press and
public abuse such as they experienced on no other policy issue
during the war, began to look favourably on a loose federation of
French political groups, including de Gaulle's, which would
decentralise French power so that at some future date various
component parts of the empire, such as Indo-China, could be
easily detached. The Foreign Office continued to receive reports
of widespread support for de Gaulle in North Africa and in France
while Giraud's stock was shown to be inexorably falling. FDR and
the State Department were convinced of the opposite.[29]

During a series of negotiations between de Gaulle and Giraud,
from March until May, the French National Committee publicly
criticised US policy and various Vichy leaders in North and West
Africa. On 3 June 1943 the Foreign Office's suspicions were confirmed when de Gaulle and Giraud announced the creation of the
French Committee of National Liberation (FCNL) with themselves as co-presidents. By the end of the month de Gaulle had
assumed effective control of the FCNL. By August the Foreign

Office informed the War Cabinet and the Defence Committee that
de Gaulle's political success was his American failure:

> His various successes in chasing out American protégés in
> North-West African theatre and his struggle to obtain command or
> control of the French Army deeply angered the President and the
> State Department. The extrusion of Boisson [Governor-General
> Pierre Boisson of West Africa] was a dear-bought victory for de
> Gaulle and aroused the fierce resentment of the President. We have
> done our best to smooth things down.[30]

By 10 November Giraud had been forced by the ascendant
Gaullists to resign from the FCNL and go into political retirement.
The Leahy–Roosevelt approach had come to a bad end: Pétain
hopelessly compromised, Darlan dead, Weygand permanently
retired and Giraud clearly outmanœuvred. The shortlist had been
exhausted.[31]

By the beginning of 1944, if not earlier, the political situation
within metropolitan France became supremely important. Even
after the purge of ultra-rightists from the FCNL during the last
months of 1943 the Committee remained relatively free of left-
wing influence since the Gaullists could be considered a left faction
only in the anomalous context of North African, or North American, politics. In France, however, the traditional parties on the
right, as was generally true throughout Europe, had been completely discredited as a result of their defeatist attitudes and collaboration with the enemy. Even the socialists, the foremost party
of the suspended Third Republic, had found it necessary to rein-
vigorate and purify themselves by expelling two-thirds of their
National Assembly members for collaborating with the Pétainists.
Unlike Italy there had been an almost total collapse of all traditional non-communist parties. Within the resistance movement,
which emerged during 1944, the communist-dominated *Francs-
Tireurs Partisans* (FTP) stood out as the most numerous and
successful component. Here was the development of a situation
which the pro-Vichy Americans in particular were incapable of
influencing or comprehending.[32]

Two factors above all others contributed to the defusing of this
potentially combustive conflict between the FCNL in North
Africa and the resistance movement. Undoubtedly the first was

the phenomenal growth of Gaullism as an essentially apolitical movement which was akin to the consensus constructed by Churchill during the war. The second factor was that Maurice Thorez and Jacques Duclos, the leaders of the French Communist Party, which by 1945 had become the largest single French party, used the same non-revolutionary tactics which Togliatti used in Italy. An early sign of this was in February 1944 when the National Council of Resistance and the FTP had acknowledged General Pierre Koenig, de Gaulle's chief military aide in France, as the commander-in-chief of the resistance—even though during this period the communist-dominated resistance was larger and more effective than the regular Free French forces. There seems little doubt that the ironic interaction of these two factors, which obviously would not have operated if American policy efforts had been successful, saved France from civil war if not a revolution.[33]

The conclusion was that when the assessments of Roosevelt and Leahy were proved wrong they were superseded by a number of disjointed, irrational, obstructionist tactics not totally dissimilar in intent to those used in the Balkan settlements. Until the last awkward moment, Roosevelt blocked American and British recognition of the FCNL. He prevented allied military authorities from concluding a post-invasion agreement with General Koenig concerning the civil administration of France and encouraged the State Department to prepare elaborate and useless schemes for the allied administration of that country. While the US had by mid-1944 become the major supplier of arms to the resistance, it delayed rearming de Gaulle's French Army in North Africa. When Colonel Rol, the leader of the Paris resistance movement, called for a general uprising on 19 August 1944, the British and Americans were without an effective communications system with the underground. For the first half of 1944, various governmental agencies in Washington interested in French affairs were forced to mark time. In the meantime none of the President's fears proved real.[34]

The outcome of these actions, which caused great mischief for several succeeding American administrations, was not just an affront to General de Gaulle and the anti-Vichy spirit of the French people, or the creation of major difficulties for the British which complicated other diplomatic problems. It was a major misallocation of diplomatic resources which inevitably contributed to American inattentiveness in such countries as Yugoslavia, Albania and Greece. It was an exercise in diplomatic fantasising which showed an enduring disregard for the objective facts. It was a sign of a pronounced American proclivity to deal with the conservative order, even when tainted with collaboration, rather than search out the new and progressive. It was a warning that when initiating, rather than grandly mediating, the Roosevelt administration was not always as enlightened and liberal as the national interest might have wished.

Notes to this chapter are on pages 202–3.

Chapter 7 THE DIPLOMATS' PEACE: GERMANY AND AUSTRIA

THE AWARENESS of an urgent need to create an equitable and secure peace settlement for the German nation, with Austria following in the wake, preceded Churchill's grand design. Neither Stalin, Churchill nor Roosevelt seriously considered bartering for interests in these nations at the last moment, nor did they contemplate allowing compromised politicians or the military progression of the war to solve their own and European political problems. Considering the vital importance of safeguarding against any sort of German recrudescence after the war, and the vivid memory of the tremendous problems of negotiating a lasting peace after World War I, it is somewhat surprising that the allies should have waited so long before setting in motion a diplomatic mechanism geared to solving German problems. The preoccupations and divisions caused by the second front and the announcement of unconditional surrender took their toll. The result was that all three governments involved were guilty of postponing important decisions until dangerously late in the war. When something was finally done, it was not surprising that the three major participants had singled out different aspects of the very large and complex problem for attention.

The British made the first move. As part of their planning for a future world organisation, on 2 July 1943 the Foreign Office handed representatives of the US and USSR a proposal for the creation of a United Nations Commission for Europe composed of the big three plus France, other European allies, and possibly some of the Dominions. A 'steering committee' composed of the US, UK, and the USSR, with France 'if she recovers her greatness', would assume 'authority in Europe to direct and co-ordinate the activities of the several Armistice Commissions, the Allied Commanders-in-Chief and any United Nations civilian authorities that may be established; and to deal with current problems, military, political and economic, connected with the maintenance of order'.[1] The Soviets were enthusiastic about this plan. When Stalin called for the creation of a big three politico-military commission in August to deal with Italian and other European problems, he was simply calling for an implementation of this idea. On 14 October, Molotov confirmed that the Soviet government wanted a commission, with France as a member, that would direct and co-ordinate all allied European affairs other than operational questions which would remain under the direction of the allied commanders. Even the British regarded this amendment, which would make the commission 'virtually an executive and governing body', with alarm.[2] Both the British and Americans were reluctant to have any tripartite body interfering in their sphere of operations in Italy. The US additionally was opposed to having the French as full members and wanted the governments of China, Yugoslavia, Greece and Brazil to have consultative rights. As has been discussed in the section on Italy, when the matter was finally sorted out the enervated Advisory Council was born.[3]

During the Moscow conference of Foreign Ministers the British tried again. They wanted a commission but not one with the powers suggested by the Soviets. The Americans wanted a commission but did not want diplomatic power to slip from their hands. None the less, by 31 October 1943, Hull, Eden and Molotov had agreed upon terms of reference for the European Advisory Commission (EAC) which was to meet in London. With the presidency to rotate among the representatives of the three powers, the EAC was to study and make recommendations to the three governments on agreed questions relating to the termination of hostilities. Eden, for one, felt a good job had been done: 'Here for the first time we have the beginnings of practical collaboration between the three powers on specific tasks of the first importance.' For perhaps the first time during the war, he felt a shared objective with the Soviets: 'The Americans are interested in talking about things. The Russians are interested in doing things. The latter should also be our objective.'[4]

By the end of 1943, before the first formal meeting of the EAC, the future shape of Germany had been strongly suggested. By mid-August, Lieutenant General Sir Frederick Morgan, Chief of Staff to the Supreme Allied Commander, had produced emergency plans for the occupation of Germany, based on his invasion planning for the Combined Chiefs of Staff, to be used in the event of a sudden German collapse. RANKIN Case 'C' was to be used if the Germans ceased organised resistance and unconditionally surrendered. The assumptions behind case 'C' were threefold: the big three would occupy Germany with the Soviets in the east, the US in the south-west and the UK in the north-west; the zones would be roughly equal in size; Berlin would be treated as an allied enclave. In principle this plan was approved by the Combined Chiefs of Staff during the first Quebec conference.[5]

By 11 October, the Post-Hostilities Planning Sub-Committee of the British Chiefs of Staff had produced a report which further clarified the proposal. It was approved by the Chiefs and the Ministerial Committee on Armistice Terms and Civil Administration. The British zone was to encompass 57,450 square miles and 22·5 million people; the Soviet zone's 76,600 square miles and 22·3 million people was to be reduced by the areas in eastern Germany which were eventually to be incorporated in Poland's new frontiers; the US zone was to include 47,100 square miles and 15·7 million people, but the Americans were to be primarily responsible for the occupation of Austria which added another 32,300 square miles and a population of some 6·7 million. Berlin was to be treated as a combined zone.[6]

Roosevelt's thinking was running in quite a different direction. Prior to the Moscow conference, he informed various State Department officials, including Hull, that he favoured the division of Germany into three or more sovereign states. After the conference, where it was decided that Germany would be deprived of her pre-war territorial gains and East Prussia, the President showed an increasing lack of confidence in Hull and the State Department and assumed a more direct interest in German affairs. Aboard the *Iowa* on his way to the Cairo and Tehran conferences, FDR had extensive talks with his military advisers about Germany without State Department advice or consultation. During these conversations, FDR indicated on a National Geographic Society map a counter-proposal to the British plan which would have given the US a large zone in the north comprising some 97,750 square miles with a population of 33·6 million. The UK's zone in the south would have covered 47,100 square miles and a population of 15·7 million; and the Soviet zone 38,300 square miles and 11·1 million. It was not clear whether Austria would fall within the British sphere or not. The British reaction to this Presidential proposal was not surprisingly negative. From their viewpoint, it was 'thoroughly objectionable', for it promised to give the US undue influence in the Netherlands, Belgium, Denmark, Norway and the German North Sea coastline, all areas of particular strategic interest to the British. The crux of their objection was that FDR's plan would force the UK to sacrifice long-term interests in Germany for short-term gains in France and Austria. They also opposed the plan because it ignored all administrative, civil, transport, military and geographical considerations.[7]

While Hull in Moscow had been opposed to suggestions that Germany be dismembered, Roosevelt during the Tehran conference proposed that Germany be divided into three to five autonomous regions, some of them becoming part of a federation composed of East European nations. Understandably, Stalin objected to this proposal. In the absence of any alternative suggestions by either the British or Soviets, the whole troublesome package was referred to the EAC.

At the EAC's first meeting in London on 14 January 1944, the representatives of the UK, US and USSR were Sir William Strang, John Gilbert Winant, US Ambassador to the UK, and Fedor Tarasovich Gusev, the Soviet Ambassador to the UK. On 27 November, René Massigli took his seat as the French representative. Of the original members only Strang was able to devote all his time and efforts to the EAC. From the beginning it was obvious that the British were exemplarily prepared and organised. They had excellent interdepartmental co-operation among their civil servants and a clear-cut chain of command; their EAC representative participated in the policy-making process, and they had a strong ministerial committee, the Armistice and Post-War Committee, presided over by Clement Attlee, which supervised and co-ordinated planning for the EAC. On 15 January Strang presented a series of proposed drafts to his EAC colleagues which in many respects were of such high quality that they fixed the direction of the EAC henceforth. One of them was the familiar 1943 British plan for zones of occupation. On 18 February Ambassador Gusev submitted a Soviet plan which was almost identical in its zonal descriptions to the British plan. It was a promising start.[8]

From the beginning, Ambassador Winant was in the extremely awkward position of being a subordinate without full agential powers who was subject to the unsettled views of several masters. The War Department attempted to subvert whatever authority Winant had by claiming that occupation and issues concerning the formation of a military government were within their sphere of responsibility. The State Department, out of touch with the President's thinking and military planning, was helplessly disorganised and lacked strong leadership. Roosevelt further complicated Winant's position by failing to appoint a task force to back him up and by expressing a strong dislike of the zone offered to the US. At other times during this period Winant found himself with no instructions at all from any source. His course of action was simply to temporise and delay.[9]

During early March Winant received FDR's pre-Tehran sketch of German zones from Washington without instructions. Both the Ambassador and his chief political adviser, George F. Kennan, advised the State Department against the plan as it failed to correspond with the traditional administrative boundaries of pre-war Germany and would largely undo what had already been tacitly agreed upon by the British and Soviets. When FDR talked with Kennan in Washington on 3 April, he reportedly was amused by the comedy of errors whereby the American military and the State Department had submitted to Winant a plan which was no longer applicable. By the end of the month the Joint Chiefs of Staff and Hull had agreed to the descriptions of the three zones in the British–Soviet plans. The allocation of zones to the British and Americans, however, remained an open question. Administrative fumbles in Washington prevented Winant from reporting the outcome of these deliberations until 1 June, which meant that work of the EAC was retarded five valuable months by FDR's ill-advised drawing.[10]

While the US and the UK had formally accepted the Soviet occupation of the eastern zone, the President, extremely reluctant to accept the south-west zone, entered into a prolonged altercation with Churchill. The Americans feared that acceptance of an occupation zone would mean keeping US troops in southern Europe well beyond the end of the war and that without a port and well-defined transportation lines their sector would be dependent on French supply routes. FDR was loath to accept either possibility. At the second Quebec conference in mid-September, however, Roosevelt, who had gained a larger point, acceded to British arguments and accepted the guarantee that the Americans would have the use of the ports of Bremen and Bremerhaven and parmanent easement through the British sector. By 14 November 1944, the members of the European Advisory Commission were able to report to their governments that complete agreement had been reached on the zones of occupation and their allocation both for Germany as a whole and for Berlin. Questions such as reparations, dismemberment, allied government, economic policy and Austria remained outstanding; obviously much remained to be done.[11]

Between February and November 1944, the EAC tackled the problems of allied control of Germany. The British envisaged an allied military government, during a short transition period of some six months, to be followed by an allied high commission. In addition to the US, UK, USSR and France, the commission would have representatives from other European and Dominion nations, especially Canada. The Soviets proposed a system whereby each zonal commander would govern his own sector with a three-power control council to supervise the local German civilian government and establish guidelines and policies for such inter-zonal problems as reparations, currency, labour and transport. The American scheme was even more extreme. It specified that the control council would have no jurisdiction outside the Berlin area, and that Germany would be divided into separate administrative areas. There would be no central administration, other than that provided by the Germans themselves, and no allied machinery for dealing with national problems, apart from that agreed upon by zonal commanders in specific cases. Like the Soviets, the Americans strongly objected to the creation of any high commission which might grow beyond the control of the big three. The compromise reached on 14 November gave Berlin a Komendatura consisting of commandants from the occupying powers, gave Germany a control council of the commanding generals in each of the country's occupation zones, and left the local commanders considerable autonomy.[12]

Meanwhile dramatic ideas were coming to the fore in Washington which threatened to overshadow, if not overturn, all the deliberations of the EAC in London. The chief protagonist in this new show was Henry Morgenthau, Jr, Secretary of the Treasury. During August he had travelled to Britain and Anthony Eden had allowed him to see the minutes of the Tehran conference. When he read the passages describing the near unanimity among the three leaders on a harsh peace and dismemberment for Germany, he was galvanised—especially since Winant and Philip E. Mosely, Kennan's successor as his political adviser, had already expressed approval for a soft peace for Germany with rapid reunification as a primary EAC objective. From this revelation, Morgenthau was able to force the first coherent discussion of the German problem in Washington. On 18 August, after his return to Washington, he informed Hull of the news. The Secretary of State was flabbergasted, for he had never been permitted to see the Tehran minutes![13]

Morgenthau promptly set about preparing a memorandum for FDR which simply, but effectively, set out in quotes, without any editorial comments by the Secretary, portions from a 'Handbook of Military Government for Germany' which had been prepared by General Eisenhower's Chief of Staff, Lieutenant General W. B. Smith. The theme of the handbook was this: 'Your main and immediate task, to accomplish your mission, is to get things running, to pick up the pieces, to restore as quickly as possible the official functioning of the German civil government in the area for which you are responsible . . .'. The following day Roosevelt shot a message to the Secretary of War, Stimson, with just the wrathful tone that Morgenthau desired. In very precise and forceful language, FDR specified that the convenient move away from unconditional surrender and Tehran was to cease. Germany was not to be treated by the military as though it were Belgium. As an alternative he suggested, as an example, a minimal diet, from army soup kitchens if necessary, so as to impress on the German people 'that the whole nation has been engaged in a lawless conspiracy against the decencies of modern civilization'.[14]

The offshoot of the handbook incident was that proposals which might never have seen the light of day were circulated and discussed, inter-departmental secrecy and bickering lessened, and the process of policy planning became more rational and systematic. A cabinet-level committee to co-ordinate German policy was formed with Hull, Stimson, Morgenthau and Hopkins as members. By 28 August, only three days after the first tremors, Henry J. Bittermann, one of Morgenthau's treasury proselytes, produced a pre-plan suggesting remedial measures which to date had not been considered by the EAC. It demanded not only that 'the industrial means for military aggression should be removed from German jurisdiction' but also that Germany be divided into two distinct north and south economic units. On 2 September, at a preliminary meeting of departmental assistants, Harry Dexter White, fresh from his struggles with John Maynard Keynes at Bretton Woods, presented what became known as the Morgenthau Plan in its maturity: Silesia and East Prussia were to be transferred to Poland and the USSR; the Saar region was to go to France; the region north of the Kiel Canal was to become part of Denmark; the Ruhr and the Kiel Canal were to be placed under international control. The remainder would be divided into north and south German nations.[15]

While White and Bittermann worked the hold, Morgenthau attempted to line up support topside. On 4 September Morgenthau held a working dinner at his home with the redoubtable Henry Stimson as the most prominent guest. The following day, in a private letter to Morgenthau, Stimson made his criticisms of the previous evening more explicit. While agreeing with the thrust of the plan, as it had been presented at the dinner and earlier at the Cabinet Committee, he objected to the proposed reduction and destruction of Germany's industrial potential. Undaunted by such intelligent and restrained criticism, Morgenthau carried his plan to the President at Hyde Park over the Labour Day weekend. After presenting one of the earlier and less inflammatory versions of the plan to FDR on 6 September, he boldly stretched the elastic idea to include the dismantling of all industrial plants and equipment in the Ruhr and the destruction of the mines. Stimson, also undaunted, continued to fight a low-keyed, persuasive rearguard action emphasising the catastrophic consequences of any plan which proposed the spoilation of a great international asset. Morgenthau continued to ride fast and hard.[16]

By the end of August the British had received garbled news of the events in Washington. In early September, Halifax reported that the Treasury was supporting a plan to artificially induce inflation in the German economy as a means of bringing about its total collapse. On 14 September the War Cabinet, acting on this report, sent a telegram to Eden, who was on his way to Quebec, expressing their opposition to the programme. At the same time, Attlee had produced an incisive memorandum for the Armistice and Post-War Committee which preceded and was in tune with Morgenthau's thinking. He pointed out that there was a 'hard core of German aggression' emanating from the Prussian Junker class, the Reichswehr, the civil service, the industrialists of Westphalia and the Bavarian interests which grew predominant after the Kapp Putsch. As the Deputy Prime Minister noted, 'These forces maintained themselves at the end of the last war, with the practical consent of the Allies, because of the fear of Bolshevism. We must not let this happen again or we shall be leaving in the ground the roots of another world war.' While Eden and members of the Foreign Office opposed this analytical approach, obviously there was support for it within the government, which called for sterner measures than those contemplated by the European Advisory Commission.[17]

When Roosevelt went to Quebec, he expressed at least partial approval for the Treasury plan by taking Henry Morgenthau as his chief adviser on economic and German affairs. The ubiquitous Hopkins, who supported the dismantling of manufacturing plants in the Ruhr, was a valuable ally. When Morgenthau presented his collection of ideas, now entitled a 'Program to Prevent Germany from Starting a World War III', the Ruhr and the Saar attracted most attention. As Churchill understood the proposal, their steel and other industries would be dismantled and an international trusteeship would then supervise the two regions. The USSR would receive most of the machinery removed, as a form of reparations, to re-equip their own manufacturing industries; the result would be primarily a rural economy for Germany as a whole.[18]

The Prime Minister's reaction to Morgenthau's presentation was initially negative, and he described the plan as one that would chain Britain and Europe to a dead body. By the end of the day, however, his attitude had changed. Perhaps he was swayed by Morgenthau's suggestion that Britain should receive $3,500 million in Lend–Lease between the end of the European and Pacific wars, supplemented by an additional $3,000 million in non-military credits. More likely he was impressed by the likelihood that Britain would be the major beneficiary of this radical shift in economics, which would place her in a position to manufacture and sell the goods previously supplied by the transformed regions. At any rate Churchill eventually drafted a memorandum, without consulting Eden or the Foreign Office, which purported to tone down the violet shades of Morgenthau's plan. None the less, it called for all the major provisions Morgenthau had enumerated at Quebec. Initialled by both Roosevelt and Churchill on 15 September 1944, Morgenthau's plan had carried the day. When Eden arrived the following day armed with his directive from the War Cabinet, he argued strongly but without result.[19]

Unquestionably one reason for the unprecedented rate of progress by Morgenthau's programme was that Soviet views had not been taken into account. Yet the Soviets had their own sources of information, and there was no special secrecy about what was going on in Washington during August and September. When Churchill went to Moscow in October to conclude his contractual agreement with Stalin, the Marshal had naturally asked him about his impressions of the Treasury plan. Though somewhat evasive about what had transpired during the Quebec conference, the Prime Minister did state during their last conversation that he favoured the isolation of Prussia, external control of the Ruhr and the Saar, and the disbursement of German machinery and tools to the USSR, Belgium, France and the Netherlands as measures equitable to both the Soviet and the British economy. Despite this rather unsatisfactory briefing, Stalin, from the record, seems not to have been disturbed. For a long time the Soviets had had only limited, but essential, demands to make. One of these unquestionably was reparations. Another was the fragmentation of Germany. Between the zonal agreements reached in the EAC, the promise of the Morgenthau plan, and the Churchill–Stalin contractual agreement of October 1944, the Soviets were satisfied.[20]

In London and Washington the long gestation period following the Quebec decisions permitted the critics time to speak out. It must have become obvious to many people that the Morgenthau plan was something of a misnomer: rather than a 'plan' it was a complex of intriguing ideas designed to exact retribution from the Germans by rendering their nation economically impotent. In Washington the opposition was led by Stimson and Hull with some help from the press. In Britain Eden's campaign progressed not quite so well. While many people in the Foreign Office regarded Morgenthau's efforts as meddlesome and ill-advised, Eden's attempts to stimulate governmental discussion on alternatives such as fragmentation, confederation and federation failed to achieve any meaningful consensus. The rub was that any drastic action, beyond the moderate measures already agreed upon in the EAC, threatened to bring the USSR even closer to the heart of western Europe. With some irony, Churchill and Attlee remained united behind the Quebec agreement. It was not until the end of the year that the Economic and Industrial Planning Staff produced any substantial rebuttal to the Treasury's programme. With only moderate pressure working upon him, Churchill had by then agreed only to the delay of any discussion or review of substantial issue until Yalta.[21]

In the USA much the same situation existed. Hull struggled, but he and the State Department none the less began to take a tougher line towards Germany. While Roosevelt wrote Hull on 20 October that 'I dislike making detailed plans for a country which we do not yet occupy', there was nothing to replace the agreement reached at Quebec. Morgenthau followed events closely and took every opportunity to remind the State Department and the President that dismemberment, restitution, reparations, agrarian reform, political decentralisation and educational reforms were all important aspects of the German settlement which had received little attention. The Soviets called for discussion of all of these items in the EAC. On 15 November, FDR let it be known that he was still in a tough mood concerning allied treatment of Germany. Little was done in terms of drafting specific policy directives for Winant to negotiate in the EAC. Part of the problem was that the Americans were uncertain about the attitude of the British and Soviets. As far as the new Secretary of State could tell, Britain was 'more interested in restraining future German competition with

British exports than in collecting large reparation', while the Soviets were more concerned with extracting in the form of reparations from current production 'the largest practicable contribution to Russian reconstruction and industrial development . . .'. So, beyond the Quebec agreements, Morgenthau produced little more than an awareness of the fundamental problems, new diplomatic complexities and profound confusion.[22]

It is fitting that Austria should be treated as a postscript to the German settlement. There was strong unanimity at the Moscow conference of Foreign Ministers that Austria was a victim of Nazi aggression and should be restored after the war as an independent state. Despite agreement on the victim theory, the British proposal of 15 January 1944 for the EAC on German zones gave the USA responsibility for all of Austria. The Soviet submission of 18 February was more in keeping with the tripartite spirit of Moscow and more realistic. It separated Austria from Germany as a diplomatic problem and provided for three-power occupation. During March FDR informed Winant that he did not want southern Germany and Austria as a zone because he suspected it was all a ruse to make the US a counter in Churchill's Balkan game. In May, when Winant saw Roosevelt in Washington, the President approved American political participation in whatever allied joint headquarters might be established in Vienna. By mid-July Roosevelt and the State Department had agreed that a token occupation force, similar to the one envisaged for Berlin, would be available for Austria. After the Soviets and British had renewed their proposals in the EAC for full zonal occupation of Austria on the German model and Winant had warned Washington that a 'token force' was insufficient, FDR and the State Department instructed Winant that 'this Government does not wish to extend its undertaking with respect to the number and location of American troops to be used in Austria'.[23]

The mainline of Washington thinking concerning Austria was somewhat indolent and reactionary: with time and the liberation of Austria the clock would be turned back, by some unknown process without American participation, to the pre-Dollfuss–Schuschnigg era (1932–8) and everything would be in good order. The British saw the problem from a different viewpoint. By mid-October they were apprehensive that, with the Axis collapse in eastern Europe, Soviet troops would occupy most of Austria while Anglo-American forces were still engaged in Italy. George Kennan, who had moved to the American embassy in Moscow, where he shared Ambassador Harriman's acute concern about Soviet expansion, warned the State Department that unless an Austrian agreement were forced on the Soviets they would dominate all of eastern and central Europe. Belying this analysis Ambassador Gusev continued to insist in the EAC that the Americans take a full and responsible role in Austrian affairs.[24]

In the end it was Winant, with a more reasonable line of argument, who persuaded Roosevelt. In a letter for the Secretary of State and the President in early December, the Ambassador initiated a very powerful line of reasoning that persisted during the Yalta discussions and beyond. After looking at the general European experience of the past few months, Winant premised, as an admirer of Churchill's grand design, that 'it is clear that failure to work out in advance agreed arrangements with the Russians and the British in areas in which we share responsibility, as in Germany and Austria, will inevitably lead to a grab as grab can policy'. As his second term, Winant observed that the Soviets were 'literal minded folk' and that they would interpret a one-third occupation of Vienna as a rejection of a one-third interest in Austria. Winant's conclusion, which was reached with considerable deductive weight, obviously had far-reaching implications: 'When Soviet and British bloc politics threaten to dominate the scene, it is perhaps wiser for us to stay on the job and to work against the bloc concept which, if left unchecked by strong outside influences like our own, may pull Europe to pieces...'. The following day the Secretary of State informed the Ambassador that FDR, in response to an earlier appeal from Winant developed along these same lines, had decided it would be wise for the US to accept a full occupation zone contiguous to Bavaria. After the details had been worked out, the EAC were so notified in January. As was the case with Germany, the first questions proved the most difficult to answer.[25]

Notes to this chapter are on pages 203–5.

Chapter 8 POLAND: THE NEGOTIATED PEACE

To SOME extent the wartime 'Polish problem' was a historical legacy; to some extent it was a creature of the personalities involved; to some extent it was an obvious product of the clash between the dynamism of events and the ossification of thought; to some extent it was the microcosmic problem of Europe moving from one era to another. The problem was certainly of such magnitude and importance to the future of Europe and the world that it demanded early and continuing negotiations between the three major powers.

When Poland was partitioned by German and Soviet armies in September 1939, a large number of Polish fighting men and politicians escaped, first to France and later to Britain. Unlike the situation in Czechoslovakia, Poland's pre-war political order had been thrice damned: its foreign policy had proved to be an unmitigated disaster; Joseph Beck, the foremost political leader and bearer of Marshal Pilsudski's mantle, had defected to Rumania; and the recognised government in London was composed, in part, of politicians long opposed to the old authoritarian system. The new London government was one sign that Poland had arisen from the ashes of defeat and that a bloodless coup had replaced a reactionary government of the 1930s.

The London Poles understandably viewed with mixed emotions the hard fact that the USSR was the only anti-fascist power on the Continent. Although they too were anti-German, the Soviets in furtherance of their own ends had joined Germany in the occupation of Poland. As had been the case throughout the preceding decade, the somewhat paradoxical reality demanded that if Poland were to have autonomous power, some accommodation with the USSR would have to be reached. There was no alternative: Britain, if not the USA, was irrevocably committed to such a course. On 23 June 1941, a few hours after the German invasion of the Soviet Union, General Wladyslaw Sikorski, the Polish Prime Minister and Commander-in-Chief, presented his government's terms for negotiating such an accommodation: cancellation of the Nazi–Soviet Pact of 1939, a political tautology, and a reversion to the provisions of the Riga Treaty of 18 March 1921, which had fixed the pre-war Polish–Soviet frontier.[1] On 5 July the Soviet Ambassador in the UK, Ivan Maisky, told General Sikorski that the Soviet Government, as ever before, was not prepared to acknowledge the validity of the Riga Treaty, but that it was willing to temporarily defer territorial questions in the interest of concluding a friendship pact.[2]

After overcoming opposition within his own government, General Sikorski concluded, later in the same month, an incomplete agreement with the USSR which provided for the recruitment of a Polish army within the borders of the USSR. In December, the agreement was further clarified and expanded. While operationally the Polish Army was subordinate to the Soviet Supreme Command, the Poles were to be represented thereon and to retain their own officers.[3] In conjunction with these agreements the Soviet Government advanced the Poles an extremely liberal, non-interest loan of some 300 million roubles.[4]

The only major unresolved difference between the Soviets and the Poles concerned the frontiers. The Polish title to the eastern territory in question rested on occupation since the 1921 Treaty of Riga. During March 1919, the Supreme Council at the Paris Peace Conference requested its Commission on Polish Affairs to recommend a frontier; by June 1917 the Commission had delineated both northern and southern sections of the eastern boundary. As Stalin was fond of saying, the Curzon Line, as it became known, was drawn dispassionately on the basis of ethnic and geographical considerations without the consent of the Soviet government. Military actions, however, had made the line little more than a diplomatic relic. In the last move of the allied intervention in the Russian Civil War, the Polish General Pilsudski, encouraged by the French and assisted by Sosnkowski and Sikorski, had advanced his armies in May 1920 to Kiev. Unlike Kolchak, Denikin, Yudenich and

Wrangel, after his defeat in July Pilsudski reappeared. Lord Curzon announced that the British government considered the Polish action nothing better than adventurism. Nevertheless, by September, Minsk had fallen for the second time to the Poles, who held most of Eastern Galicia; the nasty, costly war was over.

The French applauded the victory, but Lloyd George voiced Britain's opinion that 'the Polish army appeared to be in occupation of non-Polish territory'. As a result of this intervention Poland not only expanded geographically, contrary to the intention of the Curzon Line, but encompassed a large non-Polish population. While Molotov's 1939 estimate of ten million Ukrainians and White Russians in the eastern territory may have been high, Polish figures of the same year, which may very well have been too low, tended to support this claim. Of the 13·2 million persons in the area, the Poles estimated that 5,274,000 spoke Polish, 1,109,000 Yiddish or Hebrew, 4,529,000 Ukrainian-Ruthenian and 1,123,000 Russian. Foreign Office experts in 1944 may not have been far wrong when they estimated that only thirty-five to forty per cent of the population in Poland east of the Curzon Line were Polish. Notwithstanding the above, both Poles and Soviets had legitimate claims on the eastern territory sustained by a number of lively arguments.[5]

During the winter of 1941–2, American and British views of the Polish situation were unanimous. Both governments were in favour of Polish–Soviet negotiations, and materially assisted the Poles to rebuild their army in the Soviet Union. Neither the US nor Britain was willing to become embroiled in the territorial squabble between the two nations—a perfectly sensible attitude since nothing would be gained by academic disputes about territory which the allies were unlikely to occupy for a considerable time.

By September 1941, even before the second Polish–Soviet agreement had been signed, Polish policy had begun to shift in such a manner as to call into question its earlier constancy and appreciation of external realities. While army recruitment was in its first stages, General Sikorski instructed Lieutenant General Anders, senior Polish Officer in the USSR, that the main objective was not the early defeat of the German armies in Poland or the USSR but the preservation of the Polish Army. As he wrote to Anders, Polish troops were not to serve with the Red Army, even as an auxiliary force, in the interests 'of reaching Poland at an earlier date. . . . Enough Polish blood has been shed already, and there is no need to lavish it in order to mark Poland's active part in the camp of the fighting democracies.'[6] In accordance with this directive, in early February 1942, with no military justification, General Anders refused General Zhukov's request that the Fifth Polish Division be sent to the front.[7]

This policy shift was based on two main premises. The first was that Polish military power was going to have significance only 'in the ultimate stage of the war'. As Sikorski told his political colleagues in January 1942, this in turn would be to Poland's advantage and would enable the state, closely allied with the UK, to expand westward at Germany's expense.[8] The second premise was Sikorski's penchant for seeing the war almost exclusively in terms of World War I. As Dr Eduard Beneš was to comment after a long conversation with Sikorski, the Poles were convinced that 'the issues of war and peace would be decided by the United States and Great Britain' much as they had been at the Paris Peace Conference.[9] The product of all this was the Polish conviction that the Soviets and Germans would disembowel themselves by the end of the war while the Americans, British and Poles would emerge as the real powers in Europe.

In pursuance of their objectives the Poles proved long on boldness but short on tact. Choosing his moment carefully, when curtailed grain shipments from the USA forced the Soviets to limit rations to the Polish Army, General Anders requested permission from Stalin on 18 March 1942 for the Poles to withdraw 25,000 men from the USSR for future deployment in the UK. By the end of the month Anders was able to report their evacuation, plus thousands of Polish women and children, to Iran on the first leg of their withdrawal. At the same time, however, the Soviets insisted that the remaining 44,000 fighting men should not be further fragmented so that the Polish Army could 'be the first to enter the territory of Poland'.[10]

The second phase of the Polish operation required diplomatic action at a higher level. In June 1942 General Sikorski exploited his good relations with President Roosevelt, who had granted Poland Lend–Lease a year earlier and a handsome loan in March 1942, and asked for American assistance in securing Soviet permission to withdraw all Polish troops from the USSR to the Middle East.[11] By the beginning of July this appeal, and others to Cordell Hull and the British, had proved effective, for Sikorski was able to report to Anders and Ambassador Kot that Stalin had withdrawn his earlier objections to total evacuation.[12] The price paid by Britain and the US in the following months and years for applying pressure on the Soviets was a vastly increased responsibility for Polish affairs. With the removal of the Polish Army from eastern Europe, a vacuum had been created which ironically, as Sikorski had predicted to Beneš, could be filled only by the great powers.

The third phase of the Polish withdrawal had to do with the second trump in the Polish hand, the Home Army. Once again as early as September 1941 Sikorski had outlined the appropriate course of action: while the Home Army was not to remain, as presumably some of the London Poles suggested, completely dormant, they were to be preserved 'for the time of the outbreak of an armed rising' at an appropriate future date.[13] The Home Army consequently from 1941 to 1944 concentrated on organisational growth; and the 'armed rising' was intended for the interim period between the retreat of the Germans and the advance of the Soviet armies. The central concern clearly was to reconstitute the Polish state without Soviet assistance.

THE BREAK

1943 was a fateful year in Poland's relations with the Soviet Union. Probably in retaliation for the withdrawal of the 114,000 or so soldiers and civilians into Iran during 1942, the Soviets announced in January that they intended to exercise permanent sovereignty over all Polish territory éast of the Molotov–Ribbentrop line of 1939, ie roughly the Curzon Line. In March came the news that a Union of Polish Patriots had been formed in the USSR as an opposition government. On 13 April Radio Berlin announced that Nazi officials had discovered the bodies of 10,000 Polish officers, allegedly slain by the Soviets, in an area near Smolensk known as Katyn Forest. On the 15th the Soviet government denied the charge. The following day the Polish government-in-exile requested the International Red Cross to investigate the claim. On 21 April Stalin complained to Churchill that 'In the atmosphere of terror, with its gallows and mass extermination of peaceful population, the International Red Cross is forced [by the Polish request] to take part in the comedy of "investigation" of which the producer is Hitler'. Three days later Churchill replied to Stalin that his government would oppose such an investigation and added that it 'would be a fraud and its conclusions reached by terrorism'.[14] On 26 April the USSR broke off formal relations with the Polish government in London; two days later the hand-picked members of the German International Medical Commission arrived for an on-the-spot inquiry into the mass murders. Apparently sincerely concerned about the breach and the manner in which his colleagues had handled the matter, General Sikorski on 1 May requested W. Averell Harriman, the US Ambassador in the USSR, to mediate with the Soviets on behalf of the Polish government.[15] Unfortunately a wedge had entered Polish–Soviet relations which was never to be removed.

The aftermath of the split, which in spirit had occurred well before the Katyn tragedy, was largely predictable. In May, General Zigmund Berling, a Polish officer who had been court-martialled for refusing to exit with General Anders' troops to Iran, formed the First Polish Army, which by October was in action near Smolensk. During the same month Whitehall learned that partisans sympathetic to the Union of Polish Patriots were co-operating closely with the Red armies.[16] The deteriorating situation in London was accelerated when General Sikorski was killed in a plane crash over Gibraltar. The new government, under the premiership of Stanislaw Mikolajczyk, moved noticeably to the right, while General Kasimir Sosnkowski, a long-time friend of Pilsudski, who had temporarily resigned from the government in protest against the Sikorski–Stalin accommodation of 1941, became the Commander-in-Chief of the Polish armed forces.[17]

The Moscow conference of Foreign Ministers in October 1943 was the first major allied gathering since the Polish–Soviet split. Cordell Hull, in July, had made an ineffective effort to bring about a reconciliation over lesser issues. Eden, however, realised that the time had come for a dramatic break in the stalemate on fundamental issues. Prior to the conference he approached Mikolajczyk and requested that he be given power to enter into preliminary negotiations with the Soviets over the issue of the eastern territory. The request was refused.

In Washington meanwhile, the Poles approached Hull on the eve of his departure to the conference and attempted to convince him that the US should guarantee Poland's pre-war frontiers, her major power status in future diplomatic deliberations regarding Germany and Italy, and the occupation of Poland by the US and UK, rather than the USSR, at the war's end. If Hull's earlier reconciliation efforts had shown a certain unawareness of the intricacies of Soviet–Polish relations, his good sense saved him from making any impossible commitments to the Poles as a result of their supplication.[18] Clearly with the opening of the Moscow conference, the Poles had received the first mild warning, from both the Americans and the British, that deliverance of their country by the western powers might not follow in the natural course of events.

The disappointing build-up to the Moscow conference of October ensured that no agreement of any consequence could be reached; but at Tehran, in November, things were different, for the three major policy-makers were on the spot. When Stalin claimed that the 'ethnologically' proper line for the Polish–Soviet frontier was the Curzon Line, Churchill did not deny it; in fact the Prime Minister commented that the compensatory industrial land in the west up to the Oder River, which Stalin had suggested as early as 16 December 1941 should go to Poland, was of much greater value than 'the Pripet Marshes' in the east. Stalin's point, which was not disputed, was that the USSR was claiming only non-Polish territory.[19] While FDR remained silent about these suggestions during the discussions, in private he confided to Stalin that it was only the Polish–American bloc of six or seven million voters which restrained him from endorsing any changes in Poland's frontiers. Earlier, at Quebec, Hopkins informed Eden that FDR had already told Molotov and Litvinov that in general he would support Soviet territorial demands in Poland and eastern Europe.[20] Despite FDR's rather disappointing public reaction to the tentative agreement reached by Churchill and Stalin, the President had been exposed to the latest ideas of his counterparts and undoubtedly the situation in general had been unjammed.

The last great opportunity of 1943 for a political solution to the Polish–Soviet split came during the year's end when President

Beneš of Czechoslovakia travelled to Moscow. After preliminary discussions with the Poles in London, Beneš gained the impression that, while Pilsudski's followers were in 'a decisive majority', they would never allow Mikolajczyk to accept any reasonable Soviet proposal, even though the Polish Premier realised that territorial concessions in the east would have to be made. During conversations with Stalin concerning the Czech–Soviet treaty, Beneš sympathetically listened to the familiar arguments regarding the Soviet–Polish frontier. Additionally he learned that there would have to be a reorganisation of the Polish government in London, involving the removal of the rabid anti-communists and of reactionaries with strong ties to the policies of the Pilsudski dictatorship, such as General Sosnkowski.[21]

British policy with regard to this latest Soviet demand was unequivocal. The present Polish government was satisfactory even though the Soviets did object, from British reports, to both Anders and Sosnkowski. Merger or affiliation with the Union of Polish Patriots was out of the question unless the Union placed its fighting forces at the disposal of the London Poles.[22]

When Beneš, after his Moscow trip, conferred with Churchill in Marrakesh and Eden in London during January 1944, both British leaders could clearly see that any further delay on the Poles' part meant a strengthening of the Soviet position and a stiffening of their political demands. Notwithstanding this lack of firm British support for existing Polish policy, when Beneš talked to Mikolajczyk, with Churchill's approval, on 10 January the Polish leader could only suggest, without humour, that a mass transfer of populations in the eastern territories would be easier to arrange with his government than a change of frontiers. On the 23rd, at a meeting between Mikolajczyk, M. Romer, his Foreign Secretary, the Polish Ambassador, Churchill, Eden and Sir Alexander Cadogan, the Permanent Under-Secretary, the Poles again refused to budge from the Riga Line.[23]

The immediate climax of this mediation, so ably and tirelessly conducted by the Czech Premier, came on 26 January when Churchill attempted to secure American backing for a negotiated settlement. The plan, drafted by Churchill, was submitted to Hull by the Polish Ambassador in the US and was in the form of a letter signed by Mikolajczyk, addressed to FDR! The Polish

Government was to acknowledge the Curzon Line as a basis for negotiations and to accept East Prussia, Danzig and Upper Silesia as far as the Oder River, as compensation; Poles in the USSR were to have the right to move west of the Curzon Line. All Germans were to be expelled from the new Polish state, and the UK, USA and USSR were to guarantee the agreement. This proposal, with Mikolajczyk's private support, was strongly marked by the Churchillian tactic of skirting and elevating an impossibly congested problem. The plan's accurate appraisal of the situation was matched only by its manageable simplicity. The only significant concessions asked of the Soviets had already been granted by Stalin at Tehran and elsewhere. Perhaps more important this approach relieved Mikolajczyk of the impossible task of securing approval for the settlement from the right-wingers in his own government.

The American response to the Churchill–Mikolajczyk proposal of 26 January 1944 was perhaps the best example of fuzzy thinking during the war years. It amounted to an extremely ineffective attempt to resurrect the second point of the Atlantic Charter and the Roosevelt corollary to it, both of which had profitably rested in quiet disuse; and it attempted to introduce the extraneous spectre of what at the time was only an inchoate dream, the united nations organisation. Hull and FDR 'agreed that we should not support any definite frontier recommendation during the course of the war' for 'the United Nations organisation would get off to a better start if it were not embarrassed by individual arrangements of guarantees'. On 8 February 1944 FDR instructed the State Department, for transmission to the British, that the United States was interested in avoiding a settlement of the Polish–Soviet frontier in order to prevent 'the creation by the Soviet Government of a rival Polish Government'.[24] The suggestion that the fledgeling united nations organisation might be able to solve the Polish problem as its first order of business was exceedingly naive and a prime example of the perverse negativism which the Secretary of State, whose style marks this entire incident, was to pursue until his resignation. Hull and Roosevelt showed an unfortunate unwillingness to come to grips with unpleasant realities which indicated that the Poles eventually would have to surrender both territory and their resident reactionaries.

WARSAW: THE PRELIMINARIES

With the removal of General Anders' Polish Army from the USSR to the Middle East, and eventually to Italy, the London Poles had good reason to be careful with their second trump. As early as 27 October 1943, General Sosnkowski had issued an order to the Home Army to stay underground and not co-operate with the advancing Red Army. On 4 January 1944, the first day Soviet troops advanced into Polish territory, Premier Mikolajczyk broadcast his government's confirmation of Sosnkowski's directive. Pressures against this policy, however, rapidly increased. Many fighting units of the Home Army in the eastern territory were ignoring the order. The British too, from the Foreign Office to the Chiefs of Staff, undoubtedly brought pressure to bear, being fully aware that good Polish–Soviet relations depended on the Poles' ability 'to convince the Russians that the Polish underground movement means business and is achieving results against the Germans'.[25]

By mid-February Sosnkowski uncertainly directed his local leaders to identify themselves to the commanders of the liberating armies and to postpone any actions that would provoke or impede the Red Army. At the local level in the eastern territories this enabled a satisfactory working relationship to be established in some areas by March. The Poles were offered the same treatment as other indigenous forces serving elsewhere: while requested to reorganise into regular infantry divisions for supply and operational purposes, they retained their own officers and were treated as fighting units of an allied foreign government. Throughout the spring and summer of 1944 this profitable military co-operation continued and on several occasions the Red authorities admitted that the Poles had distinguished themselves.[26]

Politically events did not run so smoothly for the Poles. Churchill announced on 22 February that the British government had never approved of Poland's seizure of Soviet territory east of the Curzon Line and had never guaranteed any particular boundaries for the two countries. The radical and communist left had continued to organise and formed in Warsaw a National Council of the Homeland (KRN) in December 1943. In May 1944 the KRN merged with the Union of Polish Patriots, became the Polish

Committee of National Liberation (PCNL), and assumed political command of General Berling's First Army and General Zymierski's People's Army. In the United States, where support for the London Poles among Polish–Americans had hitherto been almost unopposed, Professor Oskar Lange of the University of Chicago (who subsequently became Deputy Chairman of the Council of State of the Polish People's Republic), Professor Louis Karpinski of the University of Michigan, Father Stanislaw Orlemanski, and other prominent Poles excluded from the London government formed the Kosciuszko League which supported the PCNL. Even in Washington where the London government-in-exile enjoyed warm support, Mikolajczyk found that Roosevelt had experienced a change of sentiment and refused to meet with him for several weeks.[27]

When the London Poles did secure an appointment with FDR, a most unsatisfactory and ambiguous conversation resulted. While admitting to being uncertain about the exact location of the Curzon Line, the President expressed the hope that areas such as Lvov, Königsberg and Tarnopol, which were well east of the line, might not be lost to Poland. Ironically, Stalin had already confided to the British that he was not unalterably opposed to similar exceptions. The Poles, however, always searching for means of advancing their cause, insisted on interpreting the President's remarks as a guarantee of American support for a total restitution of Poland's pre-war frontier in the east.[28] This fragile hope, coupled with the fears occasioned by the political reverses described above, resulted in a reinforcement of the Poles' desire to secure a military solution to their problems and a termination of the period of military co-operation between the Home and Red Armies.

Throughout the war years, from the early stages of their regroupment in London until the summer of 1944, the Poles never changed their military strategy. With time it became impossibly grandiose. The first blow came from the American military. In August 1943, the Polish General Staff asked the US and Britain to airlift all overseas Polish troops into Poland and for sufficient equipment to fully arm the entire Home Army, sometimes estimated to be 300,000 strong, by April 1944. The purpose of this request was to stage an uprising which was to last in isolation for about twenty days, until allied forces could come to the rescue. The US Staff Planners when confronted with this proposal reacted with incredulity: firstly, because US Army Intelligence estimated Home Army strength to be only 65,000; secondly, because to supply even this discounted number of troops would require an impossible number of air sorties over Poland; thirdly, because they could not see the strategical sense of the request since they calculated that such an uprising would not be feasible 'until such time as it is no longer needed', ie after the defeat of Germany.[29]

The second blow came in November 1943 after Sosnkowski had complained that the Special Operations Executive (SOE) and the RAF were not doing enough to assist the Home Army; the British Chiefs of Staff decided not to increase the allotment of aircraft to the Poles and thus disturb the entire supply system to resistance forces all over Europe. Most important was the crucial decision by the Combined Chiefs of Staff which specifically rejected a Polish uprising being called shortly after 'D' Day (6 June 1944) 'because it would be impossible to guarantee help by Allied forces in time to prevent their being overwhelmed'. Even after the Polish general headquarters, in Lord Selborne's words, 'boiled over with indignation, and . . . intimated that unless facilities can be materially increased they will be forced to give orders for the cessation of resistance in Poland and of transmission of intelligence', the British Chiefs of Staff decision stuck.[30]

THE UPRISING

Nevertheless, the Poles persisted in planning 'Tempest', as they named it. Mikolajczyk described the order for the calling of the uprising as being 'elastic'. Local commanders early in 1944 were given the authority 'to decide the hour and minute of each underground uprising—eruptive little waves which preceded the vast tidal wave of the Red Army as it rolled across Poland'. Given Polish logic and the isolation of the Polish General Staff, 'Tempest' was not co-ordinated with Red Army operations or with the British and Americans. By the spring of 1944, at least in the greater Warsaw area, the Home Army had ceased to be an allied military force in any sense of the word. One repercussion was that it failed to assist the allied armies at the time of the cross-channel invasion; another was one of the most avoidable tragedies of the war.[31]

During the last days of July 1944, the political and military pressures on the London Poles and their Warsaw supporters became intolerable. With the approval of Sosnkowski, who feared any sort of urban insurrection, quantities of weapons and ammunition were sent out of Warsaw to arm Home Army units in the countryside. At the same time, however, the Germans in the Warsaw area appeared particularly vulnerable. There was heavy traffic across the Vistula away from the eastern front. The Germans seemed dispirited and confused. In Warsaw, the political coalition which supported the Home Army showed increasing signs of disintegration over the question of military co-operation with the Soviets, and the left-wing parties expressed dissatisfaction with past and present Home Army policies. On 22 July, Moscow Radio announced that in the indisputably Polish town of Chelm a Polish Committee of National Liberation had been established. In the same broadcast the National Council of the Homeland was proclaimed the legitimate provisional Polish Parliament, with the PCNL as the provisional Polish government. Meanwhile, the Red Army and the First Polish Army were speeding forward.[32]

On 25 July, orders went out to Home Army units to prepare for 'Tempest'; on the 26th these were revoked. On the 25th, Sosnkowski, about to depart for an inspection tour in Italy, had instructed his Chief of Staff, General Kopanski, that the Warsaw Home Army was to stay underground while units in the surrounding area were to withdraw in a south-westerly direction. Mikolajczyk, about to set out on his own journey, this time to Moscow, gave his Deputy Prime Minister in Warsaw, Jan Jankowski, complete freedom in calling a rising on the 26th. Three days later, Kopanski also crossed the Commander-in-Chief and gave the Warsaw leaders a free hand. On the 29th, the Poles informed the British Chiefs of Staff that 'there arises the possibility of the Polish Home Army taking up operations on a big scale in the very near future'. More as a result of the situation on the eastern front than from any reliable intelligence that the Warsaw Poles possessed about the activities of either the German or Soviet armies, General Bor-Komorowski,

Commander-in-Chief of the Home Army, committed his troops on
1 August 1944.[33]

From the beginning, it was obvious that the timing of the uprising was wrong. Even before the order to attack was given, the
Germans began on the 26th to detrain south of Warsaw the special
Hermann Goering Tank-Paratroop Division, recently withdrawn
from Italy, and the Viking Grenadier-Tank Division to support
the 73rd Infantry Division. As the German Supreme Commander
of the Eastern Front, Panzer General Guderian, was later to testify
at Nuremberg, the Poles had not witnessed the withdrawal of
troops from the Warsaw front but the formation of a defensive line
behind the Vistula. Shortly after the uprising began, two other
fresh tank divisions were sent into the city to fortify the German
defence.[34]

As early as 5 July 1944, when the Red Army was a considerable
distance from Kovno, Bialystok, Brest Litovsk and Chelm, let
alone Warsaw, Molotov told Harriman that the advancing armies
intended to bypass Warsaw, isolate the German units in the city,
and then leave its liberation to the partisans, General Berling's first
Army and supplemented Soviet forces. While it is unlikely that
Harriman did not pass this information on to the London Poles,
it is possible that General Bor-Komorowski, with over-riding
political considerations in mind, may not have cared about Red
Army tactics any more than he cared about earlier disparaging
assessments of 'Tempest' by British and American military experts.
The point to be made is that the Home Army, without adequate
liaison with the Soviets, had no direct military intelligence in-
dicating that Warsaw would not be bypassed.[35]

On 5 August Stalin wrote to Churchill that he could not believe
that the Home Army with 'neither guns, aircraft nor tanks' could
take Warsaw which the Germans were defending with four
armoured divisions. A few days later an element of righteous
indignation had entered into the Soviet communications. Stalin
wrote to Churchill that the Poles' lack of co-operation with Soviet
military personnel was causing their destruction. He concluded
that 'the Warsaw action is a reckless and fearful gamble, taking a
heavy toll of the population'.[36]

At the same time the Soviet position had seemingly hardened
to the point where, though not objecting to American and British

airdrops to the Warsaw underground, they did object to these aircraft landing on Soviet-controlled territory. On 22 August, after a joint appeal from Churchill and Roosevelt to grant such permission, Stalin allowed his personal sentiments to colour his remarks: 'Sooner or later the truth about the handful of power-seeking criminals who launched the Warsaw adventure will out. Those elements, playing on the credulity of the inhabitants of Warsaw, exposed practically unarmed people to German guns, armour and aircraft.' While neither rejecting nor granting their requests for landing rights, he added: 'I can assure you that the Red Army will stint no effort to crush the Germans at Warsaw and liberate it for the Poles. That will be the best, really effective, help to the anti-Nazi Poles.'[37]

Throughout August the British, refusing to confuse Stalin's rhetoric with the military situation, retained their composure under pressure. The London Poles attacked them for not supplying enough weapons and ammunition to the partisans in Warsaw. Informed that they were losing half their aircraft on such missions, the Poles replied that the moment had arrived 'when even a 100% loss has to be incurred'. When General Sosnkowski complained about the lack of UK, US and USSR assistance for the uprising, the War Cabinet remained calm for they were reluctant to commit suicide over Warsaw. They were aware of the tremendous problems of dropping supplies into Warsaw because of the excellent German anti-aircraft defences, and that Soviet assistance to the Home Army had been delayed when the Soviet liaison officer, parachuted into Warsaw, was killed. They knew by the 25th that Stalin's attitude towards the Warsaw Poles had improved and that, as Air Chief Marshal Portal told them on 28 August, 'the Russians had suffered a setback; and all the evidence went to show that they were doing their utmost to reach Warsaw'.[38]

After the underground had been fighting in the streets and sewers of Warsaw for more than a month, the Soviets, on 9 September, agreed to co-operate with the airdrops. It was ironic that by then the British were deciding to continue using Italian airfields. They were also expressing grave doubts about the continuation of support missions over Warsaw. On 5 September Air Marshal Sir Douglas Evill, Vice-Chief of the Air Staff, had informed the War Cabinet that during the past three weeks of low altitude, slow speed operations forty aircraft had been lost and that out of 182 sorties there were fewer than three successful drops for every aircraft shot down. Evill considered high altitude missions, with only an expected ten-per-cent success rate, to be 'a gesture, the military value of which would be small'. On the 11th the War Cabinet agreed 'that the loss of 10 to 15 aircraft was a disproportionate price to pay for the delivery of equipment which could not seriously influence the outcome of the struggle in Warsaw'.[39]

The Soviets were naturally fearful that arms dropped to the partisans would fall into German hands, a fear which undoubtedly influenced their earlier attitude towards Anglo-American air support missions. Information about the exact location of General Bor-Komorowski's units, for the purposes of air drops, was not available until 12 September. As late as the 18th, when a large formation of Liberators flew over Warsaw, less than forty per cent of the total drop was accounted for. It was not until the 20th that the Soviets were able to bomb German positions in Warsaw and destroy German airfields on the outskirts of the city. In the meantime, the Germans had blown up all four bridges crossing the Vistula and continued to hold four-fifths of the city.[40]

During September units of the Red Army and the First Polish Army held a shallow bridgehead along the Vistula without tank or heavy artillery support and suffered casualties in excess of fifty per cent. The First Polish Battalion had been completely destroyed by German artillery fire. By the end of the month, the Soviet General Staff and Stalin decided that First Polish Army infantry units were no longer to be sacrificed in efforts to cross the Vistula and that General Berling's troops were to go over to the defensive. In London, Mikolajczyk was satisfied with Soviet efforts to assist the Warsaw insurgents, and those in the Foreign Office and Cabinet who read the Warsaw dispatches of SOE agent 'J. Ward', many of which were published in *The Times*, were concerned, with Deputy Prime Minister Jankowski, that unless Anglo-American efforts were dramatically increased 'all aid and its political consequences will be monopolised by the Soviets'.[41]

The larger tragedy, of course, lay inside Warsaw. When the Home Army surrendered on 2 October, more than 166,000 people —perhaps more than 250,000—had been killed, less than ten per cent of whom were members of the underground. The Germans, with 10,000 dead and 9,000 wounded, continued to hold out in Warsaw until January 1945. Any hope of a military solution by the London Poles was buried with the dead of Warsaw.[42]

THE RESOLUTION

With the arrival of Mikolajczyk in Moscow, approximately at the start of the Warsaw uprising, it was not only the military situation that had thickened. The Soviets insisted that the London Poles confer with the Polish Committee for National Liberation (PCNL), a representative body with a popular following of its own. Stalin made this point explicit in his first conversation with Mikolajczyk:

> For more than four years Poland has been under foreign occupation. In the meantime new men have become important in Poland and it would be impossible to call upon old authorities only. . . . Political trends in Poland under the burden of occupation have undoubtedly shifted to the left. One has to take into account young people, new authorities who have grown up in the heat of struggle and suffering.

As was well known to Mikolajczyk, the PCNL had a liberal platform which called for neither nationalisation of industry nor collectivisation of agriculture, although it did call for a division of land among the peasants without compensation to the landlords. Of the fifteen PCNL members, one was the brother of a former Polish premier, another a former Deputy Minister for War before the Pilsudski coup, and two, the only communists in the Committee, were members of the Supreme Council of the USSR. To emphasise the legitimacy of the PCNL, Stalin insisted at the end of their conversation that his government would discuss the question of frontiers only with a reconstituted 'united Polish Government'.[43]

When Mikolajczyk met the PCNL leaders on 8 August, they wasted no time in demanding that the Constitution of 1921, the only truly democratic constitution under which Poland had ever operated, should be the legal framework for the new government. In return the PCNL was prepared to offer the London Poles the position of Prime Minister and three other portfolios. Mikolajczyk's only substantive reply to this generous proposal was that 'the main anti-democratic stem' of the 1935 Pilsudski Constitution had already been removed by the London government.[44]

On his return to London, Mikolajczyk attempted somewhat pathetically to publicly defend the validity of the 1935 Constitution by arguing that 'it has been applied in a democratic spirit ever since 1939'. The most hopeful result of Mikolajczyk's Moscow visit came on 30 September when Sosnkowski was replaced by General Bor-Komorowski as the Polish Commander-in-Chief. This change was not made in a spirit of reform or of bettering relations with the USSR and the PCNL but to pacify feelings roused by Sosnkowski's indiscretions in the press earlier in the month when he had issued an Order of the Day attacking the British and Americans for not supporting the defenders of Warsaw adequately or bravely.[45]

After having despaired that nothing could be done for the London Poles, other than securing for them two or three portfolios in a unified government,[46] the British again took the initiative. The Foreign Secretary well understood that 'a Poland on good terms with the Soviet Union might have a chance of being strong, independent and prosperous: a Poland on bad terms with the Soviet Union would be a danger to the peace of the world and the security of these islands'. At Churchill's insistence a conference on Polish affairs was convened in Moscow in mid-October. With the exception of Roosevelt and Hull, all the major figures from past conferences were present. With Ambassador Harriman in attendance only as an observer, Churchill thus became by default, if not by his expertise and magnetism, the pre-eminent spokesman for the Anglo-American powers. From the outset he defended his Tehran position. He then declared, traversing familiar terrain, that Poland, with an eastern frontier at the Curzon Line, was entitled to territory in the west at the expense of Germany. Perhaps with an eye to FDR's reservations about the Curzon Line, Stalin added that the Poles would get Bialystok, Lomza and Przemysl. To all of this Mikolajczyk had nothing to say.[47]

On the following day the Prime Minister explained privately to Mikolajczyk, almost as one would to a recalcitrant child, that while the question of frontiers was of prime importance to the Soviets it was, in the long run, only of secondary importance to the Poles. Without an acceptance of the Curzon Line, at least in principle, the British and Americans had no currency with which to bargain with Stalin and the PCNL over the vitally important question of the composition of the Polish provisional government. When Mikolajczyk remained silent after this primary lesson, Churchill, with great bluntness, warned him that 'Unless you accept the frontiers you are out of business forever.'[48]

With something like the Tito–Shubashich agreement in mind, Churchill felt he could wring from Stalin the following concessions: the withdrawal of Soviet support for the PCNL and an optimistic sixty-per-cent representation for the London parties in the provisional government. Mikolajczyk's only significant observation and suggestion was that the three powers announce their decision without considering the London Poles. When that was done, the Polish Government would, in Mikolajczyk's words, 'make a formal protest. A government which wants to retain authority with their people cannot give up territory.'[49]

With tireless tact, and apparently disregarding Mikolajczyk's last comments, Churchill carefully drafted, during this very long conversation, a position paper which he felt would allow him to begin serious discussions with Stalin on behalf of the Poles. The two major points were the acceptance of the Curzon Line and an assertion of a willingness to enter into a unified Polish government. Churchill clearly believed that these two points alone would satisfy Stalin and the PCNL, for no mention was made of either the 1935 or 1921 Constitutions, the future role of the pro-fascist and pro-Pilsudski parties—items which had caused friction between the London Poles and the PCNL in the past—or of any reorganisation of the London government in the interim period. When Mikolajczyk refused to sign this short document, Churchill's concluding comments were merciless:

> You are no Government if you are incapable of taking any decision. You are callous people who want to wreck Europe. I shall leave you to your own troubles. You have no sense of responsibility when you want to abandon your people at home, to whose sufferings you are indifferent. You do not care about the future of Europe, you have only your own miserable interests in mind.

The interests were not Mikolajczyk's alone. On 3 November 1944 the cabinet of the Polish government-in-exile in London voted its approval of Mikolajczyk's course of action in Moscow.[50]

In mid-November Mikolajcayk attempted to find a more responsive advance in Washington. On the very day of Roosevelt's re-election to an unprecedented fourth term as President, FDR quashed the Poles' efforts to circumvent Churchill, Stalin and the PCNL. The President's letter of 17 November showed that the Roosevelt corollary and the Atlantic Charter could cut both ways when taken literally. The US position was that the Polish people were perfectly free (1) to make whatever internal political arrangements they thought best; (2) to arrange their frontiers with foreign powers as they thought best, without American guarantees; (3) to arrange for the transfer of populations; (4) to count on US economic assistance for post-war reconstruction.[51] In effect Roosevelt had decided to leave the Poles to the mercies of Churchill and Stalin.

After this rebuff Mikolajczyk had but one avenue open. The result of his first and last recorded effort to carry a substantive issue with his government helped in part to explain his negative lethargy during the August and October conferences in Moscow. On the lesser issue of frontiers Mikolajczyk failed to carry more than his own Peasant Party out of the four-party coalition. The more important question of political unification never came to the vote. On 24 November Mikolajczyk resigned and was succeeded by an even more reactionary government headed by Tomasz Arciszewski.[52]

By the end of 1944 Stalin had labelled the London government as 'incapable of helping a Polish settlement', and Churchill had attacked its composition during a House of Commons debate. The PCNL had proclaimed itself the Provisional National Government of the Polish Republic and had been recognised as such by the Supreme Soviet.[53] Yalta was the émigrés' last chance.

Notes to this chapter are on pages 205–8.

Chapter 9 THE GROWTH OF THE UNITED NATIONS CONCEPT

AMERICANS HAVE a passion for lengthy and spirited debates about legal instruments, whether they be treaties, charters or constitutions. The grander the scope and moral loftiness of the document, the more intricate and heated the debates have been. Such was the case with the League of Nations, and again during the early 1940s with the proposed creation of an international security organisation. By the end of 1942, groups such as the Commission to Study the Organisation of Peace, the League of Nations Association, the Free World Association, and the Commission to Study the Bases of a Just and Durable Peace had all had limited and local flushes of success. Nationally known figures such as Vice-President Henry A. Wallace and Under Secretary of State Sumner Welles, with FDR's quiet encouragement, were more successful and had presented the nation with both an alarm and the beginning of a bill of particulars for debate and discussion. None of these initiating groups or individuals contemplated a return to an enfeebled League of Nations incapable of dealing with the challenges of economic depression, social injustice and international aggression. None considered the creation of a new international organisation without the full participation of the United States.[1]

1943 saw the introduction of a plethora of Congressional measures, some by pre-war isolationists, concerning the ideas that Wallace, Welles and others had expressed in preceding years. Although these proposals were to die one by one in committee after subcommittee, there was little doubt that some elements of the Seventy-eight Congress were infected with the internationalist fever. On 16 March these measures were swept out of the limelight when Senator Joseph H. Ball, a Republican, introduced what the press had already named the B_2H_2 resolution. Primarily the work of Ball, with suggestions from Senators Harold H. Burton, Carl A. Hatch, Lister Hill and others, the resolution had the support of Wallace, Welles and the leading Republican of the day, Wendell Willkie. By far the most specific and controversial resolution so far offered, it called: (1) for the US to take the initiative in forming a new international organisation; (2) for the new organisation to assist in mobilising and utilising the military and economic resources of all member nations in the prosecution of the war; (3) for the new organisation to administer liberated enemy territories provisionally until new governments could be established; (4) for the organisation to create immediately an international military force.[2]

Senatorial reaction to the B_2H_2 resolution was predictable. It made little difference that many prominent Americans lent their prestige to the measure and that public support, aroused by the Citizens Council for the United Nations and the United Nations Association, was high. Isolationists, who opposed the measure, and conservatives, who were shocked by its specific proposals, tucked it safely out of harm's way in the Senate Foreign Relations Committee. During April 1943, an Associated Press poll revealed that only twenty-four senators favoured an international police force after the war while thirty-two opposed it and another forty were uncommitted. With this kind of support, the conservatives saw that they could subvert the Ball measure by proposing innocuous legislation of their own.[3]

The solution of the problem of the Ball resolution in the House came from the unwitting pen of a rookie Congressman from Arkansas, J. William Fulbright. On 5 April the young man introduced just the kind of harmless resolution that the conservatives had been searching for. 'Resolved: That the House of Representatives hereby expresses itself as favouring the creation of appropriate international machinery with power adequate to prevent future aggression and to maintain lasting peace, and as favouring participation by the United States therein.' With great ease on 21 September 1943, it passed the House by 360 resounding votes to twenty-nine. Political analysts in the British Embassy in Washington felt the vote was a triumph for public opinion. Senator Ball felt that 'the people were far in advance of Congress in these matters, though it was no use supposing that the people saw things clearly or were by any means unanimous.' In the Senate the Connally Resolution, no more instructive than the House version, was eventually reported out of the sponsor's committee by a vote of twenty to two. In the Senate it passed on 5 November by eighty-five votes to five. The internationalist position undoubtedly had been greatly strengthened by the passage of these resolutions. At the same time, neither provided a framework for future planning such as the B_2H_2 resolution contained.[4]

The administration took something less than a vigorous lead in the Congressional debates of 1943. The State Department and Hull were caught unprepared by the specificity of the B_2H_2 resolution. The closest thing that the State Department had as a guideline for comment and action was a speech delivered by Hull during the summer of 1942 which merely expressed the need for an international agency. While Hull was aware of the crescendo of internationalist expectations, he was at a loss to deal with them. He disliked the proposals of Wallace, Welles and the B_2H_2 senators; consequently, he was satisfied to wait and not see any positive action taken until he had time to think out what he did favour. Roosevelt in turn was stymied: both Hull and the Senate Foreign Relations Committee were too powerful, as Senator Ball realised, to be forced into taking more positive action. As a result, Roosevelt fought no battles on the domestic front and encouraged moderate advances.[5]

In private, Roosevelt increasingly accepted the advice of Welles, who like Hopkins had a knack for second-guessing and collaborating with the President, and developed his own programme. When Eden and Halifax consulted with FDR, Hull, Winant, Welles and Hopkins in Washington during March, the President outlined a three-tier plan for the new international organisation which showed his ability to reach original syntheses. According to Eden's understanding of the plan, there would be a general assembly of all the united nations which would meet annually for the purpose of enabling 'representatives of all the smaller Powers to blow off steam'. In the middle there would be an advisory council composed of representatives of the US, UK, USSR, China, plus six or eight others 'elected on a regional basis, roughly on the basis of population'. At the top, FDR called for the creation of an executive committee of the big four who 'would take all the more important decisions and wield police powers of the United Nations'. As Hopkins explained, regionalism was to be avoided in Europe and elsewhere 'for this would give free ammunition to isolationists here who would jump at the chance of sitting back in a similar council for the American continent . . .' and oppose truly international measures.[6]

On 22 May 1943, Churchill presented his own united nations plan, which he had been formulating for many months past, to Vice-President Wallace, Secretary of War Stimson, Secretary of the Interior Harold Ickes, Senator Connally and Under Secretary of State Welles. At the top there would be a Supreme World Council composed of the US, UK and USSR with certain elected representatives from three subordinate Regional Councils for Europe, the Americas and the Pacific. The keystone of the plan was the European Regional Council composed of sovereign states, such as the United Kingdom, and confederations: one for the Balkans, one for the Danube 'to fill the gap caused by the disappearance of the Austro-Hungarian Empire', and one for Scandinavia. When questioned by Wallace about the prospect of Belgium and Holland joining with France, the Prime Minister said they might form a Low Country confederation with Denmark. Churchill frankly hoped that the US would sit on all three regional councils while he thought 'it was quite possible that when the pressure on her western frontiers had been relieved Russia would turn her attention to the Far East'. The military blow of the organisation would come from nations dividing their military forces into two parts 'the one to form the national forces of that country and the other to form its contingent to an international police force at the disposal of the Regional Councils under the direction of the Supreme World Council'. As the Prime Minister outlined the above, he said 'special friendships devoid of sinister purpose' would not be excluded; personally 'He could see small hope for the world unless the United States and the British Commonwealth worked together in what he would call fraternal association.'[7]

In general there was 'warm assent' from the Americans on this last point. Wallace was enthusiastic about the entire discussion and called it the most encouraging 'for the last two years'. Welles told Churchill, during the same conversation, that he favoured the signing of a four-power protocol which would guarantee joint responsibility for keeping the peace after the war and maintaining adequate forces for that purpose. Meeting the following day, Churchill and FDR agreed it was 'essential that the Anglo-American combined Staff institution should be continued for a good long time after the war, at any rate until we can all be sure the world is safe'. Roosevelt was also interested in hearing about the rest of the Prime Minister's plan. By 8 June, Welles had produced a derivative plan, which he hoped FDR would approve, calling for a supreme world council of eleven members composed of the big four, two elected representatives each from the European and American regional councils, one from the Pacific, one from the independent countries of the Middle East and North Africa, and one from the Commonwealth. As reported by Halifax, the Welles plan 'would make it a condition of action by supreme world council that there should be unanimity between the four great powers. This in his view would only be recognising realities but would also be valuable from the point of view of United States opinion.' Churchill could not really have wished for a better response.[8]

This May presentation contained much that was innermost in Churchill's fecund mind and was obviously adulterated by considerations that had not yet come to the fore in American planning. Rather than trying to produce some pure, equitable, juridical construction, the Prime Minister had presented a plan aimed at redressing an emerging balance of power which he already suspected was going to be unfavourable. The objective of the plan was clear: it would neutralise Soviet power in Europe. With an independent Poland, Austria and Czechoslovakia, and pro-Western Balkan and Danubian confederations, the Soviets would be blocked. The old Europe would suffer; Belgium, Holland and Denmark, as examples, would experience some loss of sovereignty within a confederation, but the price was small in comparison to the ultimate threat.

The Soviets showed understandable indifference to the question of a united nations organisation until the British and Americans had made considerable progress with their first proposals. By the time of Churchill's visit to Washington, however, signals from

Moscow indicated a change of concerns. Realising that the Comintern, which had been dormant for nearly two decades, was still a convenient target for reactionaries everywhere, the Presidium of the Executions Committee of the Communist International proclaimed to the world on 22 May 1943 that the Comintern was dead. In part Stalin justified this action on the grounds that it cleared 'the way to future organisation of a companionship of nations based upon their equality'. Hull correctly interpreted these and other remarks as signs that the Soviets were ready to talk about an international security organisation.[9]

During the Foreign Ministers Conference in Moscow, Molotov enthusiastically called for a joint commission to study the problems relating to the formation of a post-war international organisation. Hull, fearful of the publicity such a commission would receive and the adverse reaction it might cause in Congress, requested semi-secret discussions. On more certain territory, Hull obtained immediate conference approval for his declaration on security which called for the establishment of a general international organisation 'at the earliest practicable date . . .'.[10]

Independent of Hull's initiative at Moscow, which was the only major European conference the Secretary of State attended during the war, the American position prior to November 1943 became increasingly security minded. During March FDR reflected this mood when he suggested to Eden that the international organisation should establish 'strong points' at Dakar and Bizerta, and in Formosa, Japan, Germany and Italy. Roosevelt accordingly proposed to Stalin at Tehran his 'four policemen' scheme for Europe, by which he meant the use of American planes and ships, with the UK and USSR being responsible for land forces. In addition he suggested the establishment of an advisory body of some thirty-five members, and an executive committee, to deal with all non-military matters, comprising the Big Four, two European nations, and one nation each from the Commonwealth, Far East, Near East and South Africa. Immediately after FDR made his proposal, Stalin predicted that Germany would recover within fifteen to twenty years and concluded 'we must have something more serious than the type of organisation proposed by the President'. Perhaps Stalin had in mind while making this last remark the 260 enemy divisions which he estimated were now facing the Red Armies.[11]

The upshot of this initial confrontation between Stalin and Roosevelt was of the greatest importance. The fact that FDR said that he agreed completely with Stalin meant something. While there were still the questions of Churchill's confederations and the participation of American troops in post-war policing actions, the picture seemed bright. From Stalin's comments at Tehran it was obvious that organisational questions were of little concern to the USSR. What was important was that the US, USSR and UK would have effective control of future decision making, that there would be a continuation of the anti-German military alliance after the war, and that the new international organisation, with its 'strong points', would be essentially security-orientated. On these points there seemed to be total agreement between the two leaders.[12]

PHASE II

Welles' influence over post-war security planning and Roosevelt's thinking exceeded his physical presence in the State Department by several months. As early as 1942 Hull had shown signs of unhappiness with Welles' aggressive articulation of his policy thoughts; he looked upon Welles' efforts as subverting his own authority and an abuse of Welles' personal relationship with FDR. During the spring of 1943 Hull began to regain control of his department by taking over from Welles the active chairmanship of the main planning committee, broadening its congressional membership and initiating a review of its basic objectives. This process of squeezing Welles out was a lengthy one requiring delicate and patient handling, for Hull at the time felt that he was estranged from Roosevelt. By June, however, the Under Secretary was effectively finished with the State Department. He unofficially left on 21 August; his resignation was publicly announced on 25 September. Welles told Sir Ronald Campbell that Hull 'was grossly incompetent and always thinks of public opinion before he considers administration and foreign policy'. According to Welles, he was forced out of office by Senators Connally and James F. Byrnes acting on behalf of Hull and powerful interests on Wall Street and in the petroleum industry. Be that as it may, the Foreign Office's initial reaction was that 'right-wing southerns',

'Russo-phobes', and men 'rather elderly in thought' were in the ascendancy.[13]

With such momentous, subterranean happenings in the last months of 1943 it was not surprising that the agreement reached at Tehran was to be of brief and somewhat uneasy duration. After the Moscow conference, which was Hull's greatest triumph of the war, the Secretary's popular and congressional strength was legion. He was eager to interpret his Four Power Declaration as a personal victory over the Welles–Churchill formula. By the end of the year Hull's Informal Political Agenda Group had prepared its first memorandum for FDR's perusal. The change in emphasis away from Tehran was significant: it rejected any form of regionalism, emphasised the importance of a general assembly, de-emphasised the powers of the executive council, and suggested the creation of economic, social, and trusteeship agencies. The trend was clearly towards a devolution of power from the big four to a general assembly and from a security to an omnibus international organisation. After meeting with Hull, FDR showed little resistance to this new set of policy attitudes and gave his approval to the general approach on 3 February 1944. A week later the State Department notified the UK and USSR that they were prepared to begin an exchange of papers and ideas.[14]

Hull's call was premature. Neither the British nor the Soviets were prepared for more than the consultative talks agreed upon at Moscow which were never held. The Americans themselves were not really prepared for much else. While the general plan may have taken shape, many vital cogs and gears needed machining, and some of the more important components had yet to see the drawing-board. The three main areas of imprecision were:
(1) the role and membership of the executive council;
(2) the nature of the organisation's military force;
(3) the question of the veto.

On the first matter, FDR at Tehran had suggested to Stalin that the subordinate executive committee be composed of the big four plus some six other nations. Hull's proposal at the end of 1943 recommended that the executive council, with no 'four policemen' on top, should comprise the big four or the four plus three others elected by the general assembly. By 18 July the State Department's firm suggestion was that the executive council be composed of the big four plus seven 'outside' members including France.[15]

On the question of military force the progression was less direct. Rather than allow State Department preparations to be buoyed, if not propelled, by the ground swell of public approval for the creation of an international force, Hull turned cautious. In the draft of late April, the State Department avoided a direct assault on the problem and vaguely suggested that forces and facilities would be provided by the organisation's members. It was also recommended that the precise numbers of forces could be determined after the creation of the organisation. Thus the most complicated aspect of the problem was shunted off into the future.[16]

When it came to the veto, the mainstream of American thinking was in favour of it. Breckinridge Long's Sub-committee on Security had regarded it as indispensable to the security of the United States. Welles' planning committee had concluded that neither the USSR nor the US Senate would approve a united nations charter without a veto for each of the major powers. Even Hull accepted the point. In May, before an influential bi-partisan committee of senators, he reasoned that the veto was included in the State Department's draft because it was 'chiefly for the benefit of the United States in the light of the world situation and of our own public opinion'. Senator Connally remembered that of the eight senators present at this meeting on 2 May 1944 only one opposed the idea of the US having a veto. The reactionary Senator Vandenberg, another of those present, was impressed by Hull's presentation because it was 'so *conservative* from a nationalist standpoint' and supported Hull's notions because 'no action looking toward the use of force can be taken if any one of the Big Four dissents'.[17]

The drafting of the pre-conference proposal in July produced several surprises. The first was that eleven states were to serve on the executive council, thus further diluting the power of the big four. This was well within the trend Hull had been seeking to establish for several months. The second item was not. It seemed to suggest that on non-substantive questions of security the veto safeguard would be restricted. The puzzle was why there should have been any hedging on a well-established position. Certainly in terms of public and Congressional opinion both liberals and conservatives alike were opposed, then as now, to any mitigation of the nation's veto right. When Vandenberg and La Follette warned Hull in late August that there would be a tremendous fight in the Senate on this issue, they spoke for more than their usual right-wing clique.[18]

While the Americans were clarifying their position for the Dumbarton Oaks conversations, the British were pushing ahead with their own plans. The problems were numerous, and compounded by the conflicting views of the Dominions and the vagaries of American planning. By April 1944 an interdepartmental committee reported its findings to the Armistice and Post-War Committee which in turn submitted the memoranda to the War Cabinet. The organisational scheme was familiar: a world assembly and a world council of the four powers. On the military side, the Committee rejected the creation of an international police force. In the Tentative Proposals which were circulated to the other big four nations in July, the justification was offered that 'this postulates a greater advance in international co-operation than States are yet prepared to make . . .'. In the background, however, military experts had argued that 'from the British point of view, owing to the scattered nature of the Empire we must retain the maximum strategic flexibility to switch forces from one place to another. A system by which certain forces were earmarked for tasks under the World Council might therefore prove embarrassing.' Obviously the empire mentality was still a powerful influence.[19]

After seeing these proposals, Churchill demurred, resurrected his own regional councils scheme, which had received some hard knocks from both the Americans and Soviets, and during May submitted it to the conference of Dominion Prime Ministers. Churchill immediately ran into strong opposition from the Commonwealth Ministers who saw the scheme as a prop for the sagging *British* Commonwealth. Failing to gain support for his plan outside the government proper, the Prime Minister withdrew his paper from consideration. After the conference, Eden diplomatically concluded that regional councils, especially the one for Europe, should be de-emphasised as an integral part of the international organisation's structure. Five days before the opening of the Dumbarton Oaks conference, the British tactical approach had been decided; Sir Alexander Cadogan was able to report that the British proposal was similar to the American plan in all essentials.[20]

If it was impossible to know until Tehran what the Soviets wanted, after Moscow it was possible to know what they did not want. According to Hull's recollection, Molotov at Moscow 'emphatically' attacked Churchill's plan for federations as a revival of 'cordon sanitaire' thinking. In July Harriman reported that Maxim M. Litvinov, or some equally prominent pseudonymed figure, had lofted a trial balloon in a Soviet publication calling not only, in Harriman's words, for 'a directive body composed of the great powers' which 'would act only on unanimous decision', but also for a series of documented agreements in which 'the role of each power in putting out conflagrations in this or that breeding place of aggression would be defined'.[21] This was a general formulation of the 'something more serious' Stalin had wished for at Tehran.

On 12 August 1944 the Soviet Union submitted its official Memorandum on an International Security Organisation. In comparison to those of the US and UK, it was remarkably informal, terse and muscular. The single task of the organisation was to prevent future aggression. For matters relating to 'co-operation between peoples in the economic, social, technical and other spheres' it was suggested that a separate organisation be established; with this aspect the Soviet memorandum did not deal. The principal organs of security organisation were to be the general assembly, council, international court, and secretariat general. All signatories of the Declaration by the United Nations on 1 January 1942 were to be members. The assembly was to have responsibility for determining matters of security and was also to consider questions of arms reductions, admission and expulsion of members, modifications of the charter, and allocation of expenses. Voting was to be by a simple majority on organisational questions and by a two-thirds majority on other matters. The members of the security council were to be the four major powers plus France and a limited number of other states elected by the general assembly. The council was to have prime responsibility for security matters with each nation having a veto. The only other remarkable provision of the proposal called for the creation of an international air force. In non-urgent situations the council would utilise forces placed at their disposal in accordance with prior contractual agreements.[22]

THE LONG RETREAT

The first disagreement between the US, USSR and UK during the seven-week discussions at Dumbarton Oaks was over the matter of voting in the security council. This was one of seven areas which Welles' successor, E. R. Stettinius, Jr, the chief US negotiator, informed FDR that the American delegation was ill-prepared to discuss. True to their memo of 12 August, the Soviets maintained that security questions should be decided by a simple majority with the concurrence of all the permanent members. The British position, strongly influenced by Eden's thinking, was that parties to a dispute on the council should have no vote, and that on all questions of principle there should be a two-thirds majority with the concurrence of all the great powers. Unprepared though they may have been, the Americans supported the Soviet proposal. On the question of general assembly voting there was no serious difference of opinion.[23]

On 25 August Stettinius informed the Soviets that the US, in accord with FDR's wishes as influenced by Hull's views, was going to side with the British on the matter of council voting. Three days later the Soviets objected that the Anglo-American proposal was contrary to the fundamental axiom that significant decisions were to be the product of unanimity among the powers. At this inopportune moment, Stettinius chose to announce that in addition to France, as the fifth member of the council, the US was considering proposing Brazil as a sixth permanent member—in addition to the seven non-permanent members already proposed.[24]

Ambassador Gromyko reiterated the Soviet position that the council be limited to the four powers with France later to be the fifth. It was then suggested by Mr Pasvolsky of the American delegation, with support from Sir Alexander Cadogan, that it might be appropriate for six elected members to serve for two-year periods with a divisible number elected each year. This was followed by the American proposal that thirty-four nations be included in the initial membership of the organisation, ie the original twenty-six signatories of the United Nations Declaration plus Chile, Ecuador, Paraguay, Peru, Uruguay, Venezuela, Iceland and Egypt, which had subsequently subscribed to the Declaration. The Soviet position was that these eight nations should be treated initially as 'associated' members with prospects of full membership. It was only after this suggestion that Gromyko stated that the sixteen republics of the USSR should also be treated as original members.[25]

When informed of this exchange, Hull professed to be 'amazed' that Gromyko should make such a proposal. In fact, the Soviets were merely defending themselves against the Americans' aggressive efforts to mould the international organisation for their own purposes. FDR's reaction was only slightly more reasonable: he was willing to ease the tension by not having Brazil's seat on the council mentioned in the initial draft of the charter. On the other issues he was not willing to compromise. Drawing Stettinius aside for a private conversation the following day, Gromyko accounted for his dramatic request by mentioning the US position on the two-thirds vote, which he regarded as a 'retreat', and the Anglo-American call for a restricted veto, which he considered to be a blow at four-nation solidarity. The other disputatious points that Gromyko mentioned were the international air force and the proper function of the organisation. He then promised Stettinius that no further mention of the sixteen republics would be made at Dumbarton Oaks, and that his government would agree, without condition, to original membership for the eight nations already proposed by the US.[26]

On 31 August, Roosevelt reluctantly endorsed a State Department memorandum which recommended that Brazil no longer be advanced for a permanent seat. None the less, the President maintained that 'the Brazilian matter was a card up his sleeve'. On 3 September Stettinius withdrew American sponsorship for Brazil, and the matter was settled that the big four plus France 'in due course' and six other elected members would make up a council of eleven.[27]

On 5 September Gromyko told Stettinius that he was particularly worried about the US position on voting in the security council. Hull's overdue response was that the US 'could easily return to a majority'. Like Stettinius, he could see that with a council of eleven the difference between a two-thirds and a majority vote was only one. Finally on 8 September, Stettinius told the other delegates that the US was prepared to accept a majority vote. What had been of vital importance for weeks became in a matter of hours an issue of no consequence.[28]

The fundamental question as to the proper task of the united nations organisation was disposed of more easily. On 25 August, Gromyko argued that according to Soviet estimates the League of Nations, contrary to the popular view, had spent only a third of its time considering issues directly related to the maintenance of peace; for that reason the USSR emphasised the importance of separating military from other functions. Four days later Gromyko elaborated: his government envisaged a four-power pool of aircraft to be used in emergencies; each national unit would retain its own equipment, national markings, and officers. The Ambassador added that his government also favoured similar use of troops and naval units.[29]

On 4 September, Gromyko returned to the original Soviet point. The British Joint Staff Mission at Dumbarton Oaks had asked London three times for instructions and received as many confused replies. That part of the Soviet proposal calling for small states to hand over territory to the world organisation for the use of international forces was strategically unacceptable. The question of an international air force was more difficult. The planning and military personnel strongly disapproved of it, but Churchill liked the idea and let it be known within the government that the Soviet plan 'raises very large questions of principle and cannot be decided on purely military grounds'. Cadogan informed Stettinius of Churchill's position on 5 September. There was no comparable uncertainty in the American camp. Hull and Stettinius vigorously opposed the plan and secured FDR's support for their opposition. The direct consequence of this hardening of the American position was that on the morning of 12 September Ambassador Gromyko, faced with insuperable American and British opposition, withdrew the proposal that weak nations be obliged to donate military sites or 'strong points' to the international force. More significantly, he also withdrew the Soviet plan for an international air force after British vacillation had ceased. The spirit of Tehran was finished.[30]

CONCLUSIONS

The American position on voting in the security council had wavered and shifted without any benefits accruing. In contrast, the British rejected Eden's recommendations during the Dumbarton Oaks conversations and switched to a more enlightened position. By the end of September 1944, they could see that, despite Dominion objections, the unfettered veto was essential, for peace was totally dependent on great-power co-operation. In the words of the Post Hostilities Planning Staff, 'It is therefore unnecessary to make provision for lack of this agreement, because in the absence of this unanimity the World Organisation will in any case be ineffective.' The British also began to worry about their 'special interests' in Eire, Egypt and elsewhere without a veto. On a more progressive plane they took note of Ambassador Clark Kerr's warnings that the Soviets 'fear that an exception to the unanimity rule would be used to line up the whole organisation against them'. During the second Quebec conference, Churchill, not always the most sensitive of individuals when it came to Soviet concerns, warned Roosevelt that the Soviets were aware that the two-thirds vote would ensure 'that they would be overwhelmingly defeated in a United Nations' meeting . . .'. Perhaps with an eye to his forthcoming meeting with Stalin in Moscow, and with increasing support within his own government, the Prime Minister was concerned that the Soviets 'would get sore and try to take it out on all of us on some other point'. In the end Churchill flatly refused to support the Americans in further efforts to pressure Stalin to accept a position in which they no longer believed.[31]

As a means of increasing US influence in Latin America, the matter of Brazil created nothing but distrust, especially on the part of the USSR. By any standards Brazil was not a likely candidate for a permanent seat. Its government had not declared war on Germany and Italy until August 1942, was not to declare war on Japan until June 1945, and had contributed little to the war effort. Even on the matter of the UN Declaration, Brazil had waited until February 1943 to subscribe. The introduction of the issue had no relevance to the talks in their broadest context, and acted as a divisive wedge for no other than the most suspicious bargaining purposes.[32]

It was disturbing that Cordell Hull, the acknowledged father of the United Nations, should have been, with assistance from Roosevelt, the designer of the international organisation's most fundamental weakness. More than a bitter triumph over Welles, the anti-policeman policy was a sign that Hull, and ultimately Roosevelt as well, 'tended to think of the establishment of an international organisation as a sort of talisman which would possess a powerful virtue to heal disputes among the nations'. In the end, 'instead of viewing international politics as essentially and necessarily an affair of clashing interests and struggle for power . . .', they imperfectly saw international politics as a high moral question of 'legal right and wrong'.[33] It was ironic that only a few weeks after the close of the conference the Democratic Party gained its largest Congressional majorities since the flush days of the prewar New Deal as being the more strongly internationalist of the two parties. Here was a mandate building during the conference for the administration to negotiate the strongest possible organisation, not the weakest, under the circumstances.[34]

Unquestionably one of the root causes of the deficiencies of the Dunbarton Oaks conversations was the virtual absence of adequate tripartite or inter-allied discussions. By the time of the talks the positions of the US and USSR especially had become unalterably fixed and were so fundamentally different that, even given the generous time limitations of the conference, it was nearly impossible to negotiate compromises. Unfortunately this created a situation where Anglo-American power, not reason, prevailed. The Soviets were forced to accept defeat, without compensation, on three major issues: the expansion of the general assembly from twenty-six to thirty-four members; the dilution of the security council from five to eleven powers; the acceptance of an essentially non-military international organisation. The British and Americans conceded nothing of substance.

Notes to this chapter are on pages 209–10.

Chapter 10 YALTA AND THE END OF AN ERA

IN EFFECT Yalta was the second great European peace conference of this century. Like the first grand gathering, its ostensible purposes were the diplomatic neutralisation of Germany, the dismantling of her remaining and potential capacities to make war, and the perfection of a plan to establish a world organisation capable of keeping the peace. As with other congresses, the results of the Crimea (Yalta) conference were to be widely hailed, strenuously debated and bitterly rejected by many. For the insiders there were few surprises. The issues ran deep and to predictable conclusions because they flowed naturally from the diplomatic, military, psychological, economic and political origins and consequences of the entire war.

While Roosevelt, Stalin and Churchill each brought to the Crimea many considerations, proposals and interests, the actual number discussed was quite small. Certainly the problem of the United Nations Organisation (UNO) was high on all three lists. The Americans, for whom the Dumbarton Oaks discussions had been a great success, pressed straight ahead with their advantage and once again suffered no reverses.

By February 1945, American opinion, as represented by Roosevelt, the Secretaries of War and the Navy, the Joint Chiefs of Staff and informed members of Congress, supported the view that unanimity in the Security Council on all substantive issues concerning world peace was required. When Secretary of State Stettinius on 6 February 1945 insisted on this point, no one demurred. The US was merely bringing its proposal into line with suggestions already made by both the UK and USSR during the last weeks of 1944.[1]

175

Churchill fully approved of these proposals and was quite candid about his intention to interpret the veto power in a broad manner. While understanding that the UK would be unable to keep the UNO from discussing the issues, he pointed out that he was prepared to use the veto to block any irredentist moves by China regarding Hong Kong or any anti-colonial actions relating to the Suez Canal. Stalin expressed concern that this matter of broad interpretation raised by Churchill might cause conflict between the allies, but the following day Molotov accepted Stettinius's proposals without reservations.[2]

The admission of the Ukraine, White Russia and Lithuania, 'or at any rate two', which was a vastly scaled down version of the Soviet proposal at Dumbarton Oaks, caused confusion but no problem. Although it seemed as though one might be raised when a hurriedly prepared memorandum, presumably drafted by Alger Hiss, warned the US delegation that these republics were not sovereign states in the sense of such Commonwealth nations as Australia and Canada, this warning led to naught[3] Not surprisingly, Eden and Churchill fully supported the Soviet request. On the 7th the Prime Minister told FDR and Stalin, in the words of the Soviet summary of the conversation, that the USSR 'might have reasons to look askance at the British Commonwealth of Nations if she had only one vote, despite the fact that the population of Russia greatly exceeded the white population of the British Empire'. Seeking Cabinet approval of his position, Churchill argued that it was asking a great deal of the Soviets to accept four, five or six (if India were included) Commonwealth votes in the General Assembly when they had but one. The real point was, as he informed the War Cabinet, that he wished 'to make a friendly gesture in the matter to Russia in view of other important concessions by them which were achieved or pending'.[4] Roosevelt also approved the request. As an afterthought, following the urgings of James F. Byrnes and Hopkins, FDR on 10 February also asked for additional votes. On the following day Stalin, without quibbling, suggested that the US also receive three votes.[5]

Obviously the Gromyko–Stalin request was motivated by internal political pressures since the question of compensatory votes, to establish a voting balance between the USSR and the US–UK in the General Assembly, was never an issue. Unquestionably, the British and Americans had the better of the bargain and a decisive majority in the assembly and the Security Council. While the US and UK pledged themselves to propose original member- ship for the Ukraine and White Russia at the forthcoming San Francisco conference on World Organisation, the Soviets allowed the eight 'associated nations' and Turkey, nearly all strong sup- porters of Anglo-American policies, to become original members of UNO. Stalin was fully aware that ten of the agreed original members had no diplomatic relations with the USSR.[6] By comparison, Germany proved a far more contentious item of discussion.

GERMANY AND THE FRENCH ZONE

Prior to the Crimea conference, agreement on the future of Germany in the European Advisory Commission had been limited to the drawing of the occupation zones and drafting of three- power control machinery (which simply meant that the command- ing general in each zone would control his own zone and serve on the three-nation Control Council). Beyond these points the American delegation was armed only with the spirit of the Morgenthau plan, on which there were still doubters within the State Department. None the less, FDR's resolve was reflected in the Yalta Briefing Book Paper on Germany, prepared by the State Department, which the delegation took to the conference. It recommended that Germany's self-sufficiency and potential to partake in 'economic aggression' should be abolished; it also sug- gested that Germany's entire economic surplus above a prescribed minimum standard of living should go to reparations.[7]

The Soviets were prepared to go even farther than the Ameri- cans. In January, Maisky, the Assistant People's Commissar for Foreign Affairs, told Ambassador Harriman that the USSR wanted to fragment Germany beyond the three zones agreed upon in the EAC in such a way that the Rhineland, including the Ruhr, and Bavaria would be detached. This was no more than Churchill, Morgenthau and Roosevelt, at one time or another, had proposed. On the issue of reparations, neither the British nor the Americans had any specific proposals. The Soviets were more interested in short term security, through the destruction of Germany's heavy industry, than in seeing German industries reconstructed so that larger reparations could be exacted over a longer period. In terms of labour, Maisky mentioned that the Soviets wished the use of two or three million Germans.[8]

At the second plenary session on 5 February, Maisky presented his government's most recent plan for Germany. While it did not mention any fragmentation of Germany beyond the three zones already agreed upon in the EAC, it did conform with the Assistant Commissar's earlier comments. As new items he mentioned that German heavy industry should be reduced by eighty per cent over a two-year period; that war industries be totally removed; that industries with a high war potential, such as transport, be placed under international control with the US, UK and USSR participating; and that the USSR, on the basis of military contribution and losses suffered, should receive a total of US $10 billion in removals and yearly payments in kind over a decade.[9]

British and American reactions to this presentation were diametrically opposed. Roosevelt, true to the Briefing Book, approved the Soviet proposal on the basis that 'the German standard of living should not be higher than that of the Soviet Union'. Churchill, in opposition, argued that 'at the end of the last war the Allies had also indulged themselves with fantastic figures of reparations but that these had turned out to be a myth'.[10] Maisky pointed out that pre-war Germany had spent up to $6 billion a year on armaments, but the British delegation considered the Soviet claim 'extravagant', 'fantastic' and 'hardly compatible with their proposal for the dismemberment of Germany'. Even after Maisky explained that Soviet experts calculated that $20 billion could be extracted from Germany, with the UK and US receiving $8 billion (an award highly generous to the British since the Americans had virtually no reparation damages to claim), with all other European claimants receiving $2 billion, Eden and Churchill consistently refused to accept the Soviet proposal.[11]

In fact what had happened behind the scenes was that Attlee and others of his anti-German persuasion had been defeated on several fronts. At first, after the initial shock of Morgenthau's proposals, the Chiefs of Staff had favoured a tough line on Germany as 'an insurance policy against a revival of Germany's *Rapallopolitik*, a Russo-German combination directed against the

West'.[12] The advance of the Soviet Army from the Vistula to the Oder, and its warm reception in the liberated regions, had during just a three-week period prior to the Yalta talks so visibly changed the situation that Soviet, not German, power by the time of the conference had become the prime threat.[13]

Eventually the three leaders agreed, as part of the mixed package, that they would 'take such steps, including the complete disarmament, demilitarisation and dismemberment of Germany as they deem requisite for future peace and security'. The details on the issues were to be settled in future by Eden, Winant and Gusev. While throughout the conference the British delegation was noticeably less enthusiastic about dismemberment than the US, USSR or Churchill, there was agreement that removals from Germany would be carried out for the 'purpose of destroying the war potential of Germany' within two years and that German labour, much needed in the UK as well as the USSR, was to be used as one form of reparations. An Allied Reparation Commission was established, and the Soviet and American delegations agreed on the sum of $20 billion 'as a basis for discussion' with half to go to the USSR. At the same time, the protocol registered the dissenting British view that 'no figures of reparation should be mentioned'. While these items and principles were firm, all other matters relating to Germany, many of which were to complicate allied relations in subsequent years, were postponed.[14]

When Roosevelt and Churchill proposed that France be given an occupation zone in Germany, Stalin bristled and then acquiesced. The USSR and the French Provisional Government had signed a friendship treaty during the latter part of 1944, but clearly Stalin felt that the French were getting more than they deserved when, as he expressed it during the second plenary session, 'at the present moment France only had eight divisions in the war, Yugoslavia twelve and the Lublin Government of the Poles thirteen'. Churchill compared Britain's need for a strong France with the USSR's need for a friendly Poland in their future struggles against a revitalised Germany. The point was sympathetically noted by Stalin. FDR attempted to separate the question of the French zone in Germany from French membership of the Allied Control Commission, to approve the one and not the other; the British and Soviets both saw the illogicality of this position. The concluding compromise

was that France was given a zone of occupation, to be carved from
the British and American zones, and a seat on the Allied Control
Council for Germany.[15]

POLAND

By the time of the Yalta conference, there had been a change of
sentiment within the State Department, with the President's
approval, away from the strictures of the Atlantic Charter and the
Roosevelt corollary to that document. Washington realised that
some of the more than thirty European territorial disputes would
have to be settled by the major powers before the holding of a
general peace conference. With this in mind, Roosevelt argued at
Yalta that 'the American people' favoured the Curzon Line as
Poland's eastern frontier with concessions 'in regard to Lwow and
the oil deposits in the province of Lwow'. While not regarding
frontiers 'as a question of vital importance', since the matter had
nearly been settled before the conference, Churchill, who had
moved far beyond this point in this own thinking, supported an
unrevised Curzon Line. Stalin argued that the line had been fixed
without Soviet approval, that Lenin had felt it was unfair to the
USSR, and that he and Molotov would have difficulties on their
return to Moscow if they accepted FRD's exceptions and were 'less
sure defenders of Russian interest [sic] than Curzon and Clemen-
ceau'. None the less, by the end of the conference Stalin and
Molotov had accepted FDR's views that 'the eastern frontier of
Poland should follow the Curzon Line with digressions from it in
some regions of five to eight kilometres in favour of Poland'.[16] In
the west the matter was less certain.

When on 7 February the Soviet delegation tabled a six-point
proposal on Poland, containing their acceptance of FDR's exceptions to the Curzon Line, they proposed that Poland's frontier in
the west be extended to the Oder–Western–Neisse River line.
Churchill, in the words of the Soviet minutes, replied that 'It
would hardly be the proper thing to have the Polish goose so
stuffed with German viands that it died of indigestion.' He also
worried about the expulsion of large numbers of Germans that
would be necessitated by such a frontier. The following day FDR
also disagreed with the Western Neisse line. In the end the Pro-

tocol merely stated the long-standing allied position that '. . . Poland must receive substantial accession of territory in the North and West'.[17]

When it came to the discussion of Poland's political future, Roosevelt surprisingly took the initiative and advanced what was probably the most original proposal of the entire conference. While acknowledging that the new Poland unlike the old 'should maintain the most friendly and co-operative relations with the Soviet Union', he suggested that the three leaders should create a presidential council composed of the leaders of the five major parties in Poland. The council in turn would negotiate the formation of a provisional government. Churchill's reaction was that the three leaders should create a Polish government on the spot. Stalin argued that while he was often called a dictator, he was enough of a democrat to insist that the Poles participate in the construction of their own government. By the fourth session of the conference, Churchill and Stalin had suspended discussion of their delegations' proposals and accepted FDR's plan as the appropriate starting point.[18] It was generally agreed that this plan would mean the end of the London Polish government.

Roosevelt pressed forward his proposal by suggesting that two members of the Lublin (or Warsaw, as Stalin called it) government be brought to Yalta and that Stalin select two or three other names from a Roosevelt short list of such supposedly non-political figures as the Archbishop of Cracow, Adam Sapieha. FDR felt that these four or five leaders from Poland would be able to agree on a government which undoubtedly would include leaders from London, such as Mikolajczyk, Stanislaw Grabski and Tadeusz Romer. From what Stalin had said earlier, agreement at this point was very close, for Mikolajczyk and Grabski were acceptable to both the Lublin Poles and the Soviets. Unfortunately on the following day Stalin reported that he had been unable to contact the Lublin Poles on the telephone, and that it was thus impossible to bring them to Yalta before the close of the conference.[19]

There were signs that the Soviets were not completely convinced by the President's plan. Molotov twice proposed that a better solution would be to supplement the Lublin government with Poles from London and thus by-pass the presidential committee. On the second of these occasions, Churchill proclaimed that 'we are now at the crucial point of this great Conference'. Roosevelt, well prepared for the moment, quickly submitted a plan whereby Molotov, Harriman and Clark Kerr would invite Bierut and Osubka-Morowski from Lublin, Archbishop Sapieha and Wicenty Witos, leader of the pre-war Peasant Party, from Poland, and Mikolajczyk and Grabski from London to represent the presidential office and form a provisional government.[20] Ironically, Roosevelt, who for years had allowed Churchill and Stalin to take the lead, emerged at Yalta to stamp his presence in bold letters on the ultimate solution.

On the following day, after the Foreign Ministers' meeting, FDR's plan became somewhat transformed. Churchill, Stalin and FDR eventually agreed that Molotov, Harriman and Clark Kerr would supervise the reorganisation of the Lublin government 'on a broader democratic basis with the inclusion of democratic leaders from Poland itself and from Poles abroad'. Molotov and Stalin had carried their point, with Anglo-American approval, that Lublin and not London was the location of the existing government and the starting point for the reorganisation. As far as the Soviets were concerned, even as late as April, the idea of a presidential council, while specifically not mentioned in the Protocol, still had validity. Churchill, for his part, was delighted with the result; he informed the War Cabinet that the conclusions reached at Yalta 'were on any broad and statesman-like view the best practicable, and that they were truly in the interest of Poland'. He felt that the Soviets had been reasonable and sincerely wished to build good relations with the Poles.[21]

YUGOSLAVIA, EXCEPTIONS AND OMISSIONS

After Poland, everything else was handled with considerable dispatch. The situation in Yugoslavia, as an example, was clear to everyone including the State Department. In their words, the partisans' opponents 'are reduced to sullen impotence'. When Stettinius announced the foreign ministers' decision that the Tito–Shubashich agreements should be implemented despite 'King Peter's whim', the British immediately proposed two amendments: (1) that the Anti-Fascist Assembly of National Liberation (AVNOJ) be enlarged to include members of the pre-war national assembly and (2) that all acts passed by AVNOJ during the war be ratified by a constituent assembly. Neither the Soviets nor the Americans had any objections; and none of the three leaders had any democratic scruples about imposing conditions on a settlement which had developed independently of their ministrations.[22] No one cared about the views of the partisans, whose supporters 'were particularly indignant that the AVNOJ had to incorporate members of the 1938 Assembly, which had been elected during the regime of Milan Stojadinovic, an Axis man'[23]. In this fashion, the British secured concessions from Stalin and FDR which Churchill and Shubashich had been unable to get from Tito and AVNOJ. The only other item of interest was that Stalin obviously had not one spare kopec in his store of diplomatic capital to spend in behalf of Tito or AVNOJ.

One of the last items of any significance dealt with Yugoslavia's external affairs. Prior to Yalta, Washington had been warned by Harriman that the Soviets enjoyed especially good relations with the Fatherland Front, and that the Soviet press was endorsing the idea of a Bulgarian–Yugoslav federation. During the conference Molotov confirmed this by stating that since the two nations were militarily collaborating against Germany it was only logical that political union should follow. The British took the rather legalistic position that former enemy states should not have the freedom of entering into treaties without allied permission. Molotov retorted that Churchill's Danubian Federation would have included both enemy and allied states. Eden replied with questionable candour that 'the British had never had in mind a Balkan Federation until the armistice period had terminated'. The unsatisfactory conclusion was that Stettinius proposed, and Molotov accepted, that the matter be discussed in greater detail in Moscow.[24]

In many respects Yalta, like Tehran, was the antithesis of Placentia Bay. Statements of principle were of secondary importance compared to constructive discussions of practical problems. The times had changed. The Declaration on Liberated Europe, sponsored by the American delegation, was the only noteworthy exception. It was a liberal hope for the future. It contained nothing new, but provided a useful tool in the Roosevelt administration's public relations efforts. It took up a large section of the Protocol but almost none of the conference's time. Churchill aptly commented that he would 'not dissent from the President's proposed Declaration as long as it was clearly understood that the reference to the Atlantic Charter did not apply to the British Empire'.[25] Had he been so inclined, Stalin might have expressed much the same reservation.

Two important topics were not discussed at Yalta. The first, a purposeful omission, was the Churchill–Stalin agreement of 9 October 1944. The spirit of that agreement nevertheless permeated the entire conference. The second, Spain, can be viewed only as an oversight on the part of Roosevelt and Stalin. With the Western bloc just under way, Churchill obviously did not want Spain discussed. Had the opportunity arisen, however, there can be little doubt that the Soviets would have welcomed an opportunity to remedy this aberration of the 1930s. Undoubtedly FDR's attitude had hardened during the war years. After Yalta, the President warned the American Ambassador to Spain that he could see 'no place in the community of nations' for fascist Spain. Notwithstanding this strong forewarning, time and the back-log of unfinished business did not allow the three leaders to discuss Iberia, and the matter was allowed to slip past, even by Stalin.[26]

GATHERING THE LOOSE ENDS

The Yalta conference was neither the beginning of the end of an unfortunate wartime coalition nor the end of a promising beginning for post-war co-operation. To some extent Churchill, Stalin and FDR merely confirmed during the conference the military realities of the war. While the Red Army and the converted armies of eastern Europe may have controlled less of Europe than Hitler had, there can be little doubt that they controlled more than Charlemagne or Napoleon ever had. Eighty-five per cent of all German soldiers killed during the war died on the eastern front.[27] These were the realities. Yet the USSR gained nothing during the Yalta discussions that they had not received by consent in the EAC and by Churchill's hand on 9 October 1944. The most remarkable aspect of the peace settlement at Yalta was that the military and political overlays so harmonised with other more important realities.

The Yalta decisions conformed with the post-war psychology of

Europe, or came closer to it than might have been imagined. During the war, the USSR lost $7\frac{1}{2}$ million fighting men and women, more than twice the combined losses of Germany, the UK, US and France. Altogether more than 20 million Russians died. One in every five Poles, some 6 million people, and one in every ten inhabitants of Yugoslavia, 1·5 million people, died during the war. The remaining figures are no less grim. Altogether the Germans murdered more than 12 million Europeans.[28] These tragic losses created a profound revulsion both consciously and subconsciously among the peoples of Europe, a revulsion which demanded that there be no repetition of the political and economic conditions that prevailed during the 1930s. Everywhere in the wake of the war the old order was wounded. In some parts of Europe, it was dead. The Second World War, even more than the Russian Revolution, was the starter's flag for a new thrust in twentieth-century political affairs.[29] Churchill and Roosevelt were aware of this phenomenon, Stalin was driven by it and the Yalta conference in part confirmed it by recognising that the USSR's security requirements were no longer marginal but essential to the security of Europe.

When the three leaders at Yalta refused to modify the Churchill–Stalin understanding of 9 October, when they perfected the Polish settlement and ratified the Tito–Shubashich agreements, they acknowledged that profound political changes had taken place during the war which in turn were the products and causes of the military and psychological conditions prevailing in Europe. Churchill and Smuts were perhaps the first to realise that these changes were under way. In part it was precisely because of this reforming potential that Churchill, with his rooted conservatism, had attempted to shape Europe into spheres of influence so as to eliminate as much change as possible. Even the State Department, with less political awareness and sophistication than most foreign offices, and FDR realised that Europe was not soon to return to the politics of exploitation, racism, repression and militarism. Stalin, too, realised that there was an unavoidable reformist spirit in Europe, although very likely he, like Churchill and FDR, under-estimated its universality and the challenge it constituted to his own brand of politics.[30] The important feature of Yalta was that Stalin, Churchill and Roosevelt responded to the military, political and psychological realities of the moment and saw that in the interests of stability and security a partial and temporary division of Europe was necessary.

In a sense too the three leaders moved beyond Churchill's prophylactic diplomacy and the concept of a zoned Europe. This was the ultimate spirit and meaning of Yalta. The UNO, the questions of territorial trusteeships, frontiers, and disputes; the residual problems of German policy, Austria and Poland; reparations; the trial of war criminals; German dismemberment; European disarmament; the problems of the various Control Commissions; economic reconstruction; the revision of the Montreux Convention; the diplomatic recognition of new governments; the projected meetings of the three Foreign Secretaries; all these provided ample scope for future allied co-operation. Obviously a large area of commonality was included. It was clear during the Yalta conference that these issues were intended to be resolved amicably and rationally. The most important guidelines had been drawn, and the reactionary period of the 1930s had been put to rest.

Notes and References

ALL DATES have been given in this order: day, month and year; for example, 1 October 1943 as 1/10/43. All citations preceded by letters, such as in CAB 65/19. COS (42) 33., are references to documents in the Public Record Office in London. The letters and numbers in each case are sufficient for the reader or researcher to order and locate each document. FRUS is an abbreviation for the State Department's printed series of volumes *Foreign Relations of the United States*.

INTRODUCTION THE END OF A DECADE (pages 9–11)

1 Stillman, Edmund and Pfaff, William. *Power and Impotence: The Failure of American Foreign Policy* (New York, 1966), 185
2 Roosevelt's Speech to the New York Grange in Albany, 2/2/32, *Franklin D. Roosevelt and Foreign Affairs*, I, ed Edgar B. Nixon (Cambridge, Mass 1969), note 1 (top) on 24
3 FDR quoted in the *Literary Digest* of 28/1/33, Nixon, I, top note on 28; Letter from FDR to Senator Arthur Capper, 22/3/33, Nixon, I, 28
4 Document 56, FDR's Appeal to the Nations of the World, 16/5/33, *The Public Papers and Addresses of Franklin D. Roosevelt*, II, ed Samuel I. Rosenman (New York, 1938), 187; Norman H. Davis's Speech to the Disarmament Conference, 22/5/33, *Documents on International Affairs, 1933*, ed John W. Wheeler-Bennett, assisted by Stephen A. Heald (1934), 211
5 Pratt, Lawrence. 'The Anglo-American Naval Conversations on the Far East of January 1938', *International Affairs*, 47, 4 (October 1971), 747 and note 3
6 See Zimmern, Alfred. 'The League's Handling of the Italo-Abyssinian Dispute', *International Affairs*, 14, 6 (November–December 1935)
7 For partial support for this assertion see the following persuasive and perceptive work: Nicholas, H. G. *Britain and the United States* (1963), 26–7

Note. Undoubtedly the most brilliant single volume dealing with European diplomacy during the 1930s is A. J. P. Taylor's *The Origins of the*

Second World War (1961). Unfortunately there is no work of comparable quality dealing with American diplomacy during the same time although Denna Frank Fleming's *The Cold War and Its Origins*, I (1961) is a fascinating and important source. In all respects the best single volume on the Spanish Civil War is Hugh Thomas's *The Spanish Civil War* (1961).

1   THE ALLIANCE (pages 12–24)

1   Hull, Cordell. *The Memoirs of Cordell Hull*, I (1948), 700
2   *The Shaping of American Diplomacy*, ed William Appleman Williams, II (Chicago 1967), 785, 840–7
3   Sherwood, Robert E. *Roosevelt and Hopkins: An Intimate History* (New York 1948), 249, 257–8, 352
4   CAB 65/19. War Cabinet 84(41). Churchill's Report on the Atlantic Conference, 19/8/41. For FDR's post conference follow-up on this promise see FDR's War on Submarines radio address of 11/9/41, Williams, II, 847–9
5   Joint Statement by Roosevelt and Churchill, 14/8/41, United States Department of State (eds), *Foreign Relations of the United States, Diplomatic Papers 1941*, I (Washington 1958), 368–9
6   Memo of Conversation by Welles, 10/8/41, FRUS, 1941, I, 354/5
7   Memo of Conversation by Welles, 11/8/41, FRUS, 1941, I, 363
8   Wilson, Theodore A. *The First Summit: Roosevelt and Churchill at Placentia Bay, 1941* (1969), 247. For the text of the conversation during the conference see Memo of Conversation by Welles, 11/8/41, FRUS, 1941, I, 361–3
9   Kottman, Richard N. *Reciprocity and the North Atlantic Triangle 1932–38* (Ithaca, New York 1968), 279
10 Sherwood, 264, 439; Roosevelt's War Message to the Nation, 9/12/41, and headnote, *Basic Documents in United States Foreign Policy*, ed Thomas P. Brockway (Princeton 1968), 106–8
11 Feis, Herbert. *Churchill, Roosevelt and Stalin: The War They Waged and the Peace They Sought* (Princeton 1957), 37
12 Taylor, A. J. P. *English History, 1914–45* (Oxford 1965), 536
13 Sherwood, 445–6; Stimson, Henry L. and Bundy, McGeorge. *On Active Service in Peace and War* (New York 1948), 383
14 Stimson, 414
15 Document 50, Declaration by the United Nations, 1/1/42, Brockway, 109–10
16 Sherwood, 459
17 Feis, 40
18 See Admiral Erich Raeder's comments on this fixation in Wilmot, Chester. *The Struggle for Europe* (1952), 57
19 Stimson, 417
20 See Document 207, Memorandum from Eisenhower to Gen George C. Marshall, 25/3/42, *The Papers of Dwight David Eisen-*

hower. The War Years: I, ed Alfred D. Chandler, Jr (Baltimore and London 1970), 205–7 and note 1 on 207; Pogue, Forrest C. *George C. Marshall: Ordeal and Hope, 1939–42* (1968), 314–16

21 Butler, J. R. M. *Grand Strategy*, III, Part II (1964), 563

22 Memorandum by Churchill, 16–20/12/41, FRUS. *The Conferences at Washington, 1941–1942, and Casablanca, 1943* (Washington 1968), 30

23 Butler, 563, 575–8, 617; Pogue, 317–18

24 Sherwood, 526, 536, 538, 542

25 Butler, 618–20; Doc 344, note 3, Chandler, I, 349

26 Doc 344, Minutes of an informal meeting between Gen Marshall and his staff and Sir John Dill, Gen Brooke, and Gen Ismay, 19/6/42, and note 3, Chandler, I, 348; Sherwood, Robert E. *The White House Papers of Harry L. Hopkins*, II (1949), 587, 592–3, 596; Taylor, *English*, 554

27 Pogue, 331; Doc 379, Conclusions as to practicability of SLEDGE-HAMMER, 17/7/42, Chandler, I, 389

28 Diary entry of 10/7/42, Stimson, 424

29 Sherwood, *Roosevelt*, 602, 605

30 Stimson, 425; Sherwood, *Roosevelt*, 610–11; Doc 393, Memorandum, 26/7/42, and Doc 398. Letter to B. B. Somervell, 27/7/42, Chandler, I, 417, 424

31 Churchill, Winston S. *The Second World War*, IV, *The Hinge of Fate* (1951), 598

32 Sherwood, *Roosevelt*, 624, 675, 690–1

33 Taylor, *English*, 542–3, 554; King, Cecil H. *With Malice Toward None. A War Diary*, ed William Armstrong (1970), 207–9; Pogue, 330

2 THE THIRD SIDE OF THE TRIANGLE (pages 25–42)

1 Sherwood, *Roosevelt*, 138

2 Maisky, Ivan M. *Memoirs of a Soviet Ambassador. The War: 1939–43* (New York 1967), 30, 132

3 Churchill, Winston S. *The Second World War*, III, *The Grand Alliance* (1950), 330

4 Maisky, 119; Sherwood, *Roosevelt*, 322

5 Werth, Alexander. *Russia at War* (1964), 279–80; Long, Breckinridge. *The War Diary of Breckinridge Long*, ed Fred L. Israel (Lincoln 1966), 209; Woodward, Sir Llewellyn. *British Foreign Policy in the Second World War* (1962), 155; Churchill to Stalin, 6/9/41, Ministry of Foreign Affairs of the Union of Soviet Socialist Republics (eds), *Stalin's Correspondence with Churchill, Attlee, Roosevelt and Truman, 1941–45*, I (1958), 23, hereafter cited as USSR, I; McNeill, William H. *America, Britain and Russia* (1953), 22

6 Sherwood, *Roosevelt*, 390

7   Letter from Stalin to Churchill, 18/7/41, USSR, I, 13
8   Various Messages from Churchill to Stalin, 21/7/41 to 1/8/41,
    USSR, I, 14–15
9   Stalin to Churchill, 3/9/41, USSR, I, 20–1
10 Hull to FDR, 4/2/42, FRUS, *Diplomatic Papers 1942*, III (Wash-
    ington 1961), 506
11 Ibid, 505
12 Stalin to Churchill, 8/11/41, USSR, I, 33
13 Churchill to Stalin, 22/11/41, USSR, 34–5
14 CAB 66/41. WP (43) 438. Western Frontiers of the USSR. Memo
    by Anthony Eden, 5/10/43
15 CAB 66/20. WP (42) 8. Mr Eden's Visit to Moscow. Memo by the
    Secretary of State for Foreign Affairs, 5/1/42
16 Winant to FDR and Hull, 19/1/42, FRUS, 1942, III, 495–6
17 Winant to Hull, 10/1/42, FRUS, 1942, III, 492
18 Churchill to Eden, 8/1/42, Churchill, III, 615
19 Hull to Winant, 5/12/41, FRUS, 1941, I, 194–5; Churchill, IV, 293
20 Winant to FDR and Hull, 19/1/42, FRUS, 1942, III, 502
21 Chargé in the USSR (Walter Thurston) to Hull, 5/1/42, FRUS,
    1942, III, 491
22 Maisky, 261; Butler, 592
23 Memo of Conversation by the Under Secretary of State (Welles)
    with Ambassador Halifax, 18/2/42, FRUS, 1942, III, 513–14
24 Churchill to Roosevelt, 7/3/42, Churchill, IV, 293
25 See entry of 9/3/42, Long, 253; Butler, 592; Woodward, 193–4
26 Fleming, Denna Frank. *The Cold War and Its Origins*, I (1961), 147;
    Cordell Hull, *The Memoirs of Cordell Hull*, II (1948), 1167–70
27 Memo of Conversation by the Under Secretary of State with Halifax,
    18/2/42, FRUS, 1942, III, 517
28 Memo of Conversation by the Under Secretary of State, 20/2/42,
    FRUS, 1942, III, 521
29 Maisky, 262–3
30 Butler, 592
31 Letter from Roosevelt to Stalin, 12/4/42, Ministry of Foreign
    Affairs of the Union of Soviet Socialist Republics (eds), *Stalin's
    Correspondence with Churchill, Attlee, Roosevelt and Truman, 1941–
    1945*, II (1958), 23
32 CAB 66/41. WP (43) 438. Western Frontiers of the USSR. Memo
    by the Foreign Secretary, 5/10/43
33 Sherwood, *Roosevelt*, 562–3, 569; Butler, 595
34 Butler, 595–7, 619–21; Release from the President's Office, 11/6/42,
    Documents on American Foreign Relations, eds Leland M. Goodrich,
    S. Shepard Jones, and Denys P. Myers, IV (Boston 1942), 243
35 Butcher, Harry C. *Three Years with Eisenhower* (1946), 24
36 Churchill to Stalin, 17/7/42, USSR, I, 53–5
37 Stalin to Churchill, 23/7/42, USSR, I, 56; for evidence supporting
    the Soviet experts' assertions see the following: *The War at Sea*, ed

John Winton (1967), 246, and Roskill, S. W. *The War at Sea* II (1956), 140–5

38 Stalin to Churchill, 31/7/42, USSR, I, 58

39 Churchill, IV, 428

40 Churchill, IV, 430–2, 584; Aide-mémoire from Stalin to Churchill and Harriman, 13/8/42, USSR, I, 60–1; Werth, 387, 389–90, 397, 404–5, 441–3

41 Sherwood, *White House Papers*, II, 638–9

42 Letter from Churchill and Roosevelt, 1/43, USSR, I, 87–8; Letter from Stalin to Churchill and Roosevelt, 30/1/43, USSR, I, 89; Letter from Churchill to Stalin, 9/2/43, USSR, I, 93–4; Speech by Stalin, 6/11/42, Stalin, J. V. *War Speeches, Orders of the Day, and Answers to Foreign Press Correspondents During the Great Patriotic War* (1958), 43; Letter from Stalin to Roosevelt, 16/3/43, USSR, II, 59; Churchill, IV, 674

43 CAB 80/69. COS (43) 202(o). Future Strategy. Minute by the Prime Minister for the COS, 18/4/43

44 CAB 80/69. COS (43) 256(o). Record of Chiefs of Staff meetings held on the *Queen Mary*, 6–10/5/43

45 CAB 80/70. No 281. TRIDENT. First Plenary Meeting, 12/5/43

46 Sherwood, *Roosevelt*, 730

47 CAB 80/70. No 281. Minutes of the third meeting, 19/5/43, and Final Report by the Combined Chiefs of Staff, 25/5/43

48 Stalin to Roosevelt (with a carbon copy to Churchill), 11/6/43, USSR, I, 132; for FDR's efforts see same source, 71–3; Churchill to Stalin, 27/6/43, USSR, I, 140; Woodward, 241–3; Sherwood, *Roosevelt*, 734

49 Stimson, 430–4, 438

50 CAB 80/72. COS (43) 476(o). QUADRANT. Notes on the US point of view, annex, 20/8/43; CAB 80/72. COS (Q) 13. Trident decisions in the light of Concrete 40, 11/8/43

51 CAB 80/74. COS (43) 513(o) (Part A). Record of Plenary Meetings and the proceedings of the Combined Chiefs of Staff in Quebec, August 1943; see CCS 303/1. Memo from US Chiefs of Staff, Strategic Concept for the Defeat of the Axis in Europe, 16/8/43, and CCS 319/5. Combined Chiefs Final Agreed Summary of Conclusions, 24/8/43

52 Bradley, Omar N. *A Soldier's Story* (New York 1951), 194–6

53 CAB 80/75. COS (43) 639(o). Relation of 'Overlord' to the Mediterranean. Minute from the Prime Minister to the COS, 19/10/43.

54 CAB 88/20. CCS 402. Statement of US Strategic Policy in the Balkan–Eastern Mediterranean Region, 18/11/43

55 CAB 80/77. COS (SEXTANT) 1 (Revise). Future Operations in the European and Mediterranean Theatre. Minute by the Prime Minister, 20/11/43

56 CAB 80/77. COS (SEXTANT) 1 (Revise). Minutes of first meeting, 22/11/43

57   CAB 80/77. COS (SEXTANT) 1 (Revise). Minutes of second meet-
      ing, annex I, Letter from COS to Churchill, 23/11/43
58   For the minutes of the proceedings at Cairo and Tehran from
      22/11/43 to 7/12/43 see CAB 80/77. COS (43) 791(o) (Part II),
      25/2/44
59   CAB 88/21. CCS 426. Draft report to the President and Prime
      Minister of the final agreed summary of conclusions reached by the
      CCS, 5/12/43
60   As an example of this concern see Doc 379, Memorandum. Con-
      clusions as to the Practicability of SLEDGEHAMMER, 17/7/42,
      Chandler, I, 389
61   See CAB 80/70. No 290. Appendix A. Background Notes by the
      Prime Minister, 31/5/43
62   For evidence of Smuts' influence on Churchill's thinking see Stim-
      son, 434, and Tedder, Arthur William. *With Prejudice. The War
      Memoirs of Marshal of the Royal Air Force Lord Tedder* (1966),
      Preface
63   Letter from Smuts to Churchill, 31/8/43, Churchill, Winston S.
      The Second World War, V, *Closing the Ring* (1952), 112–13

3   THE QUIET PEACE (pages 43–66)

1   See Sherwood, *Roosevelt*, 693–6
2   Mammarella, Giuseppe. *Italy After Fascism* (Montreal 1964), 1–10
3   Mammarella, 11–16; Hull, II, 1550; Feis, 154
4   Mammarella, 18–19
5   Churchill, V, 103; Mammarella, 28; Estimate of Enemy Situation
      (as of 1/11/43) by US Chiefs of Staff, United States Department of
      State (eds), *Foreign Relations of the United States. The Conferences
      at Cairo and Tehran, 1943* (Washington 1961), 222; Kolko, Gabriel.
      The Politics of War (1968), 45; Kogan, Norman. *A Political History
      of Postwar Italy* (1966), 5
6   Churchill, V, 48
7   Churchill, V, 40
8   See CAB 66/39. WP (43) 322. Post-War Settlement—Policy in Re-
      spect of Germany. Memo by Attlee, 19/7/43
9   CAB 66/39. WP (43) 339. Thoughts on the Fall of Mussolini.
      Minute by the Prime Minister, 26/7/43
10   Churchill, V, 59
11   Churchill, V, 89
12   Welles, Sumner. *Where Are We Heading?* (1947), 111
13   Churchill, V, 91
14   Feis, 156
15   Churchill, V, 92
16   Speech by FDR, 28/7/43, *Documents on American Foreign Relations*,
      eds Leland M. Goodrich and Marie J. Carroll, VI (Boston 1945),
      165

17 FO 371/35387. U 3401/324/70. Eden to Clark Kerr in Moscow, 29/7/43
18 FO 371/35387. U 3404/324/70. Clark Kerr to the Foreign Office, 31/7/43
19 Long, 320
20 Stalin to Roosevelt and Churchill, 22/8/43, FRUS,1943, I, 782
21 FO 371/35390. U 4178/324/70. Message from Attlee to Churchill, 25/8/43
22 FO 371/35390. U 4178/324/70. See the enclosed paper for Eden in a note from Gladwyn Jebb to Brigadier L. C. Hollis, 29/8/43
23 FO 371/35390. U 4179/324/70. Ivan Maisky to Eden, 1/9/43
24 FDR to Stalin, 6/9/43, FRUS, 1943, I, note 10, 784; Stalin to FDR, 8/9/43, FRUS, 1943, I, 785; FDR to Stalin, 10/9/43, FRUS, 1943, I, 785; Stalin to FDR and Churchill, 12/9/43, FRUS, 1943, I, 786
25 Chargé in the USSR to Hull, 25/9/43, FRUS, 1943, I, 787–8; FO 371/35391. U 4396/324/70. Foreign Office to Resident Minister in Algiers, 15/9/43
26 FO 371. 35391. U 4497/324/70. The Politico-Military Commission. Memo by Gladwyn Jebb, 21/9/43
27 Note 35, p. 793, and Hull to the Chargé in the USSR, 8/10/43, FRUS, 1943, I, 794
28 FO 371/35391. U 4678/324/70. Functions of the Politico-Military Commission, 30/9/43
29 FDR to Churchill, 4/10/43, *Foreign Relations of the United States, 1943*, II (Washington 1964), 382–3; Churchill to FDR, 8/10/43, FRUS, 1943, II, 384
30 Duff, Katherine. 'Italy', in *The Realignment of Europe*, eds Toynbee, Arnold J. and Veronica M. (1955), 420; McNeil, 309–10
31 Kolko, 47–8
32 Churchill, V, 89
33 Mammarella, 36–7, 62; Woodward, note 1, 234; Goodrich, *Documents*, VI, note, 173
34 The Status of Italy, 13/10/43, Bartlett, Ruhl J. ed *The Record of American Diplomacy* (New York 1960), 657
35 Mammarella, 63
36 Sherwood, *Roosevelt*, 744
37 Hull, II, 1550
38 Kolko, 46
39 Hull, II, 1550
40 Sherwood, *Roosevelt*, 752
41 Butcher, 359
42 Buchanan, A. Russell. *The United States and World War II*, I (New York 1964), 174–5
43 The Status of Italy, 13/10/43, Bartlett, 657
44 Statement by Marshal Badoglio, 13/11/43, Goodrich, *Documents*, VI, 178–9; Hull, II, 1552; Kogan, 6; Mammarella, 64

45　Churchill, V, 167, 176, 178–9
46　Goodrich, *Documents*, VI, note, 173; Mammarella, 66
47　Buchanan, 175–6; Kolko, 48
48　CAB 80/88. COS (44) 933(0). SOE Operations in Italy, 29/10/44, annex I and II
49　Goodrich, *Documents*, VI, headnote, 173; Harris, C. R. S. *Allied Military Administration of Italy, 1943-1945* (1957), 142
50　Statement by Victor Emmanuel, 12/4/44, Goodrich, *Documents*, VI, 180; Harris, 143; Welles, 113
51　Harris, 72–3, 143
52　Kolko, 55
53　Mammarella, 69–70
54　Kolko, 54
55　Mammarella, 72–3
56　FO 181/983. File No. 7. Message from Churchill to Stalin, 10/6/44, and Message from Stalin to Churchill, 12/6/44
57　For the pre-WWII period see Jakobson, Max. *The Diplomacy of the Winter War* (Cambridge, Mass. 1961) and The Finnish Ministry for Foreign Affairs, *The Development of Finnish–Soviet Relations* (Helsinki 1940)
58　CAB 66/20. WP (42) 8. Eden's Visit to Moscow. Memo by the Secretary of State for Foreign Affairs, 5/1/42
59　Chargé in the USSR to Secretary of State, 5/1/42, FRUS, 1942, III, 491; for confirmation see FO 371/35407. U 6461/516/70. V. F. W. Cavendish-Bentinck to Col C. G. Vickers, 12/11/43
60　Tehran Conference Notes (Bohlen Minutes), 15/12/43, FRUS, *Cairo and Tehran*, 848
61　Werth, 354
62　Lowery, Sidney. 'Finland', Toynbee, *Realignment*, 274
63　Churchill to Mannerheim, 29/11/41, Churchill, III, 474
64　Information Release by the Information Bureau of the Soviet Commissariat of Foreign Affairs, 1/3/44, Goodrich, *Documents*, VI, 680–2
65　CAB 66/41. WP (43) 438. Western Frontiers of the USSR. Memo by Eden, 5/10/43; CAB 81/41. PHP (43) 26C (Draft). Finland. Principles of an Armistice: Suggestions. Post-Hostilities Planning Sub-Committee, 9/11/43
66　CAB 80/81. COS (44) 259(0). Finnish Armistice Terms. Annex. Letter from the Foreign Office to the Chiefs of Staff, 14/3/44
67　CAB 80/80. COS (44) 180(0). Appendix B. Telegram from Foreign Office to Embassy in Moscow, 18/2/44
68　Mannerheim, Marshal. *The Memoirs of Marshal Mannerheim*, trans Count Eric Lewenhaupt (1953), 475–6, 481–2; Werth, 855; Mazour, Anatole G. *Finland Between East and West* (Princeton 1956), 165; Lowery, 'Finland', 267
69　State Department Announcement, 16/6/44, Goodrich, *Documents*, VI, 683; Hull to Government of Finland, 30/6/44, ibid, 684

70 Lowery, 'Finland', 268

71 Mannerheim, 495

72 CAB 80/86. COS (44) 773(o). Finland—Armistice Negotiations. Letter from the Foreign Office to the Chiefs of Staff, 27/8/44; Mannerheim, 496

73 For the complete text of the articles and annexes of the Armistice Agreement see Mazour, Appendix VIII, 249–59; Lowery, 'Finland', 274

74 CAB 80/87. COS (44) 818(o). Finland—Peace Terms. Communication from Clark Kerr to Foreign Office, 6/9/44

75 For a brief history of Finland's unassisted political shift to the non-communist left during the last weeks of the war see Lowery, 'Finland', 274, 277–8, and Mannerheim, 507

76 The most culpable of Finland's war leaders, Risto Ryti, received the harshest sentence of the handful of leaders brought to court: ten years of confinement with hard labour. See Mazour, 172–3

77 Thomson, S. Harrison. *Czechoslovakia in European History* (Princeton 1953), 375, 424; Zinner, Paul E. *Communist Strategy and Tactics in Czechoslovakia, 1918–48* (London 1963), 79; Korbel, Josef. *The Communist Subversion of Czechoslovakia, 1938–1948* (Princeton 1959), 13

78 Zinner, 81–2, 92

79 Beneš, Eduard. *Memoirs of Dr. Eduard Beneš*, trans Godfrey Lias (1954), 240

80 Speech by Beneš, November 1942, Beneš, 239–40

81 Kolko, 124–6

82 Beneš, 243

83 Beneš, 241–3

84 CAB 66/41. WP (43) 423. Proposed Agreement. Memo by Eden, 28/9/43

85 CAB 66/41. WP (43) 434. Annex C. Foreign Secretaries' Conference at Moscow. Memo by Eden, 4/10/43

86 Czech–Soviet Agreement of 12/12/43, *Documents on International Affairs, 1939–1946*, ed Margaret Carlyle, II (1954), 319; Beneš, 257

87 Churchill to FDR, 6/1/44, Churchill, V, 400

88 Soviet–Czech Agreement on Liberated Territories, May 1944, Carlyle, *Documents*, II, 321; Beneš, 263

89 Wiskemann, Elizabeth. 'Czechoslovakia', Toynbee, *Realignment*, 377–8

90 Toynbee, Arnold J. *Survey of International Affairs, 1934* (1934), 404

91 For background information on the Baltic States see the above and Toynbee's other superb surveys for 1935 and 1936; see also Spekke, Arnold. *History of Latvia* (Stockholm 1951) and Toynbee, Arnold J. and Veronica M. (eds), *The Eve of War, 1939* (1958)

92 Speech by A. A. Zhdanov to the Eighth Soviet Congress, 29/11/36, *Soviet Documents on Foreign Policy*, ed Jane Degras, III (1953), 226

93   Taylor, *Origins*, 226–9, 231; Strang, Lord. *The Moscow Negotiations
     1939* (Leeds 1968), 5–13, 17–18, 21–2

94   Elkin, Alexander. 'The Baltic States', Toynbee, Arnold J. (ed), *The
     Initial Triumph of the Axis* (1958), 43, 45; Dallin, David J. *Soviet
     Russia's Foreign Policy, 1939–1942* (New Haven Conn 1942),
     241–2

95   Beloff, Max. *The Foreign Policy of Soviet Russia, 1929–1941*, II
     (1949), 329; Dallin, 251–2; Spekke, 386

96   Dispatch from German Minister in Estonia to Berlin, 3/7/40, British
     Foreign Office, US Department of State, and French Government
     (eds), *Documents on German Foreign Policy, 1918–1945*, Series D,
     X (1957), 107–8

97   Warth, Robert D. *Soviet Russia in World Politics* (1963), 247

98   Memo of Conversation with Halifax by Welles, FRUS, 1942, III,
     513–17; CAB 66/41. WP (43) 438. Western Frontiers of the USSR.
     Memo by Eden, 5/10/43; for Norman Davis's interpretation of
     FDR's thinking on this subject see CAB 66/37. WP (43) 217. Armis-
     tices and Related Problems. Annex. Discussion with US Adminis-
     tration, 24/3/43; for evidence of FDR's unaltered thinking later in
     the year see Memo of Conversation, 5/10/43, FRUS, 1943, I,
     542

99   CAB 81/45. PHP (43) 1(0) (final). Post-Hostilities Planning Sub-
     Committee. Effect of Soviet Policy on British Strategic Interests,
     1/5/44

100 See Message from Beneš to Czech Government, 7/6/43, Beneš,
     195; Conversation between Roosevelt and Stalin, 1/12/43, FRUS,
     Cairo and Tehran, 595

4   THE GRAND DESIGN (pages 67–95)

1   Four-Nation Declaration, 10/43, Committee on Foreign Relations,
    Review of the United Nations Charter (Washington 1954), 39–40; for
    details of the Moscow conference see FRUS, 1943, I, 563ff

2   Item 119, FDR's 924th Press Conference, 29/10/43, *The Public
    Papers and Addresses of Franklin D. Roosevelt, 1943, The Tide Turns*,
    ed Samuel I. Rosenman (New York 1950), 458

3   CAB 66/40. WP (43) 389. Four-Power Declaration, annex III. Note
    from R. K. Law to Eden, 22/8/43

4   For details of the conference see FRUS, *Cairo and Tehran*

5   Memo from Hull to FDR, 25/3/44, US Department of State (eds)
    Foreign Relations of the United States, 1944, I (Washington 1966),
    584

6   Memorandum from Soviet Embassy to State Department, 29/3/44,
    FRUS, 1944, I, 588

7   Memo from FDR to Hull, 1/4/44, FRUS, 1944, I, 588–9

8   CAB 66/37. WP (43) 223. The International Horizon. Memo by the
    Secretary of State for India for the War Cabinet, 27/5/43

9 CAB 66/37. WP (43) 233. Structure of a Post-War Settlement. Note by the Prime Minister, 10/6/43

10 Summary of the Proceedings of the 8th Session of the Moscow Conference, 26/10/43, FRUS, 1943, I, 639; CAB 66/45. WP (44) 8. Record of Conversation between the Prime Minister and Marshal Stalin at Tehran on 28/11/43

11 CAB 81/43. PHP (43) 36 (final). Military Occupation in South-Eastern Europe. Report by the Post-Hostilities Planning Sub-Committee for the COS and the War Cabinet, 10/2/44

12 CAB 81/43. PHP (43) 36A (final). Military Occupation in South-East Europe, 7/3/44

13 Foreign Office Memo, 4/44, FRUS, 1944, I, 598–9

14 Churchill to FDR, 31/5/44, Churchill, Winston S. *The Second World War*, VI, *Triumph and Tragedy* (1954), 64

15 Hull, II, 1452

16 Churchill, VI, 65–6

17 Churchill, VI, 65

18 Hull, II, 1453–7; State Department Memo to European Ambassadors and Ministers, 22/6/44, FRUS, 1944, I, 611

19 Churchill, VI, 69; Hull, II, 1455

20 Churchill, VI, 69–70

21 Stalin to Churchill, 15/7/44, USSR, I, 238

22 CAB 66/51. WP (44) 304. Soviet Policy in the Balkans. Memo by Eden and Foreign Office Annex, 7/6/44

23 Churchill, VI, 90

24 Churchill, VI, 197–8

25 Hull, II, 1457–8

26 Stavrianos, L. S. *The Balkans Since 1453* (New York 1958), 697–9, 765; Sylvain, Nicolas. 'Rumania', in *The Jews in the Soviet Satellites* Meyer, Peter, Bernard D. Weinryb, Eugene Duschinsky, and Nicolas Sylvain (eds), (Syracuse 1953), 499; Wolff, Robert Lee. *The Balkans in Our Time* (Cambridge, Mass. 1967), 193

27 Roberts, Henry L. *Rumania* (New Haven 1951), 233–5; Sylvain, 'Rumania', 504

28 Stavrianos, 766

29 Ionescu, Ghita. *Communism in Rumania: 1944–1962* (1964), 65–6; Wolff, 236; Hilberg, Raul. *The Destruction of the European Jews* (Chicago 1961), 485 and Appendix III, 767

30 CAB 66/41. WP (43) 438. Western Frontiers of the USSR. Memo by Eden, 5/10/43

31 United States Department of State (eds), *Foreign Relations of the United States, 1944*, IV (Washington 1966), 134–47

32 FRUS, 1944, IV, 148–64

33 FRUS, 1944, IV, 165–84

34 Werth, 901, 903; Stavrianos, 811; Lee, Arthur Gould. *Crown Against Sickle* (1949), 69–74, 78; Harriman to Hull and FDR, 26/8/44, FRUS, 1944, IV, 196

35 Department of State to the Joint Chiefs of Staff, 2/9/44, FRUS,
    1944, IV, 208–12
36 See Welles, Sumner. *The Time for Decision* (1944), 195
37 Churchill to FDR, 11/6/44, Churchill, VI, 66
38 FRUS, 1944, IV, 213–19; United States Department of State (eds),
    Foreign Relations of the United States, 1945, V (Washington 1967),
    649–50
39 Harriman to Hull, 6/9/44, FRUS, 1944, IV, 223
40 FRUS, 1944, IV, 253–88
41 FRUS, 1944, IV, 251–2, 288
42 Ionescu, 100; Kolko, 157; Sylvain, 513; Roberts, 262; Stavrianos, 830
43 Berry to Stettinius, 12/12/44, FRUS, 1944, IV, 282; Stavrianos, 830;
    Ionescu, 103, 105; Roberts, 260, 262; Berry to Stettinius, 7/12/44,
    FRUS, 1944, IV, 278
44 Roberts, 263; Ionescu, 105–6, 109; Kolko, 405
45 Seton-Watson, Hugh. *The East European Revolution* (3rd ed 1956),
    92–3; Evans, Stanley G. *A Short History of Bulgaria* (1960), 177–8,
    180–1
46 Evans, 182; Stavrianos, 769; Estimate of Enemy Strength as of
    1/11/43, US COS, FRUS, *Cairo and Tehran*, 224; CAB 80/81.
    COS (44) 232(o). Policy Towards Bulgaria, 7/3/44
47 Wolff, 245; Seton-Watson, 96; Consul General in Istanbul to Hull,
    3/6/44, FRUS, 1944, III, 333–4
48 Winant to Hull, 25/8/44, FRUS, 1944, III, 368–9; Hull to Winant,
    5/7/44, FRUS, 1944, III, 342–4; CAB 81/42. PHP (44) 57 (Final).
    Control Machinery for Bulgaria, 19/8/44
49 Winant to Hull, 27/8/44 and 29/8/44, Frus, 1944, III, 374, 378
50 Seton-Watson, 97
51 Seton-Watson, 97; Stavrianos, 812; Wolff, 247; Lowery, Sidney.
    'Bulgaria', Toynbee, *Realignment*, 182; for perceptive comments on
    the Soviet move see Winant to Hull, 15/9/44 and 21/9/44, FRUS,
    1944, III, 424–7, 432
52 Wolff, 247; Evans, 182–3
53 Wolff, 247–8; Seton-Watson, 98; Evans, 181; Bulgarian Armistice
    Terms, 28/10/44, *Documents on American Foreign Relations*, eds
    Leland M. Goodrich and Marie J. Carroll, VII (Princeton 1947),
    241–3; FRUS, 1944, III, 415–18, 420–7, 429–32, 483, 489
54 CAB 66/37. WP (43) 240. Hungary's Relations with the Axis,
    12/6/43
55 Macartney, C. A. *October Fifteenth*, Part II (2nd ed Edinburgh
    1961), 162, 174–5; Memo by J. C. Campbell of the Division of
    Southern European Affairs, 11/44, FRUS, 1944, III, 926
56 Macartney, 271, 274, 296, 309; *The Confidential Papers of Admiral
    Horthy*, trans and ed by Miklos Szinai and Laszlo Szucs (Budapest
    1965), 289
57 Horthy, 278; Macartney, 319
58 FRUS, 1944, III, 901–10

59 Macarney, 445, 458; Kolko, 406–7
60 Chargé in the USSR to State Department, 20/10/44, FRUS, 1944, III, 916; Memo of conversation by the Associate Chief of the Division of Financial & Monetary Affairs, 21/10/44, FRUS, 1944, III, 918
61 Acting Secretary of State to Kennan, 2/11/44, FRUS, 1944, III, 922–3; Harriman to Stettinius, 30/12/44 and 31/12/44, FRUS, 1944, III, 948–50, 951–2; Stettinius to Harriman, 3/1/45 and 6/1/45, FRUS, 1944, III, 955, 963–5; for the British position see CAB 80/87. COS (44) 843(o). Armistice Terms for Hungary, 19/9/44; CAB 80/90. COS (45) 52(o). Armistice Terms for Hungary, 17/1/45
62 Macartney, 464; Harriman to Stettinius, 24/12/44, FRUS, 1944, III, 936; Kertesz, Stephen D. 'Communist Conquest of Hungary', *The Fight for Freedom*, ed Imre Kovacs (New York 1966), 49–50; Karolyi, Michael. *Memoirs of Michael Karolyi*, trans Catherine Karolyi (1956), 309, 311; Soviet–Hungarian Armistice, 20/1/45, Goodrich, *Documents*, VII, 245–8
63 For background information see Vucinich, Wayne S. 'Interwar Yugoslavia', in *Contemporary Yugoslavia. Twenty Years of Socialist Experiment*, ed Wayne S. Vucinich (Berkeley and Los Angeles 1969), 3–58
64 Tomasevich, Jozo. 'Yugoslavia During the Second World War', Vucinich, *Yugoslavia*, 67–8, 71–2; Pavlowitch, Stevan K. *Yugoslavia* (1971), 107–9; Hoffman, George W. and Neal, Fred Warner. *Yugoslavia and the New Communism* (New York 1962), 64
65 Hoffman and Neal, 71, text and note 1 on 73, 74; Stavrianos, 775
66 Stavrianos, 783; Hoffman and Neal, 75; Pavlowitch, 137–8
67 Declaration of the Jajce Congress, *Documents on International Affairs, 1939–1946*, II, ed Margaret Carlyle (1954), 334
68 Deakin, F. W. D. 'Britanija i Jugoslavija 1941–1945', *Jugoslovenski Istorijski Casopis*, 2 (1963), 45–53
69 Stavrianos, 781; Kolko, 132; Hoffman and Neal, 74; CAB 80/75. COS (43) 626(o). Support of Guerrilla Forces in Yugoslavia, Albania, and Greece. Memo by SOE, 14/10/43; Report by the OSS, 29/10/43; FRUS, *Cairo and Tehran*, 606
70 Maclean, Fitzroy. *Eastern Approaches* (1949), 390, 402; CAB 80/76. COS (43) 733(o). Situation in Jugo-Slavia—Brigadier Maclean's Report, 26/11/43; Deakin, 54–5
71 Dedijer, Vladimer. *Tito Speaks* (1953), 170, 179, 207–8; Maclean, Fitzroy. *Disputed Barricade* (1957), 241–2, 245–6; Memorandum by Harriman, 23/11/43, FRUS, *Cairo and Tehran*, 309–10; Churchill, V, 413
72 Dedijer, 170; Djilas, Milovan. *Conversations with Stalin* (1962), 12; Maclean, *Barricade*, 251
73 Dedijer, 213; Kolko, 134
74 Maclean, *Barricade*, 271; Churchill, V, 419–21; CAB 66/45. WP (44) 19. Position in Yugoslavia. Memo by Eden, 10/1/44; CAB 66/48.

WP (44) 196. Yugoslavia. Note by Brigadier Maclean, 18/3/44; Churchill to Eden, 1/4/44, Churchill, V, 421; Pavlowitch, 159; Tomasevitch, 102

75 Dedijer, 223
76 Wolff, 229; Tito-Subasic Agreement, 16/6/44, Carlyle, *Documents*, II, 335
77 Churchill, VI, 79–83; Wolff, 232; Dedijer, 234
78 Stavrianos, 814; Wolff, 267; Letter from Churchill to Stalin, 11/1/45, USSR, I, 296
79 Kolko, 136; Cankar, Izidor. 'Problems of the New Yugoslavia', *The Slavonic and East European Review*, CCIII, 62 (January 1945), 60–1; Seton-Watson, Hugh. 'Yugoslavia'; Toynbee, *Realignment*, 365; Auty, Phyllis. 'Yugoslavia's International Relations (1945–1965)', Vucinich, *Yugoslavia*, 161–2
80 Kolko, 155; CAB 66/50. WP (44) 289. Bulgaria and the Soviet Union. Memo by Sir Orme Sargent, 31/5/44

5 THE BALKAN ANOMALY: GREECE (p. 96–109)

1   Stavrianos, 785; Churchill, V, 471; Woodward, 351
2   Stavrianos, 787; Kolko, 173; Churchill, V, 472
3   Woodward, 352; Stavrianos, 788–9
4   Churchill, V, 473; Stavrianos, 790–2; Kolko, 173; Stavrianos, 788
5   Churchill, V, 473; Foot, Michael. *Aneurin Bevan*, I (1962), 482–3; Woodward, 353; National Bands Agreement, 7/43, Carlyle, *Documents*, II, 343
6   CAB 80/74. COS (43) 528(o). Policy towards Greece. Memo by the Chief of the Imperial Staff, 12/9/43
7   Churchill, V, 474–5
8   CAB 80/75. COS (43) 595(o). Policy towards Greece. Minute by the Prime Minister to General Ismay for the COS, and Annex, 30/9/43
9   CAB 80/75. COS (43) 617(o). Policy towards Greece. Minute from the FO, 8/10/43; CAB 66/43. WP (43) 518. Policy towards Greece. Memo by the Foreign Secretary, 14/11/53
10 CAB 66/43. WP (43) 522. Annex B. British Policy towards Greece. Memo by the Minister of State (resident in the Middle East), Richard Casey, 17/11/43
11 CAB 66/43. WP (43) 522. Annex A; CAB 80/77. COS (SEXTANT). Minutes of the 13th meeting held 7/12/43; CAB 80/78. COS (44) 54(o). SOE Activities in Greece, 21/1/44, Annex I and V
12 CAB 80/80. COS (44) 165(o). Annex. Copy of a minute from Eden to Churchill and Churchill's minute to Ismay, 10/2/44; CAB 80/81. Part I. COS (44) 199(o). Policy towards Greece. Copy of a Minute from Churchill to the COS, 24/2/44
13 Churchill, V, 473, 477–80, 482, 485; CAB 66/49. WP (44) 247. The Greek Crisis (April 1–25, 1944), 8/5/44

14 CAB 66/49. WP (44) 247
15 Churchill, V, 484–6
16 Woodward, note 3 on 354; Feis, 205; Woodward, 355–6
17 Stavrianos, 794, 816–17; Woodward, 356; Kolko, 180
18 Caserta Agreement, 26/9/44, Carlyle, *Documents*, II, 349; Stavrianos, 817–18
19 CAB 80/85. COS (44) 640(o). British Forces for Greece. Report by the COS, 20/7/44; CAB 80/86. COS (44) 738(o). Transfer of Allied Military Headquarters. Report by the War Office and Annex I, 16/8/44
20 Churchill to Roosevelt, 17/8/44, and Roosevelt to Churchill, 26/8/44, US Department of State (eds), *Foreign Relations of the United States, 1944*, V (Washington 1965), 133–4; Doc 1932, Letter from Eisenhower to Marshall, 4/9/44, and notes 3 and 4, *The Papers of Dwight David Eisenhower. The War Years*: IV, ed Alfred D. Chandler, Jr (1970), 2144–5; Kolko, 182–3; Stavrianos, 820; Churchill, VI, 250
21 McNeill, William H. 'Greece, 1944–1946', Toynbee, *Realignment*, 390–1; Churchill, VI, 250
22 Stavrianos, 821–2; Kolko, 183, 185–7
23 McNeil, 'Greece', 393–5; Kolko, 188; Stavrianos, 822, 824; Sherwood, 840
24 For information about the early weeks of the war see Stavrianos, 826–7; McNeill, 'Greece', 396; Kolko, 189
25 Mac Veagh to Hull, 13/6/44, and 16/6/44, FRUS, 1944, V, 121–4
26 Sherwood, *Roosevelt*, 838–9
27 CAB 80/90. COS (45) 1(o). Greek Re-armament. Note by General Ismay, 1/1/45; Sherwood, 841; McNeill, 'Greece', 396; Stavrianos, 827; Kolko, 189
28 Kolko, 181
29 CAB 66/43. WP (43) 522. Annex A. Extract from the Minutes of a Meeting of the Middle East Defence Committee held on 7/11/43; Churchill, VI, Appendix C, 617; 255; for evidence of Churchill's satisfaction with Stalin's posture at Yalta see CAB 65/5. WM (45) 22. Confidential Annex, Minute 1, 19/2/45
30 CAB 80/88. COS (44) 890(o). British Post-War Strategic Requirements in the Western Mediterranean. Copy of a letter from the FO to the COS, 7/10/44; CAB 66/53. WP (44) 433. Despatch of British Forces to Greece. Memo by the Foreign Secretary, 8/8/44
31 Foot, 485; Churchill, VI, 253–4
32 Woodward, 359–62; McNeill, 'Greece', 397
33 Kolko, 192–3; Stavrianos, 827–8; Woodward, 363; McNeill, 'Greece', 398
34 Stavrianos, L. S. 'Greece's Other History', *The New York Review of Books*, XVI No 11 (17 June 1971), 13

6 THE UNATTENDED PEACE (pages 110–25)

1   Stavrianos, *The Balkans*, 723–6; Skendi, Stavro. 'Albania', *The Fate of East Central Europe*, ed Stephen D. Kertesz (South Bend, Indiana 1956), 297, 299; Seton-Watson, Hugh. *The East European Revolution* (3rd ed 1956), 140

2   Stavrianos, 796–7; Skendi, 297; Seton-Watson, 141, 143; Wolff, 220

3   Skendi, 303; Wolff, 221–2; Stavrianos, 797; Seton-Watson, 143; CAB 80/75. COS (43) 626(o). Support of Guerrilla Forces in Yugoslavia, Albania, and Greece. Annex B. Memo by SOE, 14/10/43

4   Stavrianos, 797; CAB 80/84. COS (44) 490(o). Policy Towards Albania, 3/6/44

5   Churchill, V, 410–11; CAB 80/80. COS (44) 163(o). Supplies to Resistance Groups in the Balkans, 14/2/44; Press Release by the Acting Secretary of State, 15/11/44, Goodrich, *Documents*, VI, 873–4; Dedijer, 280

6   Crozier, Brian. *Franco: A Biographical History* (1967), 301, 304; Whitaker, Arthur P. *Spain and Defence of the West* (New York 1961), 7–9; Woodward, 374

7   Crozier, 343, 378–9; Woodward, 365, note 2 on 367; Duff, Katherine. 'Spain Between the Allies and the Axis', *The War and the Neutrals*, eds Toynbee, Arnold J. and Veronica M. (1956), 296, 302–3; Whitaker, 8–9; Estimate of Enemy Situation, 1944, by US COS (as of 1/11/43), FRUS, *Cairo and Tehran*, 226

8   See Lord Colyton (Minister at British Embassy in Lisbon 1943–4) letter to *The Times*, 29/4/70; cf Woodward, 379–83; CAB 80/70. No 281. TRIDENT Minutes of Third Meeting, 19/5/43

9   CAB 80/70. No 293. Wolfram. Report by the COS to the War Cabinet, 7/6/43; CAB 88/21. CCS 430. Appendix B. Trade with Portugal, 19/8/43, and Enclosure D. Memo by Robert P. Patterson, US Under Secretary of War, 23/9/43; CAB 66/51. WP (44) 347. Dr Salazar. Memo by Eden, 26/6/44; Acheson, Dean. *Present at the Creation* (1969), 53–4; Woodward, 383–4

10 CAB 88/21. CCS 430. 16/12/43. Enclosures D and E; CAB 80/74. COS (44) 513(o) (Part A). Minutes of Second QUADRANT Meeting, 23/8/43; CAB 80/74. CCS 321. Policy Towards Spain. Memo by British COS, 20/8/43

11 Acheson, 54; Woodward, 367–9

12 CAB 66/48. WP (44) 170. Policy Towards Spain. Memo by Eden, 23/3/44; Acheson, 54–5, 59

13 Acheson, 59–60; Woodward, 369–70, 383–4

14 Duff, 'Spain', 307–8; Churchill, V, 554

15 CAB 66/53. WP (44) 409. Duff Cooper to Eden, 30/5/44, and Eden to Cooper, 25/7/44

16 CAB 81/45. PHP (44) 26(o) (Final). Policy Towards Western Europe. Report by the Post-Hostilities Planning Staff, 6/11/44;

CAB 80/88. COS (44) 890(o). British Post-War Strategic Requirements in the Western Mediterranean, 9/10/44; CAB 80/88. COS (44) 934(o). Policy Towards Western Europe. Letter from FO to the COS, 30/10/44

17 CAB 80/89. COS (44) 955(o). Policy Towards Western Europe. Report by the COS, 8/11/44

18 Woodward, 77, 103–4, 114

19 Leahy, William D. *I Was There* (1950), 17; Langer, William L. *Our Vichy Gamble* (New York 1947), 161; Kolko, 65; Murphy, Robert. *Diplomat Among Warriors* (1964), 94

20 Woodward, 104, 106; Strang, Lord. *Home and Abroad* (1956), 72; Leahy, 23, 30

21 Murphy, 103–4; CAB 66/39. WP (43) 341 (Revise). Relations with General de Gaulle. FO Memo, 7/8/43

22 Message from Ambassador to Hull, 27/1/42, FRUS, 1942, II, 125; Langer, 211, 248; Leahy, 11

23 Murphy, 94; Feis, 89; Kolko, 66; Werth, Alexander. *France, 1940–1955* (1956), 212; Funk, Arthur Layton. *Charles De Gaulle: The Crucial Years, 1943–1944* (Norman, Okla., 1959), 33

24 Doc 586, Eisenhower to the CCS, 8/11/42, *The Papers of Dwight David Eisenhower. The War Years*: II, ed Alfred D. Chandler, Jr (1970), 670; Viorst, Milton. *Hostile Allies: FDR and Charles De Gaulle* (1965), 118; Stimson, 543

25 Viorst, 113–14, 117–18; Woodward, 209; Kolko, 66; Strang, 73

26 CAB 66/39. WP (43) 341 (Revise). Relations with General de Gaulle. FO Memo, 7/8/43

27 Woodward, 210, 212; Funk, 40–2; Viorst, 125

28 Stimson, 544; Gottschalk, Louis. 'Our Vichy Fumble', Williams, 886–91

29 Kolko, 67; Woodward, 214–18, 220; Sherwood, *Roosevelt*, 721; Langer, 382

30 CAB 66/39. WP (43) 341 (Revise). Relations with General de Gaulle. FO Memo, 7/8/43

31 CAB 66/38. WP (43) 291. The French Committee of National Liberation. Memo by Eden, 2/7/43; Kolko, 71

32 Kolko, 77–8; Woodward, 259–60

33 Kolko, 76, 84, 94, 439; Woodward, note 2 on 263

34 Kolko, 79–80, 88–9; Churchill, V, 154, 156, 161; Churchill, VI, 214; Woodward, 265; Funk, 302–3

7 THE DIPLOMATS' PEACE (pages 126–38)

1 CAB 81/41. PHP (43) 20 (Final). Annex. Aide-Mémoire, 1/7/43

2 FO 371/35392. U 5070/324/70. Clark Kerr to FO, 14/10/43

3 FO 371/35392. U 5140/324/70, 17/10/43

4 FO 371/35392. U 5432/324/70. Terms of reference for the EAC,

31/10/43; FO 371/35392. U 5433/324/70. Eden to Cadogan, 31/10/43

5   Hammond, Paul Y. 'Directives for the Occupation of Germany: The Washington Controversy', *American Civil-Military Decisions*, ed Harold Stein (Birmingham, Alabama 1963), 322

6   CAB 81/41. PHP (43) 7B. Military Occupation of Germany, 11/10/43

7   Memorandum of Conversation with Roosevelt, 5/10/43, FRUS, 1943, I, 542; Smith, Jean Edward. *The Defense of Berlin* (1963), 15–19; CAB 81/41. PHP (43) 43a (Final). American Proposals Regarding the Military Occupation of Germany, 1/1/44

8   Strang, 203; Report on the Work of the EAC, 10/9/45, FRUS, 1945, III, 545–50

9   Hammond, 325 ff; McNeill, 481–2; Feis, 358

10 Feis, 362–3; Franklin, William M. 'Zonal Boundaries and Access to Berlin', *World Politics*, I, 16 (October 1963), 16–19

11 McNeill, 455, 539; Feis, 359–64; CAB 81/45. PHP (44) 14(0) (Final). Occupation of Germany: Allotment of Zones. Report by PHP Staff for the War Cabinet, 26/6/44

12 Donnison, F. S. V. *Civil Affairs and Military Government Central Organization and Planning* (1966), 104–8; Feis, 359–60; Memo by Ambassador Gusev to the EAC, 26/8/44, FRUS, 1944, I, 299–301; CAB 81/42. PHP (44) 23 (Final). Control Machinery for Germany. US Proposals. Memo by PHP Sub-Committee, 4/5/44

13 *From the Morgenthau Diaries. Years of War 1941–1945*, ed John Morton Blum (Boston, Mass 1967), 338–42; Dictation of Secretary Morgenthau's Comments of 18/8/44, Sub-Committee to Investigate the Administration of the Internal Security Act and Other Internal Security Laws of the Committee on the Judiciary, United States Senate, 90th Congress, 1st Session, *Morgenthau Diary (Germany)*, I (Washington 1967), 415, hereafter cited as *Morgenthau Diary*

14 Memo from Morgenthau to FDR, 25/8/44, and Memo from FDR to Stimson, 26/8/44, *Morgenthau Diary*, 440, 443, 445

15 McNeill, 482; Treasury Department Inter-Office Memo, 28/8/44, *Morgenthau Diary*, 453–4; Feis, 367

16 Memo of a Dinner Conversation, 4/9/44, and Letter from Stimson to Morgenthau, 5/9/44, Memo from Stimson to FDR, 9/5/44, *Morgenthau Diary*, 503, 531, 612–13; Feis, note 40 on 368

17 Woodward, 466–7, 471; CAB 66/39. WP (43) 322. Post-War Settlement—Policy in Respect of Germany. Memo by the Deputy Prime Minister, 19/7/43

18 Woodward, 471–2; Feis, note 39 on 367

19 McNeill, 489–90; Woodward, 472; Quebec Directive on Germany, 15/9/44, *Morgenthau Diary*, 620–1

20 Woodward, 474

21 Woodward, 472–6; CAB 81/45. PHP (44) 15(0) (Revised Final). Dismemberment of Germany—Military Aspects. Memo for the War

Cabinet, 15/11/44; Watt, D. C. *Britain Looks to Germany. British Opinion and Policy Towards Germany Since 1945* (1965), 34, 37–8

22 Memo from Hull to FDR, 29/9/44, FRUS, 1944, I, 344–6; Memo from FDR to Hull, 20/10/44, ibid, 358; Memo from Morgenthau to Stettinius, 3/11/44, ibid, 379–80; Chargé in the UK to Stettinius, 12/11/44, ibid, 403–4; Memo of a Conversation with FDR, 15/11/44, ibid, 410; Memo from Stettinius to FDR, 11/11/44, ibid, 399; for confirmation of this 'suspicion' about the Soviet position see Maisky, 395; Draft Minutes of a Department of State Conference on the Work of the EAC and on Plans for Control of Germany, 13/3/45, FRUS, 1945, III, 438–57

23 Protocol of Moscow conference. Annex 6. Declaration of Austria, 1/11/43, FRUS, 1943, I, 761; Muir, John. 'Austria', *Four-Power Control in Germany and Austria 1945–1946*, by Michael Balfour and John Muir (1956), 283–4, 286; CAB 81/42. PHP (44) 12 (Final). Military Occupation of Germany—Soviet Proposals. Minute by Strang, 29/2/44; CAB 88/16. CCS 320/21. Memo by US COS, 12/7/44; Hull to Winant, 15/7/44, FRUS, 1944, I, 451; Winant to State Department, 27/11/44, ibid, 471–2; Stettinius to Winant, 5/12/44, ibid, 473

24 Memo by the Committee on Post-War Programs, 8/6/44, FRUS, 1944, I, 438–48; Aide-Mémoire from British Embassy to the Department of State, 14/10/44, ibid, 466; Chargé in the USSR to State Department, 3/11/44, ibid, 467–8; Winant to State Department, 24/11/44, ibid, 471

25 Winant to Stettinius and FDR, 8/12/44, FRUS, 1944, I, 476–7; Stettinius to Winant, 9/12/44, ibid, 478; CAB 80/90. COS (45) 49(o). Zones of Occupation in Austria. Minute from Eden to Churchill, 17/1/45

8 POLAND: THE NEGOTIATED PEACE (pages 139–58)

1 Doc 86, Broadcast by General Sikorski to the Polish Nation, 23/6/41, *Documents on Polish–Soviet Relations, 1939–1945*, I, eds General Sikorski Historical Institute (1961), 109, hereafter cited as Sikorski

2 Doc 91, Conversation between Sikorski and Maisky, 5/7/41, Sikorski, I, 117

3 Mikolajczyk, Stanislaw. *The Pattern of Soviet Domination* (1948), 289–92

4 Doc 273, Note from Bogomolov to Raczynski, 31/10/42, Sikorski, I, 449

5 CAB 81/42. PHP (44) 10 (Final). Post-War Poland and Appendix A, 5/5/44; Roos, Hans. *A History of Modern Poland* (1966), 80, 96, 173–4, 185

6 Doc 120, Letter from Sikorski to General Anders, 1/9/41, Sikorski, I, 162, 164

7 Doc 180, Telegram from Anders to Sikorski, 4/2/42, Sikorski, I, 277

8   Doc 171, Report by Sikorski to the Council of Ministers, 12/1/42, Sikorski, I, 264

9   Beneš, 148

10 Doc 193, Conversation between Anders and Stalin, 18/3/42, Sikorski, I, 301–9; Doc 199, Telegram from Anders to Sikorski, 31/3/42, ibid, 319

11 Doc 86, ibid, 112; Hull, II, 1270; Docs 229 and 230, Sikorski, I, 370–3

12 Doc 233, Telegram from Sikorski to Anders and Kot, 2/7/42, ibid, 375

13 Doc 120, Letter from Sikorski to Anders, 1/9/41, ibid, 164

14 Warth, Robert D. *Soviet Russia in World Politics* (1963), 276; Herz, Martin F. *Beginnings of the Cold War* (1966), 45, 47; Feis, 193–4; CAB 66/36. WP (43) 175. Letter from Stalin to Churchill, 21/4/43, and Letter from Churchill to Stalin, 24/4/43

15 Feis, note 1 on 193

16 CAB 66/41. WP (43) 439. Resistance in Poland. Memo by Foreign Secretary Eden, 5/10/43; Strong, Anna Louise. *I Saw the New Poland* (Boston, Mass 1946), 108

17 Warth, 277

18 Herz, 48; Hull, II, 1271–3

19 CAB 66/20. WP (42) 8. Item II. Interview between Eden and Stalin, 16/12/41; CAB 66/45. WP (44) 8. Conversation between Churchill and Stalin at Tehran, 28/11/43; as early as December of 1941, Stalin had assured Sikorski that the Soviets would help the Poles secure territorial compensation at the expense of Germany, see Doc 171, Report by Sikorski to the Council of Ministers, 12/1/42, Sikorski, I, 265

20 Herz, 52; CAB 66/41. WP (43) 438. Western frontiers of the USSR. Memo by Eden, 5/10/43; for the report of the Stalin, Churchill, FDR meeting of 1/12/43, with map, see FRUS, *Cairo and Tehran*, 599–604

21 Beneš, 264, 266

22 CAB 66/43. WP (43) 528. Possible lines of a Polish–Soviet settlement. Memo by Eden, 22/11/43

23 Beneš, 265–7; CAB 66/45. WP (44) 48. Poland. Memo by Eden, 23/1/44

24 Hull, II, 1438, 1441

25 CAB 80/78. COS (44) 1(0). Annex. Letter from the FO to the COS, 30/12/43

26 Lowery, 'Poland'; Toynbee, *Realignment*, 159–60, 164; Bruce, George. *The Warsaw Uprising. 1 August–20 October 1944* (1972) 50–1, 60–1, 66

27 Herz, 55; Lowery, 154, 165; CAB 66/47. WP (44) 128. Poles in the USA. Memo by Eden, 22/2/44; Hull, II, 1442

28 Lowery, 162, note 1 on 163; CAB 81/42. PHP (44) 10 (Final). Post-War Poland. Memo by PHP Sub-Committee, 5/5/44; *Note*: When

Eden was informed of the content of this conversation, his immediate comment was that 'the President will do nothing for the Poles, any more than Mr Hull did at Moscow or the President himself did at Tehran. The poor Poles are sadly deluding themselves if they place any faith in these vague and generous promises. The President will not be embarrassed by them hereafter . . .'. Note by Eden, 28/6/44, FO 371/30402, C8482/8/G55

29 CAB 88/16. CCS 317. Memo from the US Staff Planners to the COS, 18/8/43; see also CAB 80/75. COS (43) 633(o). Equipment and Employment of the Polish Secret Army, Annex II and III, 18/10/43, and CAB 80/77. COS (43) 780(o). Poland, plans for intensification of sabotage and guerrilla activity. SOE report for the COS, 18/12/43

30 CAB 80/76. COS (43) 689(o). Polish Resistance movement. Minute from the COS to Churchill, 5/11/43; CAB 80/76. COS (43) 660(o). Minute from Minister of Economic Warfare (Selborne) to Churchill, 21/10/43

31 Mikolajczyk, 74; Lowery, 168; CAB 80/84. COS (44) 557(o). Operations by the Polish Secret Army. Letter from Gen Smith, Chief of Staff to the Supreme Allied Commander, to the COS, 21/6/44; Bruce, 56, 59–61

32 Bruce, 70, 72

33 Lowery, 168; Woods, 61; Mikolajczyk, 76; CAB 80/86. COS (44) 670(o). Assistance to the Polish Home Army and Annex, 29/7/44; CAB 80/86. COS (44) 677(o). General Rising by the Polish Secret Army in Warsaw. Memo by SOE, 31/7/44; Strong, 157; Bruce, 73, 75–6

34 Lowery, 169–70; Kolko, 117; Bruce, 76

35 Feis, 378; CAB 80/86. COS (44) 690(o). No 30 Military Mission. Visit to the Third Belorussian Group of Armies—6–9 July 1944, 8/44; Strong, 238

36 Letters from Stalin to Churchill, 5/8/44 and 8/8/44, USSR, I, 248, 254

37 CAB 65/43. WM (44) 104. 104th Conclusions of the War Cabinet, 9/8/44; CAB 65/43. WM (44) 109. 109th Conclusions of the War Cabinet, 21/8/44; Letter from Stalin to Churchill and Roosevelt, 22/8/44, USSR, I, 255

38 CAB 80/86. COS (44) 696(o). Support of the Polish Secret Army. Memo by Major-General Gubbins, 5/8/44; CAB 80/86. COS (44) 711(o). Annex I. Letter from Sosnkowski to the Chief of the Imperial Staff, 7/8/44; CAB 80/86. COS (44) 721(o). Annex I. Letter from General Tabor to Gubbins, 7/8/44; CAB 80/86. COS (44) 711(o). Annex I. Letter from Sosnkowski, 7/8/44; CAB 80/86. COS (44) 721(o). Annex I. Letter from Sosnkowski to Ismay, 10/8/44; CAB 65/47. WM (44) 107. Confidential Annex, Minute 1, 16/8/44; CAB 65/43. WM (44) 127. 127th Conclusions of the War Cabinet, 25/9/44; for Portal's observations see CAB 65/47. WM (44)

111. Confidential Annex, Minute 7, 28/8/44; see also Hart, B. H. Liddell. *History of the Second World War* (1970), 581–4

39   CAB 65/47. WM (44) 117. Confidential Annex. Minute 1, 5/9/44; CAB 65/47. WM (44) 122. Confidential Annex, Minute 7, 11/9/44

40   CAB 80/87. COS (44) 855(o). Assistance to the Poles. Letter from the FO to the COS, 28/9/44, and Appendices I, III, IV, and V from SOE operator 'J. Ward' in Warsaw

41   Chaney, Jr., Otto Preston. *Zhukov* (Newton Abbot 1972), note on 270; CAB 80/87. COS (44) 868(o). Assistance to the Poles. Letter from SOE to the COS, 29/9/44; CAB 80/87. COS (44) 855(o). Annex I. Letter from Mikolajczyk to the US Ambassador in London, 23/9/44, and Appendix II, Message from Deputy Prime Minister to Mikolajczyk, 19/9/44

42   Feis, 388; Woods, 84–5; Herz, 59; Kolko, 117; Strong, 128, 150, 172

43   Doc 180, Conversation between Mikolajczyk and Stalin, 3/8/44, *Documents on Polish–Soviet Relations, 1939–1945*, II, eds General Sikorski Historical Institute (1967), 313, 316, 321; Dziewanowski, M. K. *The Communist Party of Poland* (Cambridge, Mass 1959), 167; CAB 66/53. WP (44) 418. Polish Committee to National Liberation. Memo by Eden, 28/7/44

44   Doc 186, Conversation between Mikolajczyk, Bierut, Osobka-Morawski, and Molotov, 8/8/44, Sikorski, II, 326

45   'Polish Attitude Defined', *The Times* (1/9/44) p. 3; Lowery, 181 and note 5; see also *The Times* (5/9/44) p. 3

46   Stettinius to Hull, 22/5/44, FRUS, 1944, III, 12

47   CAB 66/53. WP (44) 409. Letter from Eden to Duff Cooper, 25/7/44; Doc 237, Proceedings of the first session of the Moscow Conference on Polish Affairs, 13/10/44, Sikorski, II, 409, 414–15

48   Doc 239, Conversation between Mikolajczyk and Churchill, 14/10/44, Sikorski, II, 419

49   Doc 239, ibid, 419–20

50   Doc 240, First British draft proposal, 14/10/44, ibid, 422; Doc 241, Conversation between Mikolajczyk and Churchill in the presence of the Polish delegation, 14/10/44, ibid, 423; Doc 259, Resolution of the Council of Ministers, 3/11/44, ibid, 457

51   Hull, II, 1447–8; for full text see Doc 268, Letter from FDR to Mikolajczyk, 17/11/44, Sikorski, II, 468

52   Doc 272, Telegram from Winant to Stettinus, 25/11/44, Sikorski, II, 476; Herz, 62

53   Stalin to Churchill, 8/12/44, USSR, I, 282; Doc 290, Dispatch from Stalin to Roosevelt, 27/12/44, Sikorski, II, 501; Herz, 62; Doc 292, Dispatch from Stalin to Roosevelt, 1/1/45, ibid, 504–5

9 THE GROWTH OF THE UNITED NATIONS CONCEPT
(pages 159–74)

1 See Divine, Robert A. *Second Chance* (New York 1967), 29–39; Wallace, Henry A. *Democracy Reborn*, ed Russell Lord (1944); Welles, Sumner. *The World of the Four Freedoms* (1944)

2 Divine, 89–90, 92–3; B₂H₂ Resolution, 16/3/43, Goodrich, *Documents*, VI, 319

3 Divine, 95, 98–101, 110

4 Johnson, Haynes and Gwertzman, Bernard M. *Fulbright the Dissenter* (1968), 69; FO 371/34162. A 9331/144/45. Letter from Campbell to Eden, 4/10/43; FO 371/34162. A 9454/144/45. Minute by P. H. Gore Booth of a conversation with Senator Ball, 5/10/43; Connally, Tom and Steinberg, Alfred. *My Name Is Tom Connally* (New York 1954), 264

5 Divine, 32–3, 97; Radio Broadcast by Hull, 23/7/42, Goodrich, *Documents*, V, 8–9; Long, 271; Hull, II, 1642; Vandenberg, 40–1; FO 371/34158. A 479/144/45. Minute, 14/1/43; FO 371/34162. A 9454/144/45. Minute of conversation with Senator Ball, 5/10/43

6 Hull, II, 1227–9, 1638–9; CAB 66/35. WP (43) 130. Foreign Secretary's Visit to Washington. Memo from Eden to Churchill, 28/3/43

7 CAB 66/37. WP (43) 233. Record of a Conversation at Luncheon at the British Embassy, Washington, on 22/5/43

8 CAB 66/37. WP (43) 233. Annex A. Minute by Churchill and Telegram from Halifax to Eden and Churchill, 10/6/43

9 Stalin's Written Answers to Questions Put by Harold King, 29/5/43, Goodrich, *Documents*, V, 530–1; Hull, II, 1251–2

10 Woodward, 446; Four-Nation Declaration, 10/43, Committee on Foreign Relations, *Review of the United Nations Charter* (Washington 1954), 39–40

11 Long, 297; Sherwood, *Roosevelt*, 716; Roosevelt–Stalin Meeting, 29/11/43, FRUS, *Cairo and Tehran*, 530–2; First Plenary Meeting, 28/11/43, ibid, 490

12 Roosevelt–Stalin Meeting, 29/11/43, ibid, 532; Roosevelt's 11th Annual State of the Union Message, 11/1/44, *The State of the Union Messages of the Presidents*, III, ed Fred L. Israel (New York 1967), 2875–6

13 Hull, II, 1256, 1642–3; FO 371/34161. A 8102/144/45. Campbell to Cadogan, 24/8/43; see also FO 371/34161. A 8223/144/45, A 8496/144/45, and A 9064/144/45

14 FO 371/34163. A 10634/144/45. Halifax to FO. Weekly Political Summary, 21/11/43; Memo from Hull to FDR, 29/12/43, FRUS, 1944, I, 615; Note on the Hull–FDR Meeting, 3/2/44, ibid, 621; Acting Secretary of State to Harriman and Winant, 10/2/44, ibid, 622–3

15 Roosevelt–Stalin Meeting, 29/11/43, FRUS, *Cairo and Tehran*, 530;

Plan for the Establishment of an International Organisation, 23/12/43, ibid, 617; US Tentative Proposals for a General International Organisation, 18/7/44, FRUS, 1944, I, 657

16   For evidence of the ground swell see Divine, 110; Roper, Elmo. *You and Your Leaders* (New York 1957), 55, 57, 104; Hull, II, 1653

17   Long, 298; Welles, Sumner. *Where Are We Heading?* (1947), 21; Hull, II, 1662; Connally, 266; Vandenberg, 96

18   US Tentative Proposals for a General International Organisation, 18/7/44, FRUS, 1944, I, 657–8; Vandenberg, 115–16

19   CAB 81/42. PHP (44) 27 (Draft). Report of Work Done by the Post-Hostilities Planning Sub-Committee August 1943–May 1944, 17/4/44; Tentative Proposals by the UK for an International Organisation, 22/7/44, FRUS, 1944, I, 686; CAB 81/42. PHP (44) 29 (Final). World Security Discussions, 24/4/44

20   Woodward, 454–5; CAB 66/52. WP (44) 370. Future World Organisation. Memo by Eden, 3/7/44

21   Hull, II, 1298–9; Harriman to Hull, 24/7/44, FRUS, 1944, I, 694–5

22   Memo on an International Security Organisation by the USSR, 12/8/44, ibid, 707–11

Titles of FRUS documents in this section have not been given because of the multiplicity of materials. The basic source is Under Secretary of State Stettinius's personal diary and informal minutes.

23   FRUS, 1944, I, note 3 on 717, 729

24   Ibid, 730–1, 733, 737–8

25   Ibid, 739, 742–3

26   Hull, II, 1679; FRUS, 1944, I, 744, 748–9

27   Ibid, 759, 764–5

28   Ibid, 769–70, 775, 783

29   Ibid, 733, 735, 748–9

30   CAB 81/42. PHP (44) 68 (Final). World Organisation-Military Forces, 4/9/44; CAB 80/87. COS (44) 785(o). Russian Proposal for the Formation of an International Air Corps. Minute by Churchill, 26/8/44; FRUS, 1944, I, 766, 773, 795

31   CAB 81/42. PHP (44) 73 (Final). World Organisation: Proposed Charter, 27/9/44; Letter from FDR to Stettinius, 19/9/44, FRUS, 1944, I, 814

32   Baily, Thomas A. *A Diplomatic History of the American People* (5th ed New York 1955), 830

33   McNeill, 501

34   Divine, 241

10   YALTA AND THE END OF AN ERA (pages 175–86)

1   Stettinius, Jr, Edward R. *Roosevelt and the Russians* (1950), 261–2; Third Plenary Meeting, 6/2/45, US Department of State (eds), *Foreign Relations of the States. The Conferences at Malta and Yalta,*

1945 (Washington 1955), 662 (hereafter cited as the Yalta Papers); 'The Crimea and Potsdam Conferences of the Leaders of the Three Great Powers', *International Affairs* (Moscow, June 1965), 103 (hereafter cited as Yalta Minutes)

2   Third Plenary Meeting, 6/2/45, Yalta Papers, 664, 666; Fourth Plenary Meeting, 7/2/45, ibid, 712

3   Fourth Plenary Meeting, 7/2/45, ibid, 712–14; Arguments Against Inclusion of Any of the Soviet Republics Among the Initial Members, 8/2/45, ibid, 746–7

4   Yalta Minutes, No 7 (July 1965), 113; CAB 65/51. WM (45) 16. Confidential Annex, 8/2/45

5   Byrnes, James F. 'Yalta—High Tide of Big Three Unity', in *The Yalta Conference*, ed Richard F. Fenno, Jr (Boston, Mass. 1955), 12–13; Note from Marshal Stalin to Roosevelt, 11/2/45, Yalta Papers, 967–8

6   Protocol of Proceedings, 11/2/45, Yalta Papers, 976; Yalta Minutes, No 7, 115; see also Horowitz, David. *From Yalta to Vietnam* (1967), note on 39, and Clemens, Diane Shaver. *Yalta* (New York 1970), 217, 232–40

7   Winant to FDR, 28/1/45, Yalta Papers, 130–2; Clemens, 40–1; Yalta Briefing Book Paper, the Treatment of Germany, 12/1/45, Yalta Papers, 190, 193

8   Memo by Harriman, 20/1/45, Yalta Papers, 176–7; see also Clemens, 138

9   Yalta Minutes, No 6, 99–100; cf Yalta Papers, 620–1

10 Second Plenary Meeting, 5/2/45, Yalta Papers, 621–2; see also Clemens, 141–7

11 Yalta Minutes, No 6, 102; CAB 65/51. WM (45) 16. Confidential Annex, 8/2/45; Soviet Proposal on Reparations, 7/2/45, Yalta Papers, 707; Foreign Ministers Meeting and British Proposal on Reparations, 10/2/45, ibid, 874, 885; Eden, Anthony (The Earl of Avon). *The Eden Memoirs. The Reckoning* (1965), 516

12 Watt, D. C. *Britain Looks to Germany. British Opinion and Policy Towards Germany Since 1945* (1965), 38

13 CAB 65/51. WM (45) 22. Confidential Annex. Minute 1, 19/2/45; for the British economic arguments against the Soviet–American hard line see Watt, 38–43

14 Protocol of Proceedings, 11/2/45, Yalta Papers, 978–9; Yalta Minutes, No 6, 97–8; Yalta Minutes, No 8 (August, 1965), 113–14; for a discussion of the depth of these agreements see Clemens, 146–50, 162–72

15 Second Plenary Meeting, 5/2/45, Yalta Papers, 623; Clements, 152–4; Protocol of Proceedings, 11/2/45, Yalta Papers, 978

16 Third Plenary Meeting, 6/2/45, ibid, 667–9; Protocol of Proceedings, ibid, 980

17 Yalta Minutes, No 7, 114, 116; Protocol of Proceedings, Yalta Papers, 980

18   Third Plenary Meeting, ibid, 667–70; Yalta Minutes, No 7, 117–18
19   Letter from FDR to Stalin, 6/2/45, Yalta Papers, 728; Third
     Plenary Meeting, ibid, 670; Fourth Plenary Meeting, ibid, 711
20   Fourth Plenary Meeting, ibid, 716; Fifth Plenary Meeting, 8/2/45,
     ibid, 792–3
21   Meeting of the Foreign Ministers, 9/2/45, ibid, 803–4; Protocol of
     Proceedings, ibid, 980; Letter from Stalin to FDR, 7/4/45, USSR,
     I, 315; CAB 65/51. WM (45) 22. Confidential Annex, Minute 1,
     19/2/45
22   Yalta Briefing Book, Principal Yugoslav Problems, 12/1/45, Yalta
     Papers, 262; Yalta Minutes, No 8, 109; Memo from the British
     Delegation to the Soviet Delegation Regarding Yugoslavia, 6/2/45,
     Yalta Papers, 820
23   Dedijer, 237
24   Harriman to Stettinius, 10/1/45, Yalta Papers, 453; Foreign
     Ministers Meeting, 10/2/45, ibid, 876–7; Protocol of Proceedings,
     ibid, 981
25   For the full text of the Declaration see Protocol of Proceedings,
     Yalta Papers, 977–8; Sixth Plenary Meeting, 9/2/45, ibid, 848
26   FDR to the Ambassador in Spain, 10/3/45, United States Depart-
     ment of State (eds), *Foreign Relations of the United States, 1945*
     (Washington 1967), V, 667
27   Neumann, William L. *After Victory: Churchill, Roosevelt, Stalin and
     the Making of the Peace* (New York 1967), 85–6
28   Neumann, 85–6; War Statistics, *International Affairs* (Moscow,
     March 1965), 122–3
29   Kolko, 32
30   Deutscher, Isaac. 'Stalin's Dilemma', Williams, 908

Bibliography

---

1 DOCUMENTS

Transcripts of Crown copyright records in the Public Record Office appear by permission of the Controller of HM Stationery Office

Brockway, Thomas P. (ed), *Basic Documents in United States Foreign Policy* (Princeton 1968)
British Foreign Office, United States Department of State and French Government (eds), *Documents on German Foreign Policy, 1918–1945*. Series D, Vol. X (1957)
—— *Documents on German Foreign Policy, 1918–1945*. Series D, Vol. XI (1961)
Carlyle, Margaret (ed), *Documents on International Affairs, 1939–1946*. II (1954)
Committee on Foreign Relations (eds), *Review of the United Nations Charter* (Washington, 1954)
Degras, Jane (ed), *Soviet Documents on Foreign Policy*. III (1953)
General Sikorski Historical Institute (eds), *Documents on Polish–Soviet Relations, 1939–1945*. I (1961)
—— *Documents on Polish–Soviet Relations, 1939–1945*. II (1967)
Goodrich, Leland M., Jones, S. Shepard, and Myers, Denys P. (eds), *Documents on American Foreign Relations*. IV (Boston, 1942)
Goodrich, Leland M., and Carroll, Marie J. (eds), *Documents on American Foreign Relations*. V (Boston, 1944)
—— *Documents on American Foreign Relations*. VI (Boston 1945)
—— *Documents on American Foreign Relations*. VII (Princeton 1947)
Israel, Fred L (ed), *The State of the Union Messages of the Presidents*. III (New York, 1967)

Ministry for Foreign Affairs (Finland) (eds), *The Development of Finnish–Soviet Relations* (Helsinki, 1940)

Ministry of Foreign Affairs of the Union of Soviet Socialist Republics (eds), *Stalin's Correspondence with Churchill, Attlee, Roosevelt and Truman, 1941–45.* I and II (1958)

Nixon, Edgar B. (ed), *Franklin D. Roosevelt and Foreign Affairs.* I (Cambridge, Mass, 1969)

Rosenman, Samuel I. (ed), *The Public Papers and Addresses of Franklin D. Roosevelt.* II (New York, 1938)

Stalin, Generalissimo J. V., *War Speeches, Orders of the Day, and Answers to Foreign Press Correspondents During the Great Patriotic War* (1958)

Sub-Committee to Investigate the Administration of the Internal Security Act and Other Internal Security Laws of the Committee on the Judiciary, United States Senate, 90th Congress, 1st Session (eds), *Morgenthau Diary (Germany).* I (Washington, 1967)

Toynbee, Arnold J. (ed), *Documents on International Affairs, 1939–1946.* I (1951)

United States Department of State (eds), *Foreign Relations of the United States, 1941.* I (Washington, 1958)

—— *Foreign Relations of the United States, 1942.* II (Washington, 1962)

——*Foreign Relations of the United States, 1942.* III (Washington, 1961)

—— *Foreign Relations of the United States, 1943.* I (Washington, 1963)

—— *Foreign Relations of the United States, 1943.* II (Washington, 1964)

——*Foreign Relations of the United States, 1944.* I (Washington, 1966)

—— *Foreign Relations of the United States, 1944.* II (Washington, 1967)

—— *Foreign Relations of the United States, 1944.* IV (Washington, 1966)

—— *Foreign Relations of the United States, 1945.* IV (Washington, 1968)

—— *Foreign Relations of the United States, 1945.* V (Washington, 1967)

—— *Peace and War: United States Foreign Policy 1931–1941* (Washington, 1943)

—— *Foreign Relations of the United States. The Conferences at Washington, 1941–1942, and Casablanca, 1943* (Washington, 1968)

——*Foreign Relations of the United States. The Conferences at Cairo and Tehran, 1943* (Washington, 1961)

—— *Foreign Relations of the United States. The Conferences at Malta and Yalta, 1945* (Washington, 1955)

—— *Foreign Relations of the United States. The Conference of Berlin (The Potsdam Conference), 1945.* I (Washington, 1960)

Wheeler-Bennett, John W., and Heald, Stephen A. (eds), *Documents on International Affairs, 1934* (1935)

—— *Documents on International Affairs, 1935* (1936)

2 PERSONAL HISTORIES: DIARIES, MEMOIRS, AUTOBIOGRAPHIES AND BIOGRAPHIES

Acheson, Dean. *Present at the Creation* (1969)

Beneš, Eduard. *Memoirs of Dr. Eduard Benes.* Trans Godfrey Lias (1954)

Bradley, Omar N. *A Soldier's Story* (New York, 1951)

Butcher, Harry C. *Three Years with Eisenhower* (1946)

Chaney, Otto Preston, Jr. *Zhukov* (Newton Abbot, 1972)

Coffin, Tristram. *Senator Fulbright* (1966)

Connally, Tom, and Steinberg, Alfred. *My Name is Tom Connally* (New York, 1954)

Crozier, Brian. *Franco: A Biographical History* (1967)

Dedijer, Vladimer. *Tito Speaks* (1953)

Eden, Anthony (The Earl of Avon). *The Eden Memoirs. The Reckoning* (1965)

Eisenhower, Dwight D. *Crusade in Europe* (1948)

——*The Papers of Dwight David Eisenhower. The War Years*: I, Alfred D. Chandler, Jr. (ed) (Baltimore and London, 1970)

—— *The Papers of Dwight David Eisenhower. The War Years*: IV, Alfred D. Chandler, Jr. (ed) (Baltimore and London, 1970)

Foot, Michael. *Aneurin Bevan*, I (1962)

Funk, Arthur Layton. *Charles De Gaulle: The Crucial Years,* *1943–1944* (Norman, Okla, 1959)

Horthy, Admiral. *The Confidential Papers of Admiral Horthy,* Szinai, Miklos, and Szucs, Laszlo (eds and trans) (Budapest, 1965)

Hull, Cordell. *The Memoirs of Cordell Hull,* I and II (1948).

Johnson, Haynes, and Gwertzman, Bernard M., *Fulbright the Dissenter* (1968)

King, Cecil H. *With Malice Toward None. A War Diary,* Armstrong, William (ed) (1970)

Leahy, William D. *I Was There* (1950)

Long, Breckinridge. *The War Diary of Breckinridge Long,* Israel, Fred L. (ed) (Lincoln, Nebraska, 1966)

Maclean, Fitzroy. *Disputed Barricade* (1957)

—— *Eastern Approaches* (1949)

Macmillan, Harold. *Tides of Fortune, 1945–1955* (1969)

Maisky, Ivan M. *Memoirs of a Soviet Ambassador. The War:* *1939–43* (New York, 1967)

Mannerheim, Marshal. *The Memoirs of Marshal Mannerheim,* Lewenhaupt, Count Eric (trans) (1953)

Moffat, Jay Pierpont. *The Moffat Papers: Selections from the Diplomatic Journals of J. P. Moffat, 1919–43,* Hooker, Nancy H. (ed) (Cambridge, Mass, 1956)

Moran, Lord. *Winston Churchill* (1966)

Morgenthau, Henry. *From the Morgenthau Diaries. Years of War 1941–1945,* Blum, John Morton (ed) (Boston, 1967)

Murphy, Robert. *Diplomat Among Warriors* (1964)

Pogue, Forrest C. *George C. Marshall: Ordeal and Hope, 1939–42* (1968)

Pratt, Julius W. *Cordell Hull,* II (New York, 1964)

Stimson, Henry L., and Bundy, McGeorge. *On Active Service in Peace and War* (New York, 1948)

Strang, Lord. *Home and Abroad* (1956)

Strong, Anna Louise. *I Saw the New Poland* (Boston, 1946)

Tedder, Arthur William. *With Prejudice. The War Memoirs of Marshall of the Royal Air Force Lord Tedder* (1966)

Templewood, Viscount (Sir Samuel Hoare). *Nine Troubled Years* (1954)

Young, Kenneth. *Churchill and Beaverbrook* (1966)

3 SECONDARY STUDIES

Adams, D. K. *America in the Twentieth Century* (Cambridge, England, 1967)

Armstrong, Anne. *Unconditional Surrender* (New Brunswick, New Jersey, 1961)

Bailey, Thomas A. *A Diplomatic History of the American People* (5th ed, New York, 1955)

Bartlett, Ruhl J. (ed), *The Record of American Diplomacy* (New York, 1960)

Beloff, Max. *The Foreign Policy of Soviet Russia, 1929–1941*, II (1949)

Bruce, George. *The Warsaw Uprising, 1 August–20 October 1944* (1972)

Buchanan, A. Russell. *The United States and World War II*, I (New York, 1964)

Butler, J. R. M. *Grand Strategy*, III, Part II (1964)

Byrnes, James F. *Speaking Frankly* (New York, 1947)

Carsten, F. L. *The Rise of Fascism* (1967)

Churchill, Winston S. *The Second World War*. I. *The Gathering Storm* (1948)

—— *The Second World War*. II. *Their Finest Hour* (1950)

—— *The Second World War*. III. *The Grand Alliance* (1950)

—— *The Second World War*. IV. *The Hinge of Fate* (1951)

—— *The Second World War*. V. *Closing the Ring* (1952)

—— *The Second World War*. VI. *Triumph and Tragedy* (1954)

Clemens, Diane Shaver. *Yalta* (New York, 1970)

Dallin, David J. *Soviet Russia's Foreign Policy, 1939–1942* (New Haven, Conn, 1942)

Divine, Robert A. *Second Chance* (New York, 1967)

Djilas, Milovon. *Conversations with Stalin* (1962)

Donnison, F.S.V. *Civil Affairs and Military Government Central Organization and Planning* (1966)

Dziewanowski, M. K. *The Communist Party of Poland* (Cambridge, Mass, 1959)

Evans, Stanley G. *A Short History of Bulgaria* (1960)

Feis, Herbert. *Churchill, Roosevelt and Stalin: The War They Waged and the Peace They Sought* (Princeton, 1957)

Fenno, Jr, Richard F. (ed), *The Yalta Conference* (Boston, 1955)

Ferrell, Robert E. *American Diplomacy* (rev ed, New York, 1969)

Fleming, Denna Frank. *The Cold War and Its Origins* I (1961)

Graebner, Norman A. *Cold War Diplomacy: American Foreign Policy, 1945–1960* (Princeton, 1962)

—— *Ideas and Diplomacy* (New York, 1964)

Gruber, Helmut (ed), *International Communism in the Era of Lenin* (Greenwich, Conn, 1967)

Harris, C. R. S. *Allied Military Administration of Italy, 1943–1945* (1957)

Hart, B. H. Liddell. *History of the Second World War* (1970)

Herz, Martin F. *Beginnings of the Cold War* (Bloomington and London, 1966)

Hilberg, Raul. *The Destruction of the European Jews* (Chicago, 1961)

Hoffman, George W. and Neal, Fred Warner. *Yugoslavia and the New Communism* (New York, 1962)

Hoptner, J. B. *Yugoslavia in Crisis, 1934–1941* (New York, 1962)

Horowitz, David. *From Yalta to Vietnam* (1967)

Ionescu, Ghita. *Communism in Rumania: 1944–1962* (1964)

Jakobson, Max. *The Diplomacy of the Winter War* (Cambridge, Mass, 1961)

Jelavich, Charles, and Jelavich, Barbara (eds), *The Balkans in Transition* (Berkeley, Calif, 1963)

Kennan, George F. *American Diplomacy, 1900–1950* (Chicago, 1951)

Kertesz, Stephen D. (ed), *The Fate of East Central Europe* (South Bend, Ind, 1956)

Kimball, Warren F. *The Most Unsordid Act: Lend Lease, 1939–1941* (Baltimore, 1969)

Kogan, Norman. *A Political History of Postwar Italy* (1966)

Kolko, Gabriel. *The Politics of War* (1968)

Korbel, Josef. *The Communist Subversion of Czechoslovakia, 1938–1948* (Princeton, 1959)

Kottmann, Richard N. *Reciprocity and the North Atlantic Triangle 1932–1938* (Ithaca, 1968)

Kovacs, Imre (ed), *The Fight for Freedom* (New York, 1966)

Langer, William L. *Our Vichy Gamble* (New York, 1947)

Lee, Arthur Gould. *Crown Against Sickle* (1949)

Macartney, C. A. *October Fifteenth*, Parts I and II (2nd ed, Edinburgh, 1961)

Mammarella, Giuseppe. *Italy After Fascism* (Montreal, 1964)

Mazour, Anatole G. *Finland Between East and West* (Princeton, 1956)

McNeill, William H. *America, Britain and Russia* (1953)

Meyer, Peter; Weinryb, Bernard D.; Duschinsky, Eugene; and Sylvain, Nicolas. *The Jews in the Soviet Satellites* (Syracuse, 1953)

Mikolajczyk, Stanislaw. *The Pattern of Soviet Domination* (1948)

Mowat, Charles L. *Britain Between the Wars, 1918–40* (1955)

Neumann, William L. *After Victory: Churchill, Roosevelt, Stalin and the Making of the Peace* (New York, 1967)

Nicholas, H. G. *Britain and the United States* (1955)

Pavlowitch, Stevan K. *Yugoslavia* (1971)

Public Record Office: *The Second World War. A Guide to Documents in the Public Record Office* (1972)

Rauch, Basil. *Roosevelt from Munich to Pearl Harbor* (New York, 1950)

Roberts, Henry L. *Rumania* (New Haven, Conn, 1951)

Roos, Hans. *A History of Modern Poland* (1966)

Roper, Elmo. *You and Your Leaders* (New York, 1957)

Roskill, S. W. *The War At Sea*, II (1956)

Russell, Ruth B. *A History of the United Nations Charter* (Washington, 1958)

Schwartz, Andrew J. *America and the Russo-Finnish War* (Washington, 1960)

Seton-Watson, Hugh. *The East European Revolution* (3rd ed, 1956)

Sherwood, Robert E. *Roosevelt and Hopkins: An Intimate History* (New York, 1948)

—— *The White House Papers of Harry L. Hopkins*, II (1949)

Smith, Jean Edward. *The Defense of Berlin* (Baltimore and London, 1963)

Spekke, Arnold. *History of Latvia* (Stockholm, 1951)

Stavrianos, L. S. *The Balkans Since 1453* (New York, 1958)

Stein, Harold (ed), *American Civil–Military Decisions* (Birmingham, Alabama, 1963)

Stettinius Jr., Edward R. *Roosevelt and the Russians* (1950)

Stillman, Edmund, and Pfaff, William. *Power and Impotence: The Failure of American Foreign Policy* (New York, 1966)

Taylor, A. J. P. *English History, 1914–45* (Oxford, 1965)
——*The Origins of the Second World War* (Harmondsworth, 1961)
Thomas, Hugh, *The Spanish Civil War* (1961)
Thompson, Kenneth W. *Political Realism and the Crisis of World Politics* (Princeton, 1960)
Thomson, S. Harrison. *Czechoslovakia in European History* (Princeton, 1953)
Toynbee, Arnold J. *Survey of International Affairs, 1934* (1934)
—— *Survey of International Affairs, 1935* (1936)
—— *Survey of International Affairs, 1936* (1937)
Toynbee, Arnold J. (ed), *Survey of International Affairs, 1938*, I (1941)
—— *The Initial Triumph of the Axis* (1958)
Toynbee, Arnold J. and Toynbee, Veronica M. (eds), *The Eve of War, 1939* (1958)
—— *Hitler's Europe* (1954)
—— *The Realignment of Europe* (1955)
—— *The War and the Neutrals* (1956)
Viorst, Milton. *Hostile Allies: FDR and Charles De Gaulle* (1965)
Vucinich, Wayne S. (ed), *Contemporary Yugoslavia. Twenty Years of Socialist Experiment* (Berkeley and Los Angeles, 1969)
Wallace, Henry A. *Democracy Reborn*, Lord, Russell (ed) (1944)
Warth, Robert D. *Soviet Russia in World Politics* (1963)
Watt, D. C. *Britain Looks to Germany. British Opinion and Policy Towards Germany Since 1945* (1965)
Welles, Sumner. *The Time for Decision* (1944)
—— *Where Are We Heading?* (1947)
—— *The World of the Four Freedoms* (1944)
Werth, Alexander. *France, 1940–1955* (1956)
—— *Russia at War* (1964)
Whitaker, Arthur P. *Spain and Defence of the West* (New York, 1961)
White, Dorothy Shipley. *Seeds of Discord: De Gaulle, Free France and the Allies* (Syracuse, 1964)
Williams, William Appleman (ed), *The Shaping of American Diplomacy*. II (Chicago, 1956)
Wilmot, Chester. *The Struggle for Europe* (1952)

Wilson, Theodore A. *The First Summit: Roosevelt and Churchill at Placentia Bay, 1941* (1969)

Winton, John (ed), *The War at Sea* (1967)

Wolff, Robert Lee. *The Balkans in Our Time* (Cambridge, Mass, 1967)

Woods, William. *Poland: Eagle in the East* (1968)

Woodward, E. L. *British Foreign Policy in the Second World War* (1962)

Wuorinen, John H. *Finland and World War II, 1939–1944* (New York, 1948)

Zinner, Paul E. *Communist Strategy and Tactics in Czechoslovakia, 1918–48* (1963)

4 ARTICLES AND ESSAYS

Auty, Phyllis. 'Yugoslavia's International Relations (1945–1965)', Vucinich (ed), *Contemporary Yugoslavia*

Beard, Charles A. 'The Atlantic Charter', Williams (ed), *The Shaping of American Diplomacy*, II

Broz-Tito, Josip. 'On Certain Current International Questions', *Foreign Affairs*. 36, no 1 (October 1957)

Byrnes, James F. 'Yalta—High Tide of Big Three Unity', Fenno (ed), *The Yalta Conference*

Cankar, Izidor, 'Problems of the New Yugoslavia', *The Slavonic and East European Review*. 23, no. 62 (January 1945)

'The Crimea and Potsdam Conferences of the Leaders of the Three Great Powers', *International Affairs* (Moscow, June 1965, July 1965, August 1965, September 1965)

Deakin, F. W. D. 'Britanija i Jugoslavija 1941–1945', *Jugoslovenski Istorijski Casopis*, 2 (1963)

Deutscher, Isaac, 'Stalin's Dilemma', Williams (ed), *The Shaping of American Diplomacy*, II

Duff, Katherine. 'Italy', Toynbee (eds), *The Realignment of Europe*

—— 'Spain Between the Allies and the Axis', Toynbee (eds), *The War and the Neutrals*

Franklin, William M. 'Zonal Boundaries and Access to Berlin', *World Politics*. 16, no 1 (October 1963)

Hammond, Paul Y. 'Directives for the Occupation of Germany: The Washington Controversy', Stein (ed), *American Civil–Military Decisions*

Hughes, E. J. 'Winston Churchill and the Formation of the United Nations Organisation', *Journal of Contemporary History* (Autumn 1973)

Keeton, G. W. 'The Soviet Union and Great Britain', *The Slavonic and East European Review*. 23, no 62 (January 1946)

Kertesz, Stephen D. 'Communist Conquest of Hungary', Kovacs (ed), *The Fight for Freedom*

King, F. P. 'British Policy and the Warsaw Rising', *Journal of European Studies* (March 1974)

Lowery, Sidney, 'The Baltic States', Toynbee (eds), *The Realignment of Europe*

—— 'Bulgaria', Toynbee (eds), *The Realignment of Europe*

—— 'Finland', Toynbee (eds), *The Realignment of Europe*

McNeill, William H. 'Greece, 1944–1946', Toynbee (eds), *The Realignment of Europe*

Morton, Sir Desmond. 'The Free French Movement, 1940–2', Toynbee (eds), *Hitler's Europe*

Pratt, Lawrence. 'The Anglo-American Naval Conversations on the Far East of January 1938', *International Affairs* (London). 47, no 4 (October 1971)

Seton-Watson, Hugh, 'Yugoslavia', Toynbee (eds), *The Realignment of Europe*

Skendi, Stavro, 'Albania', Kertesz (ed), *The Fate of East Central Europe*

Stavrianos, L. S. 'Greece's Other History', *The New York Review of Books*. 16, no 11 (17 June 1971)

Strang, Lord. 'The Moscow Negotiations 1939' (the Twenty-Sixth Montague Burton Lecture on International Relations) (Leeds, 1968)

Sylvain, Nicolas. 'Rumania', Meyer *et al*, *The Jews in the Soviet Satellites*

Tomasevich, Jozo. 'Yugoslavia During the Second World War', Vucinich (ed), *Contemporary Yugoslavia*

Vucinich, Wayne S. 'Interwar Yugoslavia', Vucinich (ed), *Contemporary Yugoslavia*

War Statistics, *International Affairs* (Moscow, March 1965)

Wiskemann, Elizabeth. 'Czechoslovakia', Toynbee (eds), *The Realignment of Europe*

Wolff, Robert Lee. 'Bulgaria', Kertesz (ed), *The Fate of East Central Europe*

5 NEWSPAPERS

Colyton, Lord. Letter to the Editor. *The Times* (29 April 1970)

'Polish Attitude Defined'. *The Times* (1 September 1944)

'PQ 17, How the Decision Was Made'. *The Sunday Times* (1 March 1970)

Acknowledgements

THIS BOOK began in Staffordshire, at the University of Keele, as a thesis for a Master of Arts degree. My adviser, Professor D. K. Adams of the American Studies Department, generously gave his time and skilful guidance during the writing of the thesis.

While researching at the Public Record Office for the re-write of the thesis, I was fortunate in spending many British Rail commuter hours in the company of E. J. Hughes and Mark C. Wheeler who at the time were fellow students at Cambridge. Mr Hughes was very helpful in looking over my rough chapter on the United Nations and in giving me several good reasons to clarify both my thinking and my prose. The chapter's remaining vices, of course, are my own. Mr Wheeler was kind enough to let me read his excellent senior thesis on American–Yugoslav relations during the war. He also put me on to several recent sources in the field and translated the article for my use by F. W. D. Deakin which appears in my bibliography. The assistance and friendship of these scholars does not imply that they necessarily agree with either my approach or conclusions.

In the past Professors Forrest W. Frease and George G. Gates of the University of Northern Colorado and Professor Stuart B. James of the University of Denver have rendered me countless favours by fulfilling all those requests with which former students inevitably and thanklessly lumber their mentors. Because I happened to have studied English with them is no reason to suppose that my stylistic problems were ever anything but my own.

Personally I do not see how anyone finishes or starts a book without a spouse. Mine has done everything right.

Index

D5